Michel Foucault

Michel Foucault

Clare O'Farrell

SAGE Publications

London ● Thousand Oaks ● New Delhi

SAGE Publications Ltd
1 Oliver's Yard
55 City Road
London EC1Y 1SP

SAGE Publications Inc.
2455 Teller Road
Thousand Oaks, California 91320

SAGE Publications India Pvt Ltd
B-42, Panchsheel Enclave
Post Box 4109
New Delhi 110 017

British Library Cataloguing in Publication data

A catalogue record for this book is available
from the British Library

ISBN 0 7619 6163 1
    0 7619 6164 X

Library of Congress control number available

Typeset by C&M Digitals (P) Ltd., Chennai, India
Printed on paper from sustainable resources
Printed and bound in Great Britain by Athenaeum Press, Gateshead

To my mother
Deirdre O'Farrell

and to the memory of my father
Patrick O'Farrell
1933–2003

Table of Contents

Preface   ix

Acknowledgements   xi

Abbreviations   xiii

One   **A Cultural Icon**   1

Two   **Cultural Contexts**   19

Three   **Foucault's Major Works**   33

Four   **A Tool Box for Cultural Analysis**   50

Five   **The Unconscious of History and Culture**   61

Six   **Discontinuity and Discourse**   74

Seven   **Truth and Culture**   83

Eight   **Power and Culture**   96

Nine   **Ethics and Subjectivity**   109

Appendix 1   Chronology of Foucault's Life and Times   121

Appendix 2   Key Concepts in Foucault's Work   127

Bibliography   162

Index   180

Preface

The French thinker Michel Foucault, who died in 1984 aged 57, is one of the most influential sources of ideas in the humanities and social sciences today. His output was enormous, including some twelve books published during his lifetime, four 800-page volumes of his collected articles, interviews and lectures as well as seven recent and very substantial volumes of lectures with more promised. Two previously unpublished sets of interviews also appeared in 2004, 20 years after his death, one set in book form (Droit, 2004) and the other dramatised for radio (1969i). Other material is also available on video, audio tape and CD.

Such an output is daunting indeed and this book is designed as an introductory guide for people who are looking for a broad overview of Foucault's work. It is also aimed at providing some tools for students and researchers who wish to apply Foucault's ideas at more technical levels. The analysis is situated within the general field of cultural studies and is focused on the mechanics of Foucault's approach rather than towards the empirical content of his work. In addition, discussion is mainly restricted to his own work, with only limited references to what is now a very large and very diverse secondary industry.

Introducing Foucault's work is no easy matter. This book takes a layered approach, dealing with the same problems from a variety of angles in an attempt to try and deal with some of the complexities. Chapter 1 situates Foucault in the contemporary context and discusses reasons why his work is so difficult to come to grips with, write about and then apply to other domains. Chapter 2 then locates Foucault within his own social and historical setting and Chapter 3 offers brief summaries of his major works in chronological order. Chapter 4 then takes up the challenge from yet another angle, and advances the idea that Foucault's work rests on a set of five closely interrelated assumptions relating to order, history, truth, power and ethics. The remaining chapters build on this schema and examine in some detail the specific tools and concepts that Foucault has become famous for. The overall aim is to reduce some of the mystery surrounding Foucault's approach and to increase the flexibility and precision with which people can both understand and use his work.

The book also includes two appendices which are intended to function as working tools. The first is a chronology of Foucault's life, work and other major contemporary intellectual and political events. This is designed to serve as an easy set of historical reference points to ground the more theoretical analyses in the book. The second appendix provides a detailed alphabetical list of Foucault's key concepts. Brief definitions are provided, but more importantly, the aim is to guide the reader to those texts by Foucault himself where he provides definitions and illustrations of what he is trying to convey. Amongst the favorite pastimes of those engaged in the study of Foucault is trying to hunt down specific tools in his work suitable for applications to other domains, or otherwise searching for clarification of particular concepts. The intention of Appendix 2 is to make this quest a little easier. For example, someone searching for Foucault's definition of the notion of 'discourse' and how he actually puts this idea into play can look the word up in the appendix and then track down the necessary references.

The inclusion of this list of key concepts has had two consequences for the rest of the book. First of all, it has made it possible to keep the referencing structure within the text itself fairly light and unencumbered. Readers looking for a general introduction to Foucault's work therefore, need not be bothered by complex referencing, whereas those searching for more detailed information on any of his concepts can turn to the list. The inclusion of this list has also necessitated a comprehensive and custom designed bibliography of Foucault's work, in order to make it a tool that can be used not only by English speakers consulting multiple translations of the same work, but also by those working in the original French or with translations into other languages.

With regards to the translations, when the published English translation does not quite convey some of the nuances of the French original, I have modified the translation and added the annotation 'mod.' beside the reference in the text. Translations of texts not yet published in English are my own. Wherever possible, I have referred to the most recent translation of each item in English, otherwise I have listed the most accessible version in French.

Acknowledgements

This book owes much to the ongoing and generous support of many people over a number of years. I would like to begin by thanking my family, in particular my father, who died on Christmas Day 2003, and was a source of constant encouragement, support, advice and intellectual discussion, even through long-term illness. My mother has also been tremendously supportive over the years, as have other members of my family.

I would also like to thank the commissioning editor at Sage publications, Chris Rojek, and the anonymous reader who provided very helpful feedback at the proposal stage. The staff at the Foucault Archives at the Institute Mémoire Contemporaine (IMEC) in Paris helped to make my visit in 1998 a most productive one. Also in Paris, Jean-Paul and Monique Delamotte of the Association Culturelle Franco-Australienne (ACFA) were the source of generous support and hospitality. The Humanities Research Centre and Burgmann College at the Australian National University in Canberra provided excellent research facilities and accommodation in 1999. Thanks are also due to my colleagues in the School of Cultural and Language Studies in Education at Queensland University of Technology (QUT) in Brisbane for their collegial spirit. I am especially grateful to the Head of School, Jillian Brannock for facilitating work conditions in the final stages of completing this book. I would also like to mention the Foucault Reading Group at QUT whose members have provided much lively and interesting discussion.

Colin Gordon, Dominique Séglard, Chris Falzon, Jeremy Carrette, and my two fellow co-editors of the new *Foucault Studies* journal, Stuart Elden and Alan Rosenberg have all contributed in many ways with their ongoing enthusiasm for Foucault's work. I have also benefited from contact with the many researchers who have contacted me via my website on Foucault (www.michel-foucault.com). They have drawn my attention to far-flung and unexpected applications of Foucault's work across the globe. On the technical side of things, I would like to thank Peta Blackford who typed the final drafts of the manuscript and John Anderson who provided sterling assistance by entering all my bibliographical data.

Finally, I would like to dedicate this book to my mother and to my father, who even if he was not able to see the completed project, did so much to bring it into reality. His loss is sorely felt and his contribution to these pages is remembered with warm affection.

Abbreviations

Dates in square brackets refer to original date of French publication

AK   (1972) [1969]. *The Archaeology of Knowledge*. Tr. A.M. Sheridan Smith. London: Tavistock.

AN   (2003) [1999]. *Abnormal. Lectures at the Collège de France, 1974–1975*. New York: Picador.

BC   (1973) [1963]. *The Birth of the Clinic: An Archaeology of Medical Perception*. Tr. A.M. Sheridan Smith. London: Tavistock.

CS   (1990) [1984]. *The Care of the Self. The History of Sexuality: Volume 3*. Tr. R. Hurley. Harmondsworth, Middlesex: Penguin.

DE   (1994). *Dits et écrits: 1954–1988. Vols I–IV.* D. Defert, F. Ewald & J. Lagrange (eds.). Paris: Gallimard.

DP   (1991) [1975]. *Discipline and Punish: The Birth of the Prison*. Tr. A.M. Sheridan Smith. Harmondsworth, Middlesex: Penguin.

EW1 (1997). *Ethics: Subjectivity and Truth. The Essential Works of Michel Foucault 1954–1984. Volume One.* P. Rabinow (ed.) Tr. R. Hurley and others. Harmondsworth, Middlesex: Allen Lane, Penguin.

EW2 (1998). *Aesthetics, Method and Epistemology. The Essential Works of Michel Foucault 1954–1984. Volume Two.* J.D. Faubion. (ed.). Tr. R. Hurley and others. Harmondsworth, Middlesex: Allen Lane, Penguin.

EW3 (2000). *Power.* J.D. Faubion (ed.). Tr. R. Hurley and others. New York: The New Press.

FL   (1996). *Foucault Live Interviews, 1961–1984.* S. Lotringer (ed.). Tr. L. Hochroth & J. Johnston. 2nd ed. New York: Semiotext(e).

FR   (1991). *The Foucault Reader.* P. Rabinow (ed.). Harmondsworth, Middlesex: Penguin. Originally published in 1984.

FS   (2001). *Fearless Speech.* J. Pearson (ed.). Los Angeles: Semiotext(e).

HER (2001). *L'hermeneutique du sujet. Cours au Collège de France, 1981–1982.* Paris: Gallimard Seuil. [(2005). *The Hermeneutics of the*

Subject. Lectures at the Collège de France, 1981–82. F. Gros. (ed.). Tr. G. Burchell. New York: Palgrave Macmillan.]

HF   (1972) [1961]. *Histoire de la folie à l'age classique.* Revised. Paris: Gallimard.

HS   (1990) [1976]. *The History of Sexuality: Volume 1.* Tr. R. Hurley. Harmondsworth, Middlesex: Penguin.

MC   (1989) [1961]. *Madness and Civilization: A History of Insanity in the Age of Reason.* Tr. R. Howard. London: Routledge.

MIP (1976) [1954, 1962]. *Mental Illness and Psychology.* Tr. A.M. Sheridan Smith. New York: Harper and Row.

NBP (2004). *Naissance de la biopolitique. Cours au Collège de France. 1978–1979.* Paris: Gallimard Seuil.

OD   (1981) [1971]. 'The order of discourse'. In R. Young (ed.). *Untying the Text: A Post-Structuralist Reader.* Boston: Routledge and Kegan Paul.

OT   (1970) [1966]. *The Order of Things: An Archaeology of the Human Sciences.* Tr. A.M. Sheridan Smith. London: Tavistock.

P/K (1980). *Power/Knowledge: Selected Interviews and Other Writings 1972–1977.* C. Gordon (ed.). New York: Pantheon Books.

PP   (2003). *Le pouvoir psychiatrique. Cours au Collège de France, 1973–1974.* Paris: Gallimard Seuil.

PPC (1988). *Politics, Philosophy, Culture: Interviews and Other Writings, 1977–1984.* L. Kritzman (ed.). New York: Routledge.

RC   (1999). *Religion and Culture.* J.R. Carrette (ed.). Manchester: Manchester University Press.

RR   (1987) [1963]. *Death and the Labyrinth: the World of Raymond Roussel.* Tr. C. Ruas. London: Athlone.

SMD (2003) [1997]. *'Society Must Be Defended'. Lectures at the Collège de France, 1975–1976.* Tr. D. Macey. New York: Picador.

STP (2004) *Sécurité, territoire, population. Cours au Collège de France, 1977–1978.* Paris: Gallimard Seuil.

TS   (1988). *Technologies of the Self: A Seminar with Michel Foucault.* L. Martin, H. Gutman & P. Hutton (eds.). Amherst: University of Massachusetts Press.

UP   (1992) [1984]. *The Use of Pleasure. The History of Sexuality: Volume Two.* Tr. R. Hurley. Harmondsworth, Middlesex: Penguin.

ONE   A Cultural Icon

Since his death in 1984, Michel Foucault has emerged as a modern cultural icon – an iconic existence which, like his work, is plural and diverse. There is Foucault the gay saint who appears, for example, in David Halperin's work as an exemplar of a courageous champion of queer theory. There is Foucault the sinner who emerges in James Miller's biography, the tortured homosexual obsessed with death, who may or may not have deliberately infected his partners with AIDS. There is also Foucault the relentlessly erudite academic (and numbers of specialised texts testify to this), and Foucault the radical militant at demos and on protest committees (an image more widely propagated in France, particularly evident in photos, popular essays and newspaper articles). Foucault is also the quintessential embodiment of hyper intelligence and frustratingly difficult 'French thought'. His own image as a bald man – egghead – with glasses aids this perception. In the paintings and cartoons of Foucault, which appear on the covers of books or as caricatures in magazines, the bald head and glasses are the most salient features.

Foucault's status as contemporary icon is particularly in evidence in that rich yet somewhat ephemeral treasure trove for cultural analysts, the internet. Foucault cannot fail to rate a place on the 'Baldness Hall of Fame' website. Also on the net, David Gauntlett (n.d) with an application of Photoshop trickery shows Foucault and Patrick Stewart, the famously bald actor who plays Captain Picard in *Star Trek: The Next Generation*, side by side in similarly pensive pose. In the musical arena on the net, one finds a dubious rock band called The Professors, waxing lyrical with a song titled 'Foucault funk: The Michel Foucault postmodern blues' (Radford et al., 1997). On Sherry Turkle's site there is also a marvelous shockwave movie, where a caricatured Foucault seamlessly transforms into a dinosaur and a power ranger (Col and Doyle, 1995). Foucault's image becomes mysteriously one with icons of juvenile popular culture. Whether the actual content of his works and ideas can blend in so smoothly is, of course, another matter. Perhaps most extravagant of all, at the end of 2004, was German artist Thomas Hirschhorn who mounted a large and entertaining installation celebrating Foucault's persona titled '24h Foucault' at the Palais de Tokyo, one of the two major museums of modern art in Paris. [1]

The mere mention of Foucault's name has come to serve as a short-hand for intellectual pretension. In the 1998 Hollywood romantic comedy *You've got mail*, Tom Hanks' girlfriend refers to a man whose admirable intelligence is demonstrated by the fact that he can discuss Heidegger and Foucault on television. Indeed, French philosophy in general even seems to be surfacing occasionally in mainstream American film. The hero of the 1999 action blockbuster *The Matrix* hides his software in a book titled *Simulations and Simulacra*. The author's name is not on the cover, but it is of course, Jean Baudrillard.

To use Foucault's name is an efficient means of demonstrating both intelligence (one can 'understand' his work) and radicality (one is 'subverting the status quo'). Alternatively, Foucault's name is reviled by others as indicating a sea of unintelligible jargon, airy-fairy trendy French nonsense, political and moral nihilism or alternatively, a new intellectual terrorism. The use of Foucault's name can also indicate membership of an exclusive club (a 'society of discourse' to use the philosopher's own terminology). Foucault becomes another X-file, brought forward into the new millennium – stylish, scandalous, trendy, tantalizingly mysterious – the truth about his work is out there somewhere, but the academic conspirators work their hardest to limit access to that knowledge, erecting an impenetrable wall of esoteric jargon.

All of these images as much as his writings themselves combine to reinforce the continued fascination with Foucault's thought. The power of this cultural fascination can also be seen in the fact that Foucault as a persona has even entered the realms of fiction and art with the publication of novels such as Hervé Guibert's *To the Friend Who Did not Save My Life* (1990), Julia Kristeva's *The Samurai* (1990) and most fictional of all Patricia Duncker's *Hallucinating Foucault* (1996). Even more improbably, Foucault makes an appearance in the science fiction genre in a Doctor Who short story. [2] Finally one knows that Foucault has really made it when he makes an appearance in Tom Wolfe's novel *A Man in Full* (1998). The rather dim Charlie is attending the opening of an exhibition at a museum. A strange looking speaker is holding forth:

'As Michel Foucault has demonstrated conclusively in our own time – the prison – the actual *carcerel*, in his terminology – the actual center of confinement and torture – is but the end point' – Who? thought Charlie. Michelle Fookoe? He looked at Serena, who was turned about in her chair drinking in every word as if it were ambrosia.

'the unmistakable terminus – of a process that presses in upon us all. The torture begins soon after the moment of birth, but we choose to call it "education", "religion," "government", "custom", "convention", "tradition", and "Western civilization". The result is' –

Am I hearing what I think I'm hearing or am I crazy? thought Charlie. Why wasn't somebody at one of these many tables *hissing*? – or something. (1998: 435–6)

Introducing Foucault: The problems

Foucault's complex iconic status is merely the beginning of the problems faced by anyone wishing to come to grips with his work. But the seemingly overwhelming difficulties in fact provide an excellent opportunity – namely to test whether Foucault's own methods might not come to the rescue. In a discussion with some historians, Foucault draws a distinction between the exhaustive description of a period or institution and the more selective approach required by focus on a particular problem. I shall therefore begin with the obvious problem: how does one go about writing an introduction to Foucault's work? This problem is in fact frequently raised, if not necessarily addressed, by those writing introductory texts on Foucault. The first observation that one might make is that in dealing with a problem one concentrates on the parameters of the problem in hand, steadfastly ignoring, as Foucault puts it, 'the obligation to tell all, even to satisfy the jury of assembled specialists' (1980b: 13). So I will certainly not be attempting to 'tell all' in this short book. Rather, Foucault's work will be stripped of its detailed empirical apparatus in an effort to expose some of its basic underlying structures and principles (as distinct from intentions or 'hidden meanings').

The weighty volume of Foucault's output has already been mentioned but there is also the issue of the enormous range of his subject matter. His discussions range across disciplines as diverse as psychiatry, medicine, economics, linguistics, the biological and physical sciences, art and literature, law, the human sciences, geography, architecture, philosophy and ethics to mention only a few. He deals with the history of science, the history of sexuality, European legal, political and institutional history, classical Greek and Roman philosophy, early Christian, medieval and modern European philosophy, to say nothing of his interest in current events and politics. And these interests were by no means superficial: as one commentator put it, Foucault had the irritating ability to step into a new field and come up with ideas that forced specialists who had spent years in the area to significantly revise their approach (Barbedette, 1984: 53).

3

As a scholar responding to Foucault's 1970 paper on the nineteenth-century biologist Georges Cuvier remarks:

> The palaeontologists, the anatomists who have followed Cuvier's work very closely, who read it in the laboratory, who use it obviously, have never come up with such an advanced epistemological analysis. But I can tell you that they would all be very satisfied. It is very enlightening to see such a presentation. (1970c: 36)

Jeremy Carrette also refers to a meeting between Foucault and some Jesuit theologians in 1980, noting, 'This meeting began by Foucault asking the assembled theologians where the idea of "debitum", in the context of marital debt originated. The room was soon silenced by Foucault's astonishing erudition on the matter' (RC: 1). The historian Jacques Léonard also observes in relation to *Discipline and Punish*: 'It would need a squadron of competent historians to sort out the mass of interpretations that the author offers us ... Nineteenth-century scholar that I am, "specialist" in the history of medicine, I can only brush against this monument with modesty' (Léonard, 1980: 10). These illustrations also draw attention to the immense wealth of Foucault's reading. This, combined with his strong focus on social justice, prompted one commentator in the 1970s to dub him and other young researchers following his lead, as the 'National Library militants' ('les militants de la B.N.') (Donzelot, 1986: 9).

To make matters even more difficult, Foucault will sometimes refer to ideas without fully explaining them or neglect to attach names or footnotes to his sources. There are several reasons for this. Firstly, Foucault is writing within a particular cultural context which is shared by his French audience. This context, as the French sociologist Pierre Bourdieu points out, owes a great deal to the French education system, which as he argues, creates 'a whole collection of commonplaces, covering not only common speech and language but also areas of encounter and agreement, common problems and common methods of approaching those common problems' (Bourdieu, 1971: 162). These commonplaces, which are also created through historical tradition as well as public debate in the national media, may seem strange indeed to those outside the culture in question.

Secondly, Foucault often avoided naming contemporary sources through politeness and a wish to avoid polemics, a position he maintained throughout his career. He attributes this particular approach to the influence of the literary critic and novelist Maurice Blanchot. Blanchot, he explains, when he did not have something positive to say about a work preferred to say nothing, drawing a rigorous distinction between the author as a psychological entity and his or her work. As a result, the critique or analysis of a work did not become the occasion for an attack on its author. Such attacks were counterproductive in Foucault's opinion, they closed down debate rather than opened it up, creating an atmosphere of violence and terror. But Foucault was not always entirely consistent. He certainly named Jacques Derrida (1972a, 1972c) and Jean-Paul Sartre (1968d) in polemical contexts, although to be fair, in the latter case, he had not given his permission for the publication of his remarks (1968e). He was also far more willing to name names when he was not publishing in French, as his exchanges with George Steiner and Lawrence Stone demonstrate. [3]

Sometimes Foucault deliberately fails to mention his sources for strategic reasons or simply for his own amusement – to catch people out. Karl Marx is usually the target in these instances. In the 1960s to cite Marx was to make an ideological statement, to declare a position in relation to one of the reigning schools of Marxist thought which had dominated intellectual life since the end of World War II in France. Foucault did not wish to align himself with, or even directly against, any of these schools of thought. Neither did he wish to ignore what Marx's work had to offer. As for catching people out, he remarks that during the 1960s:

> it was good form ... to cite Marx in the footnotes. So I was careful to steer clear of that. But I could dredge up ... quite a few passages I wrote referring to Marx ... [I didn't cite him] to have some fun, and to set a trap for those Marxists who pinned me down precisely on those sentences. That was part of the game (1983g: 458 mod.).

Other obscurities in Foucault's work can also be explained by the fact that he often made shorthand references to his previous work. As he remarked on several occasions, his books built on each other in various ways – ideas that had been worked through in detail in previous work would be referred to in passing later on often in modified form. This can sometimes be puzzling for readers who are not familiar with the rest of his output. For example, in his 1975 book, *Discipline and Punish*, Foucault draws attention to a set of governmental regulations designed to deal with an outbreak of the plague in a town. The way the plague was dealt with, Foucault claims, set a primitive template for the later exercise of disciplinary power, in the same way as the exclusion of lepers was an early model for the Great Confinement (DP: 198). In his earlier book *Madness and Civilization*, Foucault had described the disappearance of leprosy at the end of the Middle Ages, arguing that the social exclusion suffered by lepers came to serve as a model for the exclusion and confinement of a whole category of 'unproductive' and deviant individuals such as mad people, unfrocked priests, the unemployed, libertines, people with venereal disease and so on. In short, a familiarity with Foucault's earlier work is often of considerable assistance in understanding his subsequent production.

Quite apart from all this a number of Foucault's other sources are obscure and difficult to access outside of specialised archives. To refer to *Discipline and Punish* again, sources include documents from the Bibliothèque Nationale, the Military Archives of Vincennes and the Parliamentary Archives, books, newspapers, journals, pamphlets and manuscripts in French, English and Latin dating from the seventeenth century onwards, and obscure journals such as the *Club français de la médaille*. There are also quite a number of references to contemporary research undertaken by the Annales school of historians.

Adding to the reader's difficulties, there is also the reading that Foucault does not even allude to because he considers it irrelevant to the concerns of his own work, or it has been discarded in the process of reaching his final conclusions. For example, in his exchange with George Steiner, he notes that if he did not refer to either Voltaire or the historian of ideas Arthur Lovejoy in his 1966 book *The Order of Things*, it was because Voltaire was not relevant to a history of grammar, natural history and economic history and it was a text by Daudin rather than Lovejoy which provided him with useful ideas about natural history and classification (1971o: 60). Similarly, later on when taxed with not mentioning Gaston Bachelard, he points out that it was the historian of science, Georges Canguilhem, whom he found more useful (1980e: 255–6). He concludes dryly, 'In any event, the noise from these present–absent characters which come to the doors of the book to demand redress for the injustice of which they have been victims lends to my work a fantastic atmosphere of murder, of the oubliette' (1971o: 60).

All of this might seem rather obvious and is, you may say, a factor in the production of any research, but it is in fact, quite a significant consideration in how Foucault's work has been and continues to be received and also in how the philosopher on occasions responded to his critics. With the French publication in 1994 of four volumes of collected articles and interviews, and recent and ongoing publication of his lectures, it has become increasingly apparent how much detailed empirical research Foucault conducted and discarded along the way. Entire dungeons of hidden reading under-gird the visible structures of his major books. This tends to undermine one of the major and ongoing themes in the scholarly reception of Foucault's work in the English speaking world, namely that he does not have enough footnotes, his bibliographies are not long enough and he does not refer to the right people. The aim of such criticisms is, of course, to demonstrate that Foucault's work is not valid or serious intellectual work and should as a consequence therefore be discounted. The four volumes of collected writings, *Dits et écrits*, provide an opportunity to read Foucault's work in progress and chronologically, with the result that many of the ideas that remain mysterious in his major works suddenly become quite clear. In 'The order of discourse' for example, Foucault briefly describes a transition between Hesiod and Plato when knowledge separated itself from power (OD: 54–6) but it is not until one reads Foucault's detailed analysis of *Oedipus Rex* in 'Truth and juridical forms' (1974i: 16–32) that one can appreciate the nuances of his argument. One is reminded of Henri Matisse's observations concerning his own art, that its 'apparent facility and negligence' hides a lifetime of 'slow and painful work', a detailed and secret industry that cannot be dispensed with if the final result is to be achieved (Matisse, 1994: 120–1).

Problems of translation

If in French there now exists the possibility of a careful (if not entirely complete) chronological study of Foucault's work, the English reader is not so lucky. The slow work of translation continues and Foucault's shorter writings are scattered across a number of different collections and journals in English. And of course there are the inevitable errors and omissions which go along with translation. For example, the English translation of a discussion by Foucault on the monotony of modern psychological writings on the necessary relation between art and madness includes this rather strange sentence: 'This unity makes possible such discourses of reassessment (I think of Jean Vinchon) and misery (I think of Jean Fretet and many others)' (1962c: 11). An alternative reading is suggested by the French original: 'In their repetitiveness (I am thinking of Vinchon), in their poverty (I am thinking of the good Fretet as well as many others) such discourses are only possible because of this unity' (1962b: 195). [4] In addition to this, passages are sometimes inexplicably missing, [5] and there is also the difficulty of variable translations of the same word, which is a real problem when Foucault is using a particular word in a precise technical way. Thus the French word 'dispotif' is translated as 'deployment' in *The History of Sexuality* (HS: pt. 4) but as 'apparatus' elsewhere. This makes it very difficult for scholars working in translation to accurately try and track particular concepts in Foucault's work. Less obviously there are also translation dilemmas such as 'le savoir de connaissance' (HER: 296) – both words translate as 'knowledge' in English.

Another major problem is the translation of fairly commonplace French terms with esoteric latinate words in English. 'Interdiction', a common word in French meaning prohibition gets transcribed literally as 'interdiction', a rare word in English more commonly found in legal discussion. There are bizarre translations of common locutions, for example 'brave gens' is translated on one occasion as 'grave gentlemen' rather then the more ordinary 'worthy people' or 'good folk' (1968d: 54–5).

Translations such as the latter also tend to reinforce perceptions of Foucault's male-centredness in English language discussion. Jim Jose notes of Foucault's style: 'With monotonous regularity seemingly sex-indeterminate terms like "individual", "children", "subject" and so on were automatically assumed to take the masculine pronouns' (1998: 4). The problem with this criticism is that Foucault was usually writing in French and one of the features of the French language is that, unlike English, all nouns have a formal masculine or feminine gender which is not always related to biological gender. All the nouns Jose mentions have a masculine gender and the rules of French grammar demand that the pronouns used match the gender of the noun. This feature of the French language considerably complicates matters when it comes to the detection of gender bias and also, incidentally, goes a long way towards explaining the non-existence of a gender-neutral language movement in French. As the nineteenth-century French translator of Aristophanes sums it all up rather colourfully:

> The office of the translator is similar to that of the embalmers in Ancient Egypt. We know what happened to the proudest and most delicate beauties of the time of the Pharaohs after passing through their hands. They became dried out mummies, allowing the principal lines of the bodies to be distinguished, but from which every colour and every appearance of life had vanished. (Willems, cited in Tabard, 1967: 361)

This is perhaps overstating the case but these observations concerning translation help explain the considerable differences in the way Foucault is read in France compared with the English speaking world. The distinction between a French and English-language Foucault was also considerably assisted by Foucault himself. Not only was Foucault more willing to name his contemporaries when he was outside of France, he was also far more willing to talk about his personal life and enthusiasms, generally adopting a far more relaxed and casual style. It goes without saying that a whole host of other problems are raised when Foucault's work is translated into languages such as Italian, German, Portuguese, Russian, Japanese and Norwegian. The reception of Foucault's work is further complicated in the non-English language world, for example in Scandinavia, by the fact that his work arrives already filtered by the immense Anglo-Saxon literature (Neumann, 2002: 7–38).

Applications of Foucault's work

There are still further problems facing the writer of an introduction to Foucault's work. If the scope of Foucault's own work is broad, it has been applied by others even further afield, notably in the areas of identity studies such as feminist, post-colonial and gay and lesbian studies and also in the professional disciplines such as education, accounting, business management, computing studies, architecture, urban planning, social work, health including dentistry (Nettleton, 1992) and acupuncture (Seem, 2000). Other areas in the humanities, which Foucault scarcely alluded to, have also borrowed his ideas, including sports history, studies of media and popular culture as well as others. [6]

As mentioned earlier, Foucault is frequently criticised, particularly by practitioners of identity studies, for not dealing in sufficient detail with particular issues and areas. He is frequently accused, for example, of devoting far too little space to the question of women and of being consistently gender-blind in his analyses. [7] Meaghan Morris airs the general consensus that Foucault was 'a happily Eurocentric white male who was uneasy with women and ambivalent about feminism' (Morris, 1997: 370). One of Foucault's biographers, David Macey (1993: xiv), mentions however, that accusations of misogyny in relation to Foucault's personal behaviour came from the men rather than the women who worked with him. It might also be added that when Foucault does mention feminism and the women's movement, it is to express his support. But from a feminist point of view this does little to compensate for his failure to differentiate between the situations of males and females in the rest of his social analysis. Similar accusations of neglect have been leveled against Foucault by those interested in postcolonialism (Stoler, 1995), popular culture (Horrocks and Jevtic, 1997: 171) and geography (Foucault, 1976d: 63) as well as other areas.

Foucault did not appear to be unduly intimidated by such criticisms, observing with some exasperation that the list of all the areas he should have mentioned and did not was 'practically endless' (1976d: 64), adding that he could only speak about his own interests and competencies. He regarded such criticisms as indicative of a nostalgia for the 'universal' philosopher/prophet who would pronounce the 'truth' on any and every subject, so that others might follow. Intellectuals, he argued, could only talk usefully about the 'specific' areas in which they were expert. It was up to others to borrow and modify ideas to suit their own areas of interest. He notes, 'I don't write a book so that it will be the final word; I write a book so that other books are possible, not necessarily written by me' (1971b: 162). Indeed, the sheer volume of 'other books' demonstrates how far other writers have taken him at his word.

The proliferation of applications, however, creates still further difficulties in that many secondary texts have now acquired an authority of their own and ideas invented by his followers are now frequently attributed to Foucault himself. There is a mythical Foucault that often bears little resemblance to the Foucault who appears in his own writings. Numbers of opposing schools of interpretation have arisen, complete with orthodoxies concerning the 'correct' way of interpreting Foucault's work. Foucault protested against some of these mythologies himself, mentioning for example, that the formula 'knowledge is power' was often wrongly attributed to him, complaining that he could have saved himself many long years of effort if he had indeed identified the two terms rather than studying their relation (1983g: 455). There now exist entire books which purport to be about Foucault, but which scarcely refer to his original work – focusing instead on what others have had to say about him. This is something which later in his career Foucault found particularly irksome, referring to the problem on a number of occasions. He saw no difficulties with a variety of different readings of the same book as long as people took the trouble to actually read the book. 'What is serious', he says 'is that, as you continue to write you are no longer read at all and readers going from one distortion to another, reading books on the shoulders of others end up with an absolutely grotesque image of your book' (1984r: 453 mod. Cf. 1980i: 323).

The writer of an introduction to Foucault cannot ignore either the fact that there already exist a significant number of other introductions to Foucault's work – indeed they form a sub-industry in themselves. Amongst the most notable features of these texts is that a large proportion of them could scarcely be described as 'introductory' and would test the comprehension skills and knowledge of even the most advanced student. Another notable feature is that if Foucault's own work is exciting, these volumes singularly fail to convey this quality. The overwhelming temptation for the writer of an introduction to Foucault's work seems to be to use it as a platform to demonstrate the writer's own academic prowess while at the same time, more often than not, sinking into a quagmire of semi-digested paraphrase and summary or desperate reliance on secondary sources as the sheer enormity of dealing with an output such as Foucault's slowly dawns in all its awful splendour.

Introducing Foucault: Strategies

So, finally, what strategies can be adopted to deal with these complexities? How can one reduce the task to manageable proportions and at the same time not simply repeat what has gone before? My first strategy is, in effect, generated by the fact that this is an introduction which is aimed specifically at situating Foucault's wide-ranging work in relation to one admittedly amorphous discipline, namely cultural studies. This immediately limits the task, even if only slightly. But this preliminary move scarcely begins to resolve the problems. One must then decide whether to organise one's treatment of Foucault's work chronologically or thematically. Given the diversity and changeability of Foucault's work it has been fairly common practice to deal with it chronologically, dividing it into three distinct periods, covering roughly the 1950s–1960s, the 1970s and finally the 1980s. I will be following this conventional model, at least to some extent, but if the more common (but not the only) approach has been to emphasise the radical breaks in Foucault's work, the emphasis here will be on its coherence. With the passage of time and the publications of Foucault's collected writings and lectures, it has become increasingly apparent that for all the diversity and changeability of this work, there are certain problems he returns to again and again even if he completely reformulates their context, emphasis, appearance and technical vocabulary. This constant reinvention endlessly annoyed and confused his critics – just as they were satisfied that they had finally worked out what he had to say and reduced it to a convenient slogan, they found they had to start all over again from scratch. Foucault, from his side of the fence, found these attempts to pin him down equally irritating and alludes to the problem several times throughout his career. As he said somewhat testily to a German interviewer in 1972:

> Don't keep going back to things I said in the past. When I utter them, they are already forgotten. I think in order to forget. Everything I have said in the past is of absolutely no importance. You write something when you've already worn it out in your head; drained bloodless thought, you write it and that's that. What I have written doesn't interest me. What interests me is what I could write and what I could do. (1972d: 304–5) [8]

Foucault's frequent changes of subject matter, and technical vocabulary, not to mention declarations of this kind, often obscured the fact that he remained consistently interested in the same structural problems, namely how human beings seek to impose order on the world via their social structures and knowledge, the points at which these orders break down and how they change with the passage of time. He was also fascinated by the fact that there is always something that escapes our every attempt to immutably fix any order. Foucault, after early attempts to come to a definite conclusion on these matters, eventually decided late in his career that no firm theories were indeed necessary and that assigning a fixed concrete content to thought was neither possible nor desirable. He notes in an interview that even before finishing *The Order of Things* he realised that this and his proceeding books raised a large number of problems which meant he would have to write another book:

I was very disappointed when I became aware of this. When writing one always dreams that it's the last time, but in fact it's not true. The questions raised and the objections made have forced me to go back to work, reasonably stimulated, either out of amusement or interest, and sometimes out of irritation. (1969g: 65 mod.)

As is evidenced by the rest of his career, Foucault never in fact reached a point where he was satisfied that he had said it all in a form that he was happy with. Thus, my second strategy is to emphasise those themes common to all of Foucault's work.

The third strategy, which is closely related to the second, is to focus on the methodological and philosophical structures of Foucault's work with a view to providing an understanding of the general principles Foucault applies to ordering his material. Readers might then glean some clues as to how they might apply Foucault's ideas themselves, without getting too bogged down in technical jargon and complex empirical details or the problems occasioned by his frequent shifts of emphasis. Fourthly, to minimise confusion, I shall be concentrating almost exclusively on Foucault's own work with only occasional references to other interpretations of his ideas. The secondary literature on Foucault is now overwhelming and an adequate treatment of it within the confines of this work would be impossible.

Cultural studies: History

Having somewhat lengthily set the parameters of my project, I would now like to turn to a more detailed explanation of my first strategy, namely the location of Foucault's work in relation to cultural studies. This immediately raises a number of particular problems quite different to those posed by dealing with his work in the context of well-established disciplines such as history, philosophy, sociology or specialised disciplines such as the history of science or the history of ideas. All disciplines, or as Foucault prefers to call them, 'discursive formations', have particular rules about how they 'form groups of objects, enunciations, concepts or theoretical choices' and include or exclude material (AK: 181). [9]

But if one can ask in relation to the more traditional disciplines, such as philosophy or history, how far Foucault's work either fits into or modifies their existing structures, one must ask different questions in relation to cultural studies. This is for two reasons. Firstly, cultural studies is a new academic discipline which did not even begin to become a significant force until after Foucault's death. The Centre for Cultural Studies at the University of Birmingham was indeed established in 1964 and published its first issue of Working Papers in 1972, but cultural studies in its present form did not start to emerge until well into the late 1970s and 1980s. Secondly, the examination of many current definitions, not to mention current applications, of cultural studies reveals the overwhelming influence of Foucault's thought on the very formulation of definitions, even if this is not spelled out directly or is derived second hand from other theorists. [10]

Stuart Hall, in his famous 1981 essay 'Cultural studies: Two paradigms', goes so far as to say that Foucault's work is in fact one of the primary foundations of British cultural studies and one could certainly argue the same for cultural studies in other countries including Australia, Canada and North America. Hall argues that 'Foucault and Gramsci between them account for much of the most productive work on concrete analysis now being undertaken in the field' (1981: 35). There are of course many other theoretical influences at work in the raging controversies over what cultural studies actually is or should be. It is still very much a discipline in the process of creating its own institutional form and structures.

If these questions about disciplinary definition appear unduly academic, as both Foucault and Bourdieu point out, such debates are in fact manifestations of a struggle for ownership over interpretations of the world (Bourdieu and Adamson, 1990: 143–4). Those who set the rules regulating truth and falsity, valid and invalid knowledge and ways of acquiring knowledge are in position to exercise considerable power. Again, this may seem a statement of the obvious and has certainly been repeated often enough, but it often seems to be forgotten by those grandstanding about truth and disciplinary rigour.

Foucault's reception in France

If one needs confirmation of these arguments and of the link between Foucault's work and the growing discipline of cultural studies, one need only turn to the issue of the current reception of Foucault's work in France and the English-speaking world. In English, to list a book by Foucault (usually *Discipline and Punish*) in one's bibliography, or to bandy around words such as 'discourse', 'power/knowledge', 'genealogy' or 'governmentality' is considered the *nec plus ultra* of academic style in trendy intellectual circles. The contrast with the current situation in France is extreme, although there are signs of a renewed interest in his work, marked by the 20th anniversary of his death in 2004.

By the end of the 1990s in France, Foucault had become a historical figure, just one of the distantly revered but neglected pantheon of a post-1960 generation of thinkers. There were few scholars applying his ideas, and his work was not studied at university or other tertiary institutions. Books about him, if continuing to appear in a slow trickle, were also relatively scarce in comparison with output in English. In France, those who had written university theses on his work had great trouble, in fact, they found it impossible to procure university jobs. Aspiring scholars complained that even to cite his works was to invite exclusion from the university career structure. In addition, if one consults that barometer of enthusiasms and trends, the internet, one also notes that the most important (and until recently the only) French website on Foucault, www.foucault. info, is a site which is predominantly in English. The choice of English as the language of the site reflects the recognition that most of Foucault's readership is English speaking.

Why this extraordinary difference? One factor is to do with the institutional politics relating to education. Up until 2002 the most recent author studied in the school philosophy program, which had remained relatively unchanged since 1973, was Sartre. This meant that more recent thought was not taught at tertiary level or set as a topic for preparation for the prestigious competitive exams which qualify teachers in France: the Agrégation and the CAPES. In the late 1990s resistance to newer thought remained strong and Luc Ferry, president of the National Curriculum Council and subsequent Minister for Education published a book putting forward a number of proposals in relation to government attempts to reform the teaching of philosophy in schools and universities. In this book, Foucault emerged as a regrettable ideologue of philosophical historicism, the product of a 'strangely distant era' (Ferry and Renaut, 1999: 37, 56). Foucault, Deleuze, Althusser, Lacan and other representatives of the so called 'thought of 68' were all signs of the decadence of contemporary philosophy. They were figures who marked 'an exhaustion, a disappearance of the grandiose' which could only be found in the great philosophers of the past such as Nietzsche, Heidegger, Marx or Freud, questionable as even these thinkers were, if one compares them to Plato, Descartes, Kant or Hegel (Ferry and Renaut, 1999: 281, 275).

In addition, after the post 1968 explosion of radicality that lasted until the 1980s, the French tertiary system arguably reverted to the well-tried traditions and strictures of the classical canon. University systems once again ossified into philosophy, history and literature departments. Traditional university historians and philosophers in France continued to reject Foucault's work as outside their canons of orthodoxy, although his work could still be found in the philosophy section of bookshops in France and continued to sell well. Unspoken disapproval surrounding Foucault's political and anarchist radicality, as well as his homosexuality, were also factors in this silence.

After intense political protest by philosophy teachers, Ferry was forced to accept a revised program for schools in 2002, which included Foucault's work (the suggestion of noted historian of science Michel Fichant) which of course also meant the introduction of the study of his work for the competitive teacher qualification examinations and its study at tertiary level. The public exam also included a new feature which replaced one of the general essays with a commentary on a text. This reinforced the candidates' need to engage with specific texts on the program. Apart from this, there are also some signs that with the changed global political situation, Foucault's wide adoption outside his country of origin is becoming a matter of pride, a symbol of the continuing presence of France on the world scene. There are now a number of smaller French web pages relating to his work – previously none had existed. 2004, the 20th anniversary of Foucault's death, marked the appearance of three books of previously unpublished work and a book containing a corrected version of an article (2004a) only available until then in incomplete form in an obscure journal. A previously unreleased book length interview was also dramatised for radio (1969i). Books were published about Foucault and a number of wide circulation journals and newspapers all featured special issues on his work in this anniversary year, notably *Le Point*, *Magazine Littéraire*, *Vacarme*, *Libération*, and *Le Monde*. The annual Festivale d'automne in Paris showcased his work with radio talks, art installations (by a German artist) and other presentations. 2004 also saw a small number of conferences on Foucault's work in France, but an examination of the lists of speakers at the most high profile of these revealed a preponderance of non-French presenters. It is early days yet and if there are a number of younger French scholars who are starting to swell the ranks of an existing but sparse field of Foucault studies, in general, French scholarship has not as yet had time to catch up with an industry that has been flourishing quite spectacularly elsewhere for some years. [11]

In the English-speaking world, the resounding success of cultural studies has created and maintained a space for the reception of Foucault's hard-to-classify work. Cultural studies has also provided an avenue for the dissemination of Foucault's work towards the applied disciplines and professional studies such as education, social work, health studies, business and architecture. Of course, the subject of precisely why cultural studies has become so popular in the English-speaking world would require a scparate study, which I do not have the space to embark on here. It is cultural studies departments and the cultural studies sections of sociology, history and literature departments that run courses on Foucault, not traditional philosophy departments. In addition to this, the politics of identity in the forms of feminism, postcolonialism and the gay and lesbian movements have achieved a far greater success in the Anglo-Saxon world than in France. These movements have used Foucault's work extensively as a theoretical basis for their own activities. Thus the fortunes of Foucault's work and those of cultural studies would seem to be indissolubly linked at a number of levels. Just how far cultural roles have been reversed in the last decades can be seen in a discussion with Foucault in 1979 while he was in the USA. The American interviewer asks Foucault to account for the fact that if his work was part of 'popular culture' in France, it was only known in 'academic circles' in the USA. Foucault replies by explaining that in France the university had been in crisis since 1964 and that there was a rebellion by students against the purely academic life, a movement which had affiliations with other movements such as feminism and gay rights. Academics had likewise rejected traditional academic life by publicising their ideas in the mass media (1979p: 298). It is only now in France that Foucault's work is beginning to take its place once again in the public arena and for the first time in the educational curriculum.

Cultural Studies: Definitions

At this point it might be useful to offer some further precisions concerning cultural studies. One can identify five major strands which adopt this disciplinary description. These strands simultaneously overlap and war with each other; there are considerable struggles over which group has most right to 'own' the label cultural studies. First of all, there is the strand instigated by the original Birmingham Centre for Cultural Studies which tends to use a framework heavily determined by classical sociological methodologies and Marxist ideology to examine subjects such as youth and popular subcultures. A second strand of cultural studies engages in more literary analysis of popular culture, everyday practices, film and media. This strand often tends to focus most closely on cultural 'representation' or the 'world as representation', or as Roger Chartier puts it, 'a world fashioned by means of the series of discourses that apprehend and structure experience' (Chartier, 1988: 11). Cultural history might also be included in this strand. A third strand could perhaps be described as the 'identity studies' school which focuses on analysing, creating and maintaining the identities of groups oppressed by the mainstream, in particular ethnic minorities, postcolonial cultures, women and homosexuals. [12] A fourth strand, the most recent, focuses on the analysis of institutions and policy in the way they produce and 'govern' cultural practices. Much of the work of this school uses Foucault's idea of 'governmentality'. In this context, many of the professional disciplines are finally beginning to discard the dusty empiricism and pseudo-Marxism that so often characterise their theoretical foundations and are looking to Foucault as a replacement theorist, generally in this 'governmental' incarnation. The fifth strand could perhaps best be described as encompassing 'cross-cultural studies' as well as anthropology. The object of analysis here is the comparative study of different national/cultural groups and their 'cultural practices' and institutions. This is the point at which the label cultural studies starts to become confusing and one would perhaps have to exclude studies in this area which are simply empirical, without any extended analysis of the effects of power, as most current definitions see the analysis of power as an essential part of the new discipline.

For all their differences these strands do have important things in common. The first of these is their general understanding of what culture is and second, that culture exists in an unavoidable relation with power. Traditional notions of 'culture' see it as a kind of icing on the cake of the more fundamental levels of the economic and social. This is still very much a current perception and cultural studies analysts are often perceived as dilettante purveyors of the frivolous in comparison to the 'serious' disciplines of economics, sociology or history. This, of course, is a Marxist or a materialist schema which perceives the economic as the fundamental infrastructure with culture and ideology as superstructures floating above this.

However, cultural studies is distinguished by the fact that it adopts a far more comprehensive view of the notion of culture. Foucault himself offers a useful definition which many cultural theorists might make their own. In 1967 he describes the task of the philosopher and by extension his own, as being to analyse the present 'cultural conjuncture'. 'Culture being understood here', he says 'in the widest sense, not only of the production of works of art, but also of political institutions, forms of social life, prohibitions and diverse constraints' (1967c: 582. Cf. HER: 173). Thus culture, in this sense, could be defined as the way a society constructs and organises knowledge about the world and social relations and defines particular behaviours and knowledges as either acceptable or unacceptable. Culture can be seen in the most mundane practices and material objects as well as in the products of high art and high culture. The experience of 'culture', of something that could be called the study of culture(s), lies at the very heart of Foucault's own work. It is a body of writing thoroughly permeated with the recognition of the strangeness, the non-naturalness of human cultural expression in all its forms. And it is this same general recognition – that nothing produced or perceived by humans at any level – conceptual, social or material – is 'natural' or self-evident; everything is fodder for analysis – that also underpins cultural studies as a discipline. Foucault himself, when asked in an interview published in Italian in 1967 to provide a disciplinary location for his work, remarked:

It is hard for me to classify a form of research like my own within philosophy or within the human sciences. I could define it as an analysis of the cultural facts characterising our culture ... I do in fact seek to place myself outside the culture to which we belong, to analyse its formal conditions in order to make a critique of it, not in the sense of reducing its values, but in order to see how it was actually constituted. (1967e: 91)

How exactly Foucault conducts his cultural analysis will be examined in later chapters.

End Notes

[1] The installation was on display from October 2004 to January 2005. For a review see Léfort, 2004.

[2] In this Avengers/Doctor Who crossover story, the Doctor and one of his companions, Mrs Jones, visit Paris in the 1960s. 'Mrs Jones got herself involved in various student uprisings. She came back to tell them that she's been throwing bricks into the barricades alongside none other than Michel Foucault. The Doctor gave her a hard stare' (Magrs, 1999: 333). Perhaps the Doctor and his companions were visiting a parallel universe as in real life Foucault was in Tunisia at the time.

[3] See 1971h and 1971q on Steiner. As well as taking Lawrence Stone to task for his misinterpretations of Madness and Civilization, Foucault also criticises Stone's assessment of the French historian Philippe Ariès. See 1983h and 1984i: 647.

[4] See Morris (1979) and the Michel Foucault resources website for additional examples of mistranslation. (www.michel-foucault.com)

[5] See, for example, 1962f which omits most of pages 209–10 of the version which appears in Dits et écrits (1962e). See also 1983b: 367 which omits a question and response crucial to the argument. See also 1971g. In this case the omission of the last third of the interview is all the more puzzling, as it originally appeared in English in Partisan Review (1971f).

[6] For examples of some of these far-flung applications see O'Farrell (1997).

[7] See for example, Carrette, 2000: 64; McNay, 1992: 9, 11–12; Mills, 2003: 123; Stoler, 1995: 93. Many feminist writers like Vikki Bell while cautiously acknowledging the usefulness of some of Foucault's ideas hasten to add that he 'was by no means a feminist writer' (1993: 4).

[8] Cf. Foucault, 1983g: 455–8; 1984c: 376.

[9] To be precise, Foucault argues that 'discursive formations' and disciplines are not entirely equivalent (AK: 178–9).

[10] Michael Meadows (1999: 44) for example, offers an extended definition, which even if it does not mention Foucault's name, includes such magic words as 'discursive', 'practices', 'articulation', and 'multiple sites of power' – all characteristic of Foucault's own terminology.

[11] For a confirmation of some of these observations concerning the reception of Foucault in France see Potte-Bonneville (2004). I would also like to thank Dominique Séglard for drawing my attention to information concerning the teaching of philosophy in France.

[12] See for example David Halperin's lively and readable account which boasts the immortal lines: 'So let me make it official. I may not have worshipped Foucault at the time I wrote One Hundred Years of Homosexuality but I do worship him now. As far as I'm concerned the guy was a fucking saint' (1995: 6).

TWO   Cultural Contexts

Foucault's life and death

Foucault's work is itself, of course, the product of his own life in a particular culture, intellectual context and time. Foucault's personal biography and the general social and intellectual backdrop to his work have been dealt with extensively in a number of books, notably in the three biographies of Foucault, in the excellent chronology in volume I of *Dits et écrits* (1994) and also in my own earlier work *Foucault: Historian or Philosopher?* (O'Farrell, 1989). But any introduction to Foucault's work needs to provide at least some account of his historical context in order to assist in providing some understanding of why he addressed particular sorts of problems in particular ways.

The question of Foucault's personal biography and its relation to his work is an especially interesting one for a number of reasons, and has been an issue of particular controversy since his death. Foucault was the first to admit that there was a close relation between the events of his personal life and his work, commenting that he had always seen his books as 'fragments of autobiography. My books have always been my personal problems with madness, the prison, sexuality' (1984t: 747–8). But for all that, he was notoriously reticent about discussing those links in a public forum. On numerous occasions he made it quite clear to interviewers that he was unwilling to provide details of his personal life, but he did relent slightly towards the end of his career, but then generally only in interviews and articles published outside of France. Even then he preferred to refer to well-defined concrete events rather than to the emotional or psychological aspects of his existence. However there are some very lengthy interviews which were not published during his lifetime where he is more forthcoming. One set of these interviews with Roger-Pol Droit was finally published towards the end of 2004 (Droit, 2004). Another series of interviews with Claude Bonnefoy (1969i), where he describes his interior life as a writer, was aired in dramatised form on radio in France in October 2004. In the latter series of interviews he describes his early difficulties with handwriting at school, and his discovery, during his three-year posting as cultural attaché in Sweden, that writing could be enjoyable (1968c: 651–2). It was during this time, he says, while he was obliged to speak in Swedish and English, neither of which he felt comfortable with, that he began to understand that his own language was not totally transparent and natural but had its own concrete existence and structure. His own language, French, became a refuge. Foucault explains that he built himself a kind of comfortable home out of writing and that it was at that point he began to discover a pleasure in writing. He already felt an outsider in terms of his homosexuality. As he explains:

> In my personal life, it happened that after the awakening of my sexuality, I felt excluded, not really rejected, but belonging to the shadows of society. All the same, it is a distressing problem when you discover it for yourself. Very quickly, it was transformed into a kind of psychiatric threat: if you are not like everybody else, then you are abnormal, you are sick. (2004c: 94–5)

But it was perhaps the profound cultural and language shock experienced in Sweden that persuaded Foucault to fix that experience in an ongoing way in writing and to extend his ideas of the non-naturalness of all human culture. As he remarked later during a visit to North America: 'The further I remove myself from my natural and habitual centres of gravity, the greater my chance of grasping the foundations I am obviously standing on ... It is always good for me to change language and country' (1971g: 73).

Foucault's love of intellectual pursuits in general can perhaps be traced back further to his childhood. In an interview originally published in English, he notes that while growing up in the difficult world of occupied France he came to see knowledge as a way of ordering and understanding the chaos of the exterior world and 'as a protection of individual existence' (1983l: 125). Writing for Foucault was a way of no longer having a face (AK: 17). He dreamt of being nothing more than what he wrote, fully aware that this was an impossible dream. But this desire for the self-protection and order that knowledge and writing could bring was also combined with a formidable curiosity and a willingness to test the limits of order. This can be seen in the story his mother tells of him as a small boy wanting to be a goldfish just to see what it was like, even though he absolutely loathed cold water (Macey, 1993: 14). Thus writing for Foucault was both a form of self-protection and a way of escaping from himself, so that he no longer had to remain identified with his own life or indeed even with his own past writings (1980e: 241–2). His reticence about his personal life was also a way of allowing readers the freedom to simply interact with a text rather than having it all tightly framed – 'explained' by the psychological persona of the 'author'. As Foucault says in his anonymous interview 'The Masked Philosopher':

> If I have chosen anonymity ... it's a way of addressing the potential reader, the only individual who is of interest to me, more directly: 'Since you don't know who I am, you will be more inclined to find out why I say what you read; just allow yourself to say, quite simply, it's true, it's false. I like it or I don't like it. Period'. (1980i: 323)

Besides a desire to preserve his own freedom and that of the reader, Foucault had a number of theoretical reasons for his position. The first of these was to do with his view that no one system of order could be used to explain another and that accepted categories of organising knowledge should all be questioned. In this instance, the psychological entity designated as the 'author' did not operate according to the same rules as the text produced by that author. This separation of author and text is also closely related to Foucault's criticism of traditional notions of the 'subject' by which he means an entity which is the irreducible source of truth and authenticity from which all action and knowledge proceed. This does not mean, as Foucault responds dryly to outraged critics who took him to task for declaring the death of the author and the death of man, that all authors should be thrown into prison and that the human race is dying out (1969i: 145), rather, it is a matter of calling into question accepted categories for organising knowledge. Finally, and this was to emerge more particularly in Foucault's later work, confessing the details of one's own life means that one is more susceptible to being ensnared in and manipulated by networks of power (HS: 59–63). The complexities of these notions of freedom, the subject and power will be dealt with in more detail in later chapters. Suffice it to say at this point that these discussions in Foucault's work have made things rather difficult for the biographers who have all alluded at some length to the problem. But perhaps the fact that there have been no less than three biographies since Foucault's death (and a sequel to one of them) indicates that biographers see their subject's reservations more as a challenge than as an insurmountable obstacle.

Didier Eribon's biography of Foucault was the first to appear in French in 1991 and has been extensively translated. A competent and useful account, it has nonetheless been criticised in some quarters for being overly respectful and for providing merely a superficial treatment of Foucault's work, but as Eribon explains, he is writing a biography not a critique of Foucault's work. David Macey's 1993 biography *The Lives of Michel Foucault* provides a comprehensive yet at times strangely bland account of Foucault's life and times placing him in his intellectual and social context in France. As an overview and source of information on Foucault's work, life and intellectual setting it is an invaluable text.

However, by far the most notorious biography of Foucault and the one that has excited the most controversy is James Miller's *The Passion of Michel Foucault* (1993). Well publicised even before its appearance on bookshop shelves, this biography is more a reflection of the social pre-occupations of the early 1990s than of Foucault's work. Miller in the dramatic prose of investigative journalism exposes Foucault's alleged obsession with death and self-destruction which he claims is clearly evidenced by his treatment of the subject matter in *Birth of the Clinic* in particular. He also makes much of Foucault's homosexuality and experiments with drugs and S/M.

Miller also publicly airs a rumour that the philosopher, knowing he was dying of AIDS, deliberately infected his partners in Californian bath-houses in the early 1980s. The context and details of Foucault's death from AIDS are extremely controversial and have been the subject of widespread discussion in several languages. Miller's biography has been widely criticised by experts on Foucault's work as well as by those who knew him personally. In particular, Didier Eribon, takes strong exception to Miller's approach in an interesting sequel to his first biography titled *Michel Foucault et ses contemporains* (1994). Eribon also makes the pertinent observation that the debates around Foucault's biography all seemed to boil down to one issue: how to write a biography of a philosopher who was also homosexual (1994: 11). It is a controversy that refuses to die – its most recent incarnation being in *The Times Literary Supplement* at the end of 2001. Raymond Tallis claimed in a review that 'Foucault, as every schoolchild knows, denied that there were such things as objective truths' (2001: 3), going on to suggest that Foucault had knowingly and deliberately spread AIDS. Strong exception to both statements was taken by a number of correspondents in the letters to the editor section over the two months following this review. Given the seemingly perennial nature of such discussions, it is worth pausing to look a bit more closely at the allegations surrounding Foucault's death.

Even Miller has to admit that he believes the rumour about Foucault's alleged behaviour to be 'essentially false' (Miller, 1993: 375). One of the further problems with Miller's interpretation is that it provides a some-what anachronistic reading of events. One might draw attention, for instance, to the fact that a reliable test for AIDS was not available in France until the Spring of 1984 and if Foucault may have indeed suspected that he had the disease, no positive diagnosis of his condition was ever made by doctors. As Macey, a more reliable biographer of Foucault remarks: 'Days before his death, his doctors were still saying: "If it's AIDS"' (1993: 475).

Neither were doctors in a position in the early 1980s to offer much useful advice on the subject of HIV/AIDS or on safe sex. It is certainly true that many gay men, including Foucault, expressed initial disbelief in the existence of a disease that specifically targeted gay men, seeing this as yet another ploy by the medical establishment to exercise social control. But as Michael Bartos points out in a well-informed article on the evolution of AIDS in relation to public health policies and the gay community, this attitude changed as firmer medical evidence came to the fore. And as Bartos further notes these kind of controversies fall into well-worn patterns:

> [T]he accusation that an HIV infected person deliberately sought to infect others through anonymous sex is one of the most common tropes of the epidemic ... The rumour that Foucault had gone to American bath-houses to deliberately spread HIV should be seen for what it is: a commonplace of the demonisation of people with HIV and an iteration of the standard myths of the malevolent importation of HIV/AIDS. (1997: 687–8)

Those who knew Foucault also argue that his rumoured behaviour is simply not consistent with his other views on social and political responsibility. Far from limiting himself to writing, he worked hard at the most practical organisational level on committees advocating the rights of prisoners, immigrants and the politically oppressed in countries such as Tunisia, Spain and Poland, and on occasions put himself at some physical risk in doing so (Macey, 1993: 204–5).

Thus for all Foucault's theoretical insistence on the idea that the work of an author cannot be explained simply in terms of his or her personal life or psychology, he was unable to escape this fate himself, but as he points out in his well-known article 'What is an author?', if the author function is definitely changing in contemporary society, it hasn't quite disappeared yet. As he argues, the category of the author is a way of limiting what can and cannot be said and organising the huge field of available discourses into manageable portions for general consumption (1969h: 221). The confusion between the order of the text and the order of the author's psychological persona has yet to be resolved in the critical or popular consciousness, and Foucault is just one more addition to a long line of thinkers who have been the subject of heated controversy over whether their personal life disqualifies their intellectual work. As another example, at regular intervals of every ten years or so, the more serious issue of the German philosopher Martin Heidegger's affiliation with Nazism and the implications that this has for the acceptance of his thought becomes the subject of discussion in French newspapers and journals. The theme of Foucault as a scandalous homosexual with a penchant for whips, chains and leather continues to be perpetuated in such texts as Horrocks and Jevtic's *Foucault for Beginners* (1997), on the principle perhaps that the only way to interest contemporary students in the intellectual content of his work is through a liberal smattering of sex and scandal, four letter words and racy cartoons.

Foucault's social and historical context

P ersonal and psychological issues of biography aside, it must not be forgotten that Foucault produced his work in a quite specific historical and social setting. One of the features of modern Western thought since the end of the eighteenth century and since the Enlightenment, has been its tendency to think in terms of revolution and progress. No new progressivist movement in philosophy, art or politics was worth its salt unless it relegated all that went before to the scorned and dusty recesses of history. This cultural necessity, indeed capacity, to shock, to completely discard the old, to transgress social and cultural taboos has lost its force in recent years, but when Foucault started writing in the 1950s, it was still very much on the agenda of any radical intellectual or artist seeking to make a name. Neither was it simply a purely technical exercise in name-building. The reality of post-war France was one of rapid change on a multitude of fronts – technological, social, political, intellectual and cultural – and a number of intellectuals who started writing in the 1950s and 1960s felt that older styles of thought were simply no longer adequate to the task. As Foucault notes in an interview in 1980:

> The experience of war had shown us the urgent need of a society radically different from the one in which we were living, this society that had permitted Nazism that had lain down in front of it ... A large sector of French youth had a reaction of total disgust toward all that. We wanted a world and a society that were not only different but that would be an alternative version of ourselves: we wanted to be completely other in a completely different world. (1980e: 247–8)

Foucault goes on to say that this same generation rejected the view of history as the triumphal march of progress and reason and likewise rejected phenomenology and existentialism which tied experience to a universal and unchanging subject.

Post-war humanist thought

A fter World War II, there were a number of schools of thought in France, all of which could be roughly grouped under the umbrella of 'humanism'. These schools of thought were made up of both left and right-wing intellectuals and Catholic and atheist intellectuals who subscribed to a variety of philosophies and political ideologies, including phenomenology, Marxism and existentialism and Gaullism (a form of right-wing political thought). It was this general movement of humanist thought which was called into question by Foucault and a number of others designated by the media as 'structuralists'. The main assumptions of post-war humanism thought ran as follows: First of all, there was a thing called 'human nature' which determined how people existed and acted in the world. This 'human nature' which, depending on your point of view, was either God-given or a natural biological occurrence, remained essentially the same throughout history and was something that could be gradually discovered and defined via science at the empirical objective level, or through philosophical introspection at the personal subjective level. The weaknesses of human nature could be addressed and eventually eliminated via the use of science – although a number of humanist thinkers, including Jean-Paul Sartre, demonstrated a very ambivalent attitude towards science which they saw as existing in a fundamental dehumanising opposition to art, philosophy and human creativity. If there was very broad agreement on certain general principles, different schools of thought had vastly different takes on how humanism might be enacted.

Phenomenology, originally represented by Edmund Husserl and Maurice Merleau-Ponty, and then taken up by many others, argued that it was through the meticulous examination of everyday lived experience that we could discover the truth about ourselves as human beings and the 'meaning' of the world. This philosophy is still flourishing today, forming notably the basis of ethnomethodological methods in the social sciences. These methods are premised on the idea that if one observes a sufficient number of people in their everyday work or domestic settings and examines their subjective experiences within these settings, then one can discover the truth about how humans live and act in the world. Once enough data has been accumulated, then one day, science will eventually be able to form a complete picture of human nature and make valid predictions on that basis. Existentialism, as represented by Sartre, who borrowed and modified the ideas of German philosophers Husserl and Martin Heidegger, argued that we are thrown into the world and abandoned to our fate. It is through our decisions about how to act that we create ourselves as viable human beings, but this must still be in accordance with an authentic core of humanity (even if this remains undefined), otherwise we are acting in 'bad faith', deceiving ourselves about who and what we really are.

Another strand of thought, humanist Marxism (in line with Karl Marx's original ideas) argued that the essence of man was work. Human nature was defined by human beings' need and desire to work. A large section of the population, however, was alienated from the product of its own labour, or to put it another way, the working classes slaved to produce goods that the ruling classes then appropriated as their own. The only way to restore things to their proper natural order, to reunite humans with their real nature, was via revolution, which would produce a Communist society where everyone owned goods in common and no-one was alienated from the products of their own labour. Catholic and Protestant forms of humanism argued that God had created human nature and that human nature had become flawed as the result of original sin. It was our task both to face the depths of our depravity and allow God to redeem that fallen human nature. On the subject of religion, it is now often forgotten what a large influence both religious institutions and religious forms of thought exerted in intellectual life in general before the 1970s. In the contemporary era religion as a viable intellectual force has been largely discredited in the Western world.

None of these forms of thought existed in isolation and there were many hybrid forms, such as Catholic existential Marxism. These ideas were also linked in complex ways with historical, political and social events in Europe. Also, of course, looming large as a backdrop in the late 1940s and 1950s was the general aftermath of World War II and the Nazi occupation of France. The Communist Party which had aided in the resistance (at least during the later years of the war) gained much prestige as a result of its stance. It attracted members of the working class and also intellectuals who felt guilty about their middle-class privileges. The Absurdist movement, a literary movement which included such writers as Nobel laureate Albert Camus, argued that existence was absurd – who could make sense of the horrific results of the war? If Sartre argued on the contrary, that everything no matter how absurd had a meaning, this meaning had to be found and created in the face of dreadful odds whilst the searcher was overwhelmed by the nausea induced by confrontation with the void. Phenomenology suggested that the only way to deal with the massive dislocation and destruction caused by the war was to focus on the miniscule events of the everyday in one's own local setting.

Structuralism

Towards the end of the 1950s, things began to change. As Europe started to rebuild, an optimism regarding the technological achievements of science began to come to the fore. At the same time there arose an awareness of the dangers of new forms of social regulation, via the subtle and complex intertwining of mechanisms of scientific technology, bureaucracy and various forms of social education. It was at this point that a movement described as 'structuralism' by the media and spearheaded in France by the anthropologist Claude Lévi-Strauss began to emerge.

What structuralism rejected was the whole notion of an unchanging and universal human subject or human nature as being at the centre and origin of all action, history, existence and meaning. Styles of thought characterised as structuralist were also notable for the fact that they adopted linguistics – in the form developed by the noted Swiss linguist Ferdinand de Saussure who died in 1913 – as a methodological model, and applied it to a very diverse range of disciplines. Practitioners of structural linguistics, instead of examining language in terms of speaking subjects or groups, studied the internal organisation and structure of language. They also argued that meanings were determined by the relations that existed between different elements, not located within those elements themselves. In the place of research centred around an unchanging and introspective human subject, the structuralists advocated the exploration of the unconscious structures underlying culture, knowledge, society and language – in short the structures underlying all human endeavour. They examined structures of cultural production without linking them back to a central human agency or to individual psyches, to consciousness or to individual lived experiences of existence.

So, for example, the literary critic Roland Barthes, instead of analysing literature in terms of the psychology of the author and his or her intentions and personal biography, looked at how the work itself was structured. Psychoanalyst Jacques Lacan argued that the unconscious was structured like a language, Claude Lévi-Strauss posited that it was not people who dreamt up myths, but rather it was the myths that structure the way people think and act. Marxist thinker, Louis Althusser suggested along similar lines, that it was not people who made history, but that history was a process that people simply acted out. Literary analysts and writers who belonged to the 'New Novel' movement such as Alain Robbe-Grillet, claimed that the author was not at the centre of his or her own creation, but was simply the conduit of a language that already bore its own meanings and structures. Thus structuralism in general shied away from the kind of ontological speculations about consciousness and existence that had been the focus of phenomenological and existential thought. It was no surprise therefore that humanist thinkers protested long and loudly at the ideas put forward by these new thinkers, characterising them as inhuman and abstract.

But one of these new thinkers, Foucault, in an impassioned defence of the new movement, countered that it was in fact the older forms of thought that were deficient on this front:

It is humanism that is abstract! It is all these cries from the heart, all these claims concerning the human person and existence that are abstract: that is, cut off from the scientific and technical world which is actually our real world ... Well, the current effort being made by people of our generation, is not to set up man *against* science and *against* technology, but precisely to show that our thought, our life, our way of being, right down to our most everyday way of being, are a part of the same systematic organization, and thus emerge from the *same* categories as the scientific and technical world. It is the 'human heart' which is abstract, and it is our research which seeks to link man to his science, to his discoveries, to his world, which is concrete. (1966d: 517–18)

This view of the undue abstraction of phenomenological and existential forms of thought is one Foucault maintained throughout his career. In an interview conducted in 1983, he says (while conceding that he is perhaps being somewhat harsh) that even if phenomenology claimed to be dealing with the concrete, this concrete domain tended to be 'a bit academic and university-oriented ... the perception of a tree through an office window' (1988d: 408).

Much has been made of Foucault's protests that he was not a structuralist, but up until the late 1960s, he was quite willing to identify himself with the movement. He also provided some definitions of structuralism that were to all intents and purposes simply descriptions of his own work – as evidenced by the statement above for example. He pointed out, however, that the label 'structuralism' was generally a label used by those who opposed these ideas, adding 'you must ask Sartre who the structuralists are, since he thinks that Lévi-Strauss, Althusser, Derrida, Lacan and me constitute a coherent group, a group constituting some kind of unity that we ourselves don't perceive' (1968d: 53). He admits however that this is a 'rather common phenomenon' and the existentialists themselves suffered from the same kind of reductive labelling (1968c: 653).

Most of Foucault's positive remarks in relation to structuralism occur in interviews or lectures originally conducted outside of France, where Foucault felt he did not have to oppose media misconceptions. The persistence in English of the idea that Foucault was completely opposed to structuralism is also no doubt perpetuated by the fact that most of his extended and positive treatments of the movement have not as yet been translated. For all his later insistence that he was not a structuralist (Foucault did not like being labelled – he felt it tied him down and confined his thought within a limited set of parameters), he offered a number of excellent definitions and historical accounts of the movement (Cf. 1968c: 653). There is no doubt that Foucault was, and in fact, always remained, closely aligned to the structuralist movement, if we define 'structuralism' as a movement focused on the examination of the relations between things and their structures at every level of culture and knowledge, as opposed to attempts to describe things in their essence.

But, where he parted company with the structuralists, and one of the major reasons for his insistence that he was not associated with the movement, was his rejection of the ahistorical formalism often adopted by those espousing structuralist method. If many practising this method in literary studies, linguistics and other social sciences were seeking to discover formal structures which they could then apply as templates to a variety of situations, Foucault was only interested in describing orders as they already existed and had already occurred in quite specific historical situations. He was not interested in deducing and applying a universal order, structure or formal logic.

Just as existentialism and phenomenology had flirted with the political ideology of Marxism, so too did certain forms of structuralist thought. The 1960s also saw a growing global interest in the status of socially disadvantaged groups – women, ethnic minorities, mad people, prisoners, homosexuals and others. The events of May 1968 in France, with major student uprisings, a general strike and the subsequent fall of the government, marked the explosion on to the scene of the 'political' and a general awareness and criticism of the oppressive and unjust excesses of the mainstream 'establishment'. 1968 also saw other student uprisings on a global scale: in Tunisia, Japan, Poland, Germany, the USA and Mexico. It was a year that marked the beginning of over a decade of general social contestation and the politicisation of intellectuals, workers, students and a variety of socially disadvantaged groups.

The events of 1968 also marked the beginning of the decline of structuralism in France with the radical politicisation of many intellectuals, including Foucault. Foucault was living in Tunisia in 1968 and it was his experiences of the very real physical risks taken by students during uprisings in March of that year and the risks he himself took to support their cause that convinced him to adopt a more politically engaged stance. He notes in an interview originally conducted in 1975, that in March 1968 he witnessed a student strike 'which literally bathed the university in blood', with students being badly beaten (2004c: 120). When he returned to France at the end of that year he was determined to try and do things that 'required a personal, physical, and real involvement, things that would address problems in concrete, precise and definite terms in a given situation' (1980e: 281).

Social activism and the 1970s

In the 1970s, Foucault appeared at the forefront of militant and intellectual activity in France drawing attention to social injustice. In particular, he supported groups which advocated better conditions for prisoners, health workers, immigrants and inmates of asylums. His work with the Groupe d'Information sur les Prisons (GIP) which sought to draw attention to conditions in prisons and his history of the prison, *Discipline and Punish*, attracted a great deal of attention. The analysis of 'power' replaced structuralism in France as the focus of media attention in the intellectual arena.

The 1970s also saw the rise of extreme left-wing terrorism in Europe, a history often forgotten in the wake of the terrorist attacks on New York and the Pentagon in September 2001. Groups such as the Red Brigade in Italy, the Baader Meinhoff group in Germany, and other terrorist groups such as the IRA and the UDF in Northern Ireland and the Basque separatists in Spain and France all made their presence felt. In France, the Maoists, notably under the auspices of a group known as the Gauche Prolétarienne, seemed initially groomed to occupy this role, but somehow France managed to avoid, for the most part, the bloody excesses of left-wing terrorism. There was much discussion in France at the time as to why this was the case, with some arguing that it was the moderating influence of intellectuals such as Foucault, amongst other factors, that had saved French leftism from travelling down this route. As Thierry Pfister (1981: 400), the author of an article titled 'What has protected France from terrorism' observed in 1980, although a number of intellectuals 'admitted to the legitimacy of the revolt expressed by the extreme revolutionary left, they contributed at the same time towards moderating its expression'. He cites Maurice Clavel (a well-known journalist and essayist) and Michel Foucault, in particular, as expressing 'numerous reservations', especially when it came to death threats against people accused of being police informants and other forms of incitation to violence.

Nonetheless, in the early 1970s, Foucault willingly advocated somewhat dubious notions of spontaneous and unregulated 'popular justice', but after incidents involving violence committed by people who had attended meetings at which Foucault had been present, and after discussions with friends, he changed his position. Claude Mauriac, the novelist and journalist who was also involved in many of the same militant activities as Foucault, reports that at a particular meeting in 1975: 'When it was a question of "popular violence" (against fascist violence), I remained silent. Daniel Defert laughed. He said, "You'll come around ...". I said, "No, never, I don't think so." And Michel solemnly, "You made me change position on this subject. That is a great achievement on your part"' (Mauriac, 1976: 576). [1] Eribon notes that the friendship between Foucault and fellow French philosopher Gilles Deleuze probably ended over the question of terrorism. He draws attention to a passage in Mauriac's journal where Foucault observes in relation to a person Mauriac designates as 'X' (Eribon, 1991: 260): 'We don't see each other any more ... not since Klaus

Croissant ... It's quite simply that I couldn't accept terrorism and blood and I didn't approve of Baader and his gang ...' (Mauriac, 1986: 388).

A number of young radical Maoist intellectuals were also later to become well-known in the late 1970s for their anti-Marxist position and their criticisms of the repressive regimes of Communist states. These intellectuals, dubbed 'the new philosophers' by the press, made an appearance on the cover of *Time* magazine in 1977 with the caption 'Marx is dead' and were, at least initially, supported by Foucault in the form of a positive review of André Glucksmann's work (1977q). Very quickly however, the 'new philosophers' came under attack from other intellectuals for being far too cavalier in their research and also for being far too light-weight on the intellectual front.

The 1980s

I n the late 1970s and the early 1980s interest in the work of Foucault and other French thinkers was starting to grow outside France, particularly in the English language world. Foucault made a number of trips to North America, to deliver lectures and discuss his work with other intellectuals. There was also considerable interest at the beginning of the 1980s in the work of members of the Frankfurt School, and its most recent major representative Jürgen Habermas, with a particular focus on their ideas on 'rationality'. Foucault alluded to their works on a number of occasions in the 1980s, particularly in response to interview questions.

In the early 1980s Foucault also surprised those who followed his work by turning his attention to the early Christians, the Ancient Greeks and to ethics and notions of the self and the subject in his lectures with publications starting to appear on these subjects in 1982. The beginnings of an interest in these areas had already become apparent in his 1978 lectures in an extended discussion on pastoral power and forms of conduct (STP: 119-232). In 1982 he declared: 'It is not power, but the subject, that is the general theme of my research' while at the same time admitting, with somewhat notable understatement, that 'it is true that I became quite involved with the question of power' (1982b: 327). This change of interest provoked a number of commentators to argue that Foucault had lost the plot, abandoned the good fight and retreated into an academic and apolitical quietism. It is a point of view that still persists widely in contemporary criticism. The reality of the situation was in fact that Foucault remained closely involved in various practical activities in support of those suffering from political and social oppression. For instance, he was treasurer for the international branch of the trade union movement Solidarity which was opposed to the military dictatorship in Poland. He visited the country and was interviewed on a number of occasions both in the press and on television about events there. On a lower key, after a serious terrorist attack on a well-known Jewish restaurant in Paris in 1982, Foucault dined there as often as possible 'as a sign of resistance to terrorism' (DE I: 61). He was also involved in other activities involving human rights and refugees, notably in relation with the plight of the boat people. But leaving aside now this brief account of the social and political context of Foucault's work and his participation in that context, we will turn to focus more directly on his writings in the next chapter.

End Note

[1] For detailed accounts of Foucault's militant activities during these years see Mauriac, 1976; Macey, 1993: 290–322; Eribon, 1991: 238–62. For a different perspective and somewhat contentious take on these years, see Miller, 1993: 203–7.

THREE   Foucault's Major Works

In keeping with the introductory mission of this book, this chapter will provide a series of short summaries of Foucault's major works. The descriptions will be fairly brief and the detail of Foucault's ideas will be expanded on more fully in later chapters. Once again we are faced with a series of complex problems. If, as we have already seen, the category of the 'author' is far from being straightforward, the category of the author's 'work' also generates a number of significant difficulties.

In the first chapter of his methodological work *The Archaeology of Knowledge*, Foucault begins by questioning the various categories that are commonly used to organise written material, namely the author, the 'work' and the book. These categories might appear to be obvious, but on closer examination, this is far from being the case. For instance, are a novel, a mathematical text book, or a road map all the same kind of object? Can we simply lump together texts which have been published by an author under his own name, under a pseudonym, or his collected works published after his death, his laundry lists or his insane jottings after he has gone completely mad? By drawing attention to these kinds of uncertainties and the fluidity of categorisation, Foucault aims to demonstrate that the categories we take for granted could quite well be replaced by others based on different organisational principles and assumptions.

As a number of commentators have observed, these kinds of considerations are particularly pertinent to Foucault's own work. Foucault has written anonymous and pseudonymous texts (1980i; 1984g) and there have been protracted battles over the status and publication of the typescripts and audiotapes of his lectures and other material. Seven books of these lectures have appeared to date with more to come. What is their status in the canon of 'books by Foucault'? There are also novelised accounts of things Foucault may or may not have said. In what sense is Foucault the 'author' of these statements? In addition to this, three pieces which originally appeared as articles have also been published as short books in French. [1] Are we to describe these works as books or articles? Further complications emerge in English in relation to the category of the book. For example, 'The orders of discourse', which was originally a lecture, was published in French as a book, but in English has only ever been published as an article and as an appendix to the first edition of *The Archaeology of Knowledge*. The first translation of this work into English also contained serious errors and omissions which were rectified in a subsequent translation.

With the publication of his lectures which began in 1997, another unexpected problem arises. If the material in *Dits et écrits*, which was published in 1994, can be slotted into a chronological account of his production fairly easily, the lectures often provide unexpected and different kinds of material which have not as yet been assimilated into the general reception of Foucault's work. This poses the dilemma of whether one should deal with the lectures chronologically alongside Foucault's other production, or after that work in the order of publication. Nit-picking as some of these examples may seem, they are perfect illustrations of Foucault's point about the dangers of taking particular ways of ordering knowledge and texts for granted. It is bearing these problems in mind that I now offer brief summaries of Foucault's most recognised works.

Dream, imagination and existence (1954)

Foucault's first publication, 'Dream, imagination and existence' (1954), if not one of his better known texts, is worthy of inclusion by virtue of it being his first. Unfortunately, it is by no means an easy read and only the most valiant of scholars have persisted with it. It was published in 1954 as an introduction to the German psychologist's Ludwig Binswanger's essay *Dream and Existence*. Foucault's text was almost twice the length of the main text, and as he freely admitted, bore only a marginal resemblance to the material it was introducing (1954: 33). Essentially it offered a brief history of Western dream interpretation and an analysis of the image and the imagination in Western history. Interestingly, Foucault's last publication before his death, Volume 3 of *The History of Sexuality: The Care of the Self*, included a lengthy opening section on Ancient Greek dream interpretation. He had come full circle.

Although the influences of phenomenology and existentialism are clear in this text, already certain themes and structures characteristic of all of Foucault's work are in evidence. For instance, we can already see his view that the best way of understanding human existence and experience as well as notions of truth and order, is through a reflection on the concrete events of history whether these events are physical, cultural or at the level of ideas or psychology. But at the same time, he is interested in where the orders of history break down – the margins and limits of orderly experience. It is dreams which signal that point where people become aware that everyday orderly existence is not all there is. Foucault writes: 'Man has known since Antiquity, that in dreams he encounters what he is and what he will be, what he has done and what he is going to do, discovering there the knot that ties his freedom to the necessity of the world' (1954: 47). This piece is also notable for its scathing attack on Freud's reduction of dreams to a mere pathology. In Freud's work, Foucault argues, dreams become no more than a set of symptoms – no longer the sign of another world. Throughout his career Foucault was to remain consistently hostile to any attempts to reduce historical complexity to one term, to one foundation, or to one explanation. He also remained opposed to attempts to silence alternative versions of accessing the truth.

Mental Illness and Psychology (1954)

It is with some relief that one leaves the arcane intricacies of 'Dream, imagination and existence' to turn to Foucault's first book which also appeared in the same year, 1954. This small volume was commissioned by the Presses Universitaire de France and titled *Maladie Mentale et personnalité*. It subsequently reappeared in a new edition and retitled in 1962 as *Mental Illness and Psychology* (MIP). In this book, Foucault examines how it is that madness comes to be defined as an illness. He argues that organic pathology and mental pathology form two separate orders and the attempt to reduce them to the same thing poses a number of significant problems. He briefly examines the social functioning of madness in non-Western societies, and offers a historical account from the Middle Ages to the present of the Western view of madness. He also addresses the relation between madness and truth in Western history. The characterisation of madness as 'mental illness' is a phenomenon, he says, that dates only from the nineteenth century. In many ways *Mental Illness and Psychology* provides a very useful potted summary of Foucault's much longer and more elaborate work on madness published in 1961.

Madness and Civilization (1961)

Foucault wrote *Madness and Civilization* (MC), his first major work, while he was posted in Sweden and presented it for a *doctorat d'état* in France. A full translation is only due to be published in English in 2005 – the existing translation being of the abridged French version with some additions. In this enormous and complex volume which comes to some 690 pages in the original French, Foucault examines the ways in which a certain experience of the limits of human experience – namely madness – has been given cultural form from the thirteenth century to the beginning of the nineteenth century in European history. He deals with the economic, institutional, medical, philosophical, ethical, political, literary and artistic practices which have helped define madness as a cultural and social category and also as an object of knowledge and science.

Foucault argues that during the Middle Ages and Renaissance, madness formed a kind of general conduit for what he terms the 'tragic experience' (MC: 31) – namely an awareness of death, truth, other realms and the general fragility of ordinary everyday life. People who were mad were as a consequence granted a kind of grudging respect. However, this was to change in the seventeenth century with what Foucault terms the 'Great Confinement', a movement across Europe which saw the establishment of institutions which locked up people who were deemed to be 'unreasonable'. This not only included mad people, but the unemployed, single mothers, defrocked priests, failed suicides, heretics, prostitutes, debauchees – in short anyone who was deemed to be socially unproductive or disruptive.

Foucault nominates 1656, the date of the decree which founded the Hôpital Général in Paris, as a symbolic landmark date to indicate this general movement of confinement. He then traces the gradual separation of mad people from other 'unreasonable' populations and the final emergence of madness as an object of science towards the end of the eighteenth century. By this stage, madness is no longer a voice reminding all people of the frailty of human existence, but is the silent object of medical science shut away and invisible in institutions. No longer madness, but mental illness. In Foucault's account, if the avowed aim of psychiatrists and others was to render the treatment of mad people more humane, in removing the physical chains, they merely substituted the far more insidious chains of science and moral training.

Foucault commented, on several occasions throughout his career, on how disappointed he was by the initial reception of this work, although one might argue that the lack of critical quantity was more than made up for by the critical quality. Literary critics Roland Barthes, Maurice Blanchot, historians Fernand Braudel, Philippe Ariès and philosophers of science Georges Canguilhem and Michel Serres all viewed the book with favour. But after a slow start, by the end of the 1960s, sales of the book had increased dramatically. This can be attributed to a number of factors: Foucault's best selling status with *The Order of Things* in 1966; his reputation as one of the leaders of the trendy new 'structuralist' movement; and the success of the anti-psychiatry movement, as well as a general growth of interest in marginal groups and experiences. The book was also met with outrage by traditional psychiatrists with an entire conference being convened in 1969 to denounce its pernicious effects. [2] Foucault put this anger down to the unwillingness of certain 'soft' sciences to face their less than glorious pasts. *Madness and Civilization* has now become a standard (if still controversial) text in the history of psychiatry and the notion of the 'Great Confinement' has found wide application in a number of historical treatments dealing with the seventeenth century.

The Birth of the Clinic (1963)

In 1963 Foucault published two books: firstly a history of French clinical medicine and secondly an essay on the obscure French surrealist writer Raymond Roussel. As Foucault remarked later in his career, *Raymond Roussel* (RR) is a highly personal book. It deals with his then current obsessions with representation, the arbitrary nature of the links between words and things, and also with the experience of that limit which is death. Indeed, some have argued (with good cause) that this book is personal to the point of total obscurity. Like many of Foucault's other writings on literature in the 1960s, it is more notable for its poetic rather than its explanatory value. The same themes emerge in *The Birth of the Clinic* (BC) and if this book on the whole lacks the gothic attractions of *Madness and Civilisation*, opting for a more restrained approach (notwithstanding a few notable literary outbursts), it has also become a standard text in the history of medicine.

The Birth of the Clinic traces the origins of modern clinical medicine in France at the end of the eighteenth century during the period 1769–1825. Traditional histories of medicine have argued that at this time dubious medical practices based on superstition, magic and a blind reliance on ancient texts were replaced by an enlightened empirical science based on the observation of the real world and data to hand. Foucault, however, provides a different account. What changed, he says, was both how illness and how the doctor were defined and how these two terms were related. It was not that the new doctor suddenly saw what had been invisible to those blinded by superstition and an over reliance on ancient texts, rather, the new doctor started looking in a different way at a differently constructed object of scientific knowledge, namely illness.

If, in *Madness and Civilization*, Foucault focuses primarily on the changes in the way a particular object (madness) is historically constructed, in *The Birth of the Clinic*, he also focuses in addition on the way knowers (that is doctors) are constructed. He traces this transformation by examining medical theories and practices as well as political, institutional and social changes in Revolutionary France. As he does in *Madness and*

Civilization, he accompanies his account with frequent references to works of art and literature. Later, in an interview conducted in 1975, Foucault claimed that these literary allusions were more decorative than argumentative (1986a: 150), but this did not prevent him from elevating literature in his early work to a place of honour as an alternative conduit to truth in modern culture and thought.

In parallel to his examination of the formation of medical knowledge, Foucault also looks at the political, social and institutional changes which occurred at the same time. It is important to emphasise that in Foucault's analysis it is not a question of one set of changes 'influencing' or 'causing' others, but of a complex series of interactions which allow the production of possible objects of knowledge. For example, although institutional and funding structures might favour the development of a particular type of research, these structures in themselves do not determine the eventual research findings. The political and economic situation in France at the end of the eighteenth century produced a radical change in the general social and political status of medicine. From being ' "The dry and sorry analysis of millions of infirmities" the dubious negation of the negative' (BC: 34) medicine became linked to the positive political task of establishing a population and a nation State, healthy and productive in mind, body and behaviour. These were themes that Foucault was to develop at length in his work during the 1970s.

In addition to his discussion of the transformation of medical knowledge and of social, political and economic factors, Foucault draws attention to the limits of human experience and knowledge. If in *Madness and Civilization* madness had been tamed and stripped of its capacity to point to another world, and to extreme experience and to truth, the same fate is in store for 'death' in *The Birth of the Clinic*. Death, in Foucault's account, became the foundation of the new medical science and of the human sciences. If human bodies were of only vague amorphous interest while they were alive, when they died and were dissected, each body became individualised, an object of scientific interest and knowledge. Death, instead of marking the end and limits of illness and life, became the instrument of understanding life itself. Foucault notes poetically: 'Death left its old tragic heaven and became the lyrical core of man: his invisible truth, his visible secret' (BC: 172). Illness is a disorder, a dangerous limit to everyday orderly existence. Science attempts to deal with this disorder by making illness and those who are ill the object of orderly categories of knowledge. Foucault had earlier described an identical process in relation to madness which became the foundation of a new science of psychiatry which also sought to reduce the dangers such limit-experiences represented.

The key term that commentators and researchers have retained from *The Birth of the Clinic* is 'the gaze', a notion that resonates with Foucault's later popular idea of a society centred around surveillance. In clinical medicine, knowledge was ordered around visible structures. Illnesses displayed themselves in concrete physical symptoms that could be observed and read by doctors who had been taught how to read them. 'The gaze' at the end of the eighteenth century was aimed at revealing what had hitherto remained hidden and unseen not only in the physical body but also in the social and political body. Visibility could dissipate both disease and political and social tyranny.

When Foucault wrote *The Birth of the Clinic*, structuralism was beginning to come to the fore in France. The word 'structure' recurs frequently in *The Birth of the Clinic*, so much so, that Foucault was to make an effort to remove some of this terminology in later editions of the book in an attempt to distance himself from the associations with the movement.

The Order of Things (1966)

B y the time Foucault published his next major work *The Order of Things* (OT), the structuralist movement was in full swing and this work was hailed by the media as a major contribution to the new movement. Although a bestseller on its publication, *The Order of Things* is probably one of Foucault's most difficult works and it is doubtful that many of those who purchased it actually read beyond the first chapter. Indeed, there were numerous remarks to this effect at the time. A copy of *The Order of Things* on one's coffee table was *de rigueur* in certain circles and the book discreetly tucked under one's arm had certain advantages in picking up members of the opposite (or the same) sex. As well-known historian Michel de Certeau suggested facetiously in 1967, useful additions could be made to the array of literary buttons or badges worn by trendy people about town in Paris. Badges could include, for example, 'I am mad about Foucault' ('je suis fou de Foucault') and also, 'I've actually read *The Order of Things*' (Certeau, 1967: 344). The truth is that not much has changed – except perhaps that these slogans would now probably appear on tee-shirts rather than on buttons and would also be more likely to appear in English.

The Order of Things, subtitled *An Archaeology of the Human Sciences* deals with the history and pre-history of the modern disciplines of linguistics, biology and economics from the Renaissance to the nineteenth century, with a concluding chapter on the human sciences which include history, sociology, psychoanalysis and ethnology. Foucault was to say later that the book was aimed at a specialist audience of historians of science and scientists (1974e: 524. Cf. 1980e: 267, 270) and there is no doubt that it is hard going for non-specialists – but it was not his specialist findings that made the book famous.

Using historical analysis, he launched a full-scale attack on established post-war philosophies namely humanism, Marxism, phenomenology, existentialism and scientific rationalism. He caused a media storm by declaring that 'man was dead' and that Marxism was a mere storm in a children's paddling pool (OT: 262). As a further aggravation, in the later foreword to the English edition, Foucault heaped scorn on those 'half-witted "commentators"' in France who had tried to explain his outrageous critiques of so many ideological icons as one of the hallmarks of 'structuralism' (OT: xiv).

Aside from these claims, Foucault argues in his book that different periods of history organise and order their formal systems of knowledge according to different principles. These principles of order can be found simultaneously across very diverse fields of knowledge during the same period. Foucault calls this arrangement of knowledge in each period an *episteme*, a notion that critics have often compared to Kuhn's paradigm. Foucault later remarked, however, that he had been unaware of Kuhn's work when he wrote *The Order of Things* (1971r: 60). He was also taken to task by critics for the abrupt and unexplained discontinuities between epistemes. Sartre (1966: 4) famously accused him of replacing 'cinema by the magic lantern, movement by a succession of immobilities'. In Sartre's view, this was clearly an attack on Marxism which of course supported the view of an inexorable march of history towards world Communism.

In more specific terms, Foucault focuses on the historical transformations affecting three areas of knowledge which up until the end of the eighteenth century were described as general grammar, the analysis of wealth and natural history. In the nineteenth century, these areas were systematised according to the conceptual apparatus of 'science' and became philology, political economy and biology. These very diverse areas were organised in very similar ways at the same points in history, and also underwent major reorganisations at roughly the same points in history. Foucault argues that until the end of the sixteenth century in Europe, it was the notion of resemblance that structured knowledge. So, in medicine for instance, if a plant (such as aconite) looked like an eye then this was a sign that it was good for diseases of the eye, just as walnuts which looked like brains were good for head wounds and the brain (OT: 27). All of nature was one huge book which could be read and interpreted by those who knew how to decipher the signs and marks God had left in nature. The scriptures and the books left by Antiquity were on an equal footing with the Book of Nature (OT: 33–4). This structure of knowledge which required people to seek out signs and resemblances and then to interpret them, was replaced by a different system in the seventeenth century which ordered things into tables and compared and measured them against each other. Identity and difference, rather than resemblance, became the way of relating different objects to each other.

If the Renaissance had seen the whole world as a kind of primary language which needed to be made to speak through the secondary languages of commentary and exegesis, the Classical Age which followed it, did away with this 'massive and intriguing existence of language' (OT: 79). Hence, argues Foucault, language is no longer a secondary commentary on a primary text, instead it becomes *discourse*, a way of speaking, arranging and presenting representations of the world in a logical order.

Another shift occurred at the beginning of the nineteenth century and history became the new principle of ordering knowledge, and 'science' started to come into its own. Foucault's discussion of this new configuration is difficult and complex. Knowledge was organised on the principle of stripping away the history that hid its true origins. At the centre of this knowledge was the essence or nature of 'man' which could gradually be uncovered by science. The problem with this, Foucault says, is that the idea of a human nature or essence is a metaphysical one – a belief – yet at the same time it has been set up as the object of empirical knowledge – a fact. Foucault argues that because the human sciences rest on this shaky foundation, they are fundamentally flawed in their approach to knowledge. He maintains that another break in knowledge is occurring in the contemporary era and the essence of man as the centre and foundation of all knowledge is dissolving.

Foucault was to later argue that *The Order of Things* was somewhat of an anomaly in his production in that it didn't deal with the limits and margins of existence or with social institutions. He notes in an interview in 1980:

> I've already spoken about limit-experiences and that's the theme that really fascinated me – for me, madness, death, sexuality and crime are more intense things. By contrast, *The Order of Things* was a kind of formal exercise for me … it's a marginal book in terms of the passion that runs through the others (1980e: 267 mod.).

But one is under no obligation to agree with Foucault's retrospective assessment here. There is considerable passion in his attacks on a bankrupt 'humanism' and also in his advocacy of an idea of 'literature' which following dreams, madness and death had become Foucault's preferred conduit for a 'tragic' experience of that other world which exists beyond the boundaries of orderly knowledge and mundane existence, and of an alternative way of accessing truth.

The Archaeology of Knowledge (1969)

After *The Order of Things*, readers eagerly awaited a similar effort, but Foucault's response was to publish in 1969 what some felt was a disappointingly dry and formal text, namely *The Archaeology of Knowledge*. But for those interested in historiography and method it is a rewarding read. Foucault describes traditional ways of organising 'discourse' such as the work, the author, the great man, the unifying universal subject, cause and effect, and influence, and then systematically takes these categories apart and proposes alternative methods of organisation. He also advocates a principle of discontinuity, by which he means that difference at every level in history should always be drawn attention to, not explained away. In addition to this book Foucault also published a number of very useful articles on historical method in the late 1960s and early 1970s.

'The order of discourse' (1971)

In 1970, Foucault was appointed to a Chair at the Collège de France and his inaugural lecture 'The order of discourse' (OD) was published in 1971. This short work is usually recognised as the text that marks the transition between Foucault's works on 'discourse' and those on 'power'. Once again, it is a methodological work and continues Foucault's attack on traditional ways of writing history. It deals with the way discourse is controlled, limited and defined by exercises of power and draws attention to the way boundaries between the true and the false are erected within this context. The idea of a link between knowledge and power (or various political, economic and institutional arrangements) had always been a theme in Foucault's work even if it is not overtly stated, but this text marks his first extended use of the word power.

Discipline and Punish (1975)

Foucault was not to publish his next book until 1975, but in the meantime he continued to write articles, give interviews and deliver his annual series of lectures at the Collège de France as well as conduct militant activity in support of a variety of socially marginalised groups. His next major work *Discipline and Punish* (DP) draws indirectly on his experience in this domain and famously opens with a lurid account of the torture and execution of the regicide Damiens in 1757. This is followed by a far more sedate description of a prison timetable in 1838. Foucault's point is that in the intervening period, spectacular corporal punishment disappeared to be replaced by new forms of punishment in the shape of imprisonment and the deprivation of liberty. Traditionally, historians have argued that this change occurred because people and society had become more humane and 'civilized'. Foucault rejects this kind of explanation and suggests instead that the old methods of punishment had simply become inefficient. Too many wrong-doers were escaping the arm of the law and public executions were no longer acting as a salutary warning to the rest of the populace. Instead public executions were actually inciting people to crime and public disorder, providing the occasion for riots, and all sorts of other minor crimes such as pick-pocketing.

Foucault argues that prison was chosen as the preferred method of punishment in Western Europe, not because it was the most effective means of punishment, but rather because it fitted in best with the emergence of what he describes as a 'disciplinary society'. By this, he means a certain way of acting upon and training the body and behaviour so that the individuals who make up populations could be easily controlled. This training was enforced and practised through a number of institutions, many of which appeared at the same time as the prison – namely schools, military training institutions, factories, hospitals and so on. The smooth functioning and enforcement of this 'disciplinary society' was guaranteed by a system of social surveillance. Foucault uses Jeremy Bentham's model prison, the Panopticon, to serve as a metaphor for the way this system of surveillance operated and continues to operate within the social body.

Foucault's book appeared on the scene in the context of severe unrest in prisons in a number of countries, and also amidst intense theoretical discussion focussing on both power and the body – it made a key contribution to these debates. If the book concludes its history in 1840 with the official opening of the model prison camp of Mettray in France, it was read as a damning indictment of the contemporary social order. As Foucault said himself five years after its publication: 'the research ends in the 1830s. Yet ... readers, critics or not, saw it as a description of contemporary society as a society of confinement' (1980e: 243–4 mod.). *Discipline and Punish* is now, along with volume 1 of *The History of Sexuality* Foucault's most consulted work. Its ideas on power, surveillance and social regulation have been adopted by theorists working not only in the humanities and social sciences, but also in vocational and applied disciplines such as education, the social services, accountancy, planning theory, management and architecture as well as many others.

Lectures: 1973–6

*D*iscipline and Punish however was not Foucault's first attempt to theorise the disciplinary society. With the 2003 publication of his

1973–4 lectures *Le pouvoir psychiatrique* (PP), it emerged that he first applied his ideas on disciplinary power, normalisation and panopticism to the history of the psychiatry. Across these somewhat uneven lectures, for all the interest of a number of the discussions, one gains the impression that psychiatry and the asylum are not quite adequate to Foucault's task and it is not until he focuses on the prison for his work *Discipline and Punish* that the whole conceptual apparatus really falls into place. Nonetheless, *Le pouvoir psychiatrique* contains invaluable analyses of sovereign power (vested in an authority figure and the king) versus disciplinary power and also on the ambiguous role of the family as a point of intersection between these two forms of power. There are also some extremely interesting pages outlining a brief history of truth in the West which we shall return to in later chapters.

Reading the lectures originally delivered at the Collège de France and noting their variable quality, one can understand Foucault's reported reticence with regards to the publication of such material. The lectures are frequently very much works in progress rather than the polished products which appear in his many books, articles and interviews. But for all this, the publication of these lectures has been absolutely invaluable on a number of fronts. Firstly, they provide a fascinating insight into the kind of research, experimentation and logic that allowed Foucault to construct the conceptual apparatuses for which he is so well-known. Secondly, they add extra empirical detail to discussions that only appears in abbreviated form elsewhere in his work. Thirdly, the lectures show dead ends that Foucault did not pursue, for example, the detailed discussions on anomalous behaviour and 'monsters' in his 1975 lectures *Abnormal* (AN), and of course his development of the ideas of a disciplinary society in relation to psychiatry.

The 1975 series of lectures adds little to Foucault's opus with its accounts of some of the more obscure and unpleasant byways of human behaviour, while lacking much of his customary insight. This material aside, however, it contains invaluable discussions relating to the history of confession and penitence, discussions which complement and flesh out his discussions elsewhere on the topic, notably in his 1976 Volume 1 of *The History of Sexuality*. Also of interest in these particular lectures are his comments relating to the uneasy relationship between medical and legal models of power which came into being in the nineteenth century.

Foucault's 1976 series of lectures, *Society Must be Defended*, is more consistently interesting. It provides a wealth of ideas on the history of notions of race, war and on what Foucault terms 'biopolitics' – all ideas which appear in far more abbreviated terms in Volume 1 of *The History of Sexuality*.

The History of Sexuality: Volume 1 (1976)

Leaving aside the lectures, further volumes of which are as yet to be published, in 1976 Foucault published the first volume of what was intended to be a six volume work on *The History of Sexuality* (HS). The initial reception of this book was poor: one outraged American reviewer proclaimed: 'my main purpose here is to persuade you not to read this book', adding further, 'this book is an intellectual embarrassment. Worse than that ... it comes very close to being a fraud' (Robinson, 1978: 30, 32). Not all reviews were so universally damning however, and over time this book has become as popular as *Discipline and Punish*. It is popular for a number of reasons: first of all, it is short and fairly straightforward reading, with easy to follow and interesting examples. Foucault's argumentation is also relatively simple in comparison with some of his other books and he also offers simple and point-by-point definitions of what he means by power (HS: 94–97). In addition to this, to state the obvious perhaps, the subject matter is of wide interest, even if Foucault was to somewhat provocatively declare later on, that 'sex is boring' (1983c: 253).

Foucault begins his book by noting that according to current received wisdom, the end of the seventeenth century marked the beginning of a repressive regime of censorship and prudishness with regards to sexuality. Reversing this argument he suggests instead that never before had there been so much attention focused on sexuality, and the nineteenth century in fact saw the emergence of an enormous proliferation of knowledge and the development of multiple mechanisms of control in relation to sexuality. Foucault also develops a number of influential theses about power, resistance to power and the management of populations that have been widely adopted by those applying his work. He argues notably that power is not something that simply forbids and represses, but is something that produces particular kinds of knowledge.

Much affected by the poor reception of his book, Foucault decided it was time for a change of direction. Reflecting later on the way he wrote his book, he commented that he had thought that he had reached a point where he could simply rest on his laurels. Instead, he found that not only was this boring for himself, but that his readers also noticed: '[The reader] can easily tell when you have worked and when you merely talk off the top of your head', he says, also adding, 'to work is to undertake to think something other than what you thought before' (1984l: 455 mod.). He was not to produce another book until 1984. In the early 1980s, French critics and the media began to talk about the 'silence' of Foucault and of intellectuals in general. But even if he was not publishing books,

Foucault was more prolific than ever in his production of articles, interviews and lectures.

Lectures: 1978–9

In 1978 Foucault published what was to become an enormously influential article titled 'Governmentality' (1978v). This piece, originally delivered as a lecture, provides a brief history of the origins of the modern State and describes the formation of particular ways of efficiently governing and organising populations. It is a work which has been used widely by researchers across a whole range of disciplines as a source of ideas for the analysis of the operations of institutions and bureaucracies. An excellent and informative collection of essays titled *Foucault, Cultural Studies and Governmentality* published in 2003, makes the extent and the sheer range of these connections particularly clear (Bratich et al., 2003). Indeed 'governmentality studies' now constitutes such a large field that conflicting schools of thought exist within its ranks. [3]

The appearance of Foucault's 1978 and 1979 lectures in 2004, however, mark a very significant addition to Foucault's previously published ideas on governmentality and the State. A number of the obscurities of the original 1978 publication are finally dispelled and fleshed out. For instance, at the end of the original article he briefly and somewhat mysteriously refers to three major elements which have produced the modern State, namely, 'the pastoral, the new diplomatico-military technics, and finally the police' (1978v: 222). If clues as to what these things might be can be gleaned from some of Foucault's other work, *Sécurité, territoire, population* finally offers extended historical clarifications in relation to all three elements.

The modern State, Foucault argues, consists of the convergence of a very particular set of techniques, rationalities and practices designed to govern or guide people's conduct as individual members of a population and also to organise them as a political and civil collective. This idea of 'governing' people at a political level, of organising their day to day conduct, he says, is borrowed from the metaphor of the care of a shepherd for his flock and originated in Egyptian, Assyrian, Mesopotamian and Hebrew cultures. The notion of leading and guiding people in the same way as a shepherd who cares for his flock and for each member of that flock, was then adopted and completely transformed by European Christianity and given institutional form by the Church. It meant taking care of every aspect of people's lives from birth to death in order to guide them to salvation. These techniques of what Foucault describes as 'pastoral power' started spreading from religious to secular contexts from the

Middle Ages onwards in Europe. It is the adoption and modification of these practices of pastoral government, he argues, that most uniquely characterises the exercise of power in the Western world (STP: 134).

He then goes on to explain the important role of diplomatic and military techniques in maintaining the balance of power between the newly conceived European States (STP: 304–18). He also offers a detailed history on the role of the 'police' in the seventeenth and eighteenth-century sense of the word, meaning the general maintenance of social order which promotes the everyday subsistence and happiness of the citizens of the State (STP: 318–55; Cf. 1978zl: 70). [4] In addition, he puts forward some interesting theories concerning 'counter-conducts' – namely forms of resistance to the conducts imposed by pastoral and governmental forms of the exercise of power.

Foucault's lectures for 1979, *Naissance de la biopolitique*, further develop the idea of what it means to govern within the context of political sovereignty. This collection of lectures also offers something which is quite unique in Foucault's work, that is a detailed history of neo-liberal 'arts of government' in the post-World War II period in France, Germany and the United States. It also provides a very useful critique of economic rationalism, and an interesting discussion of the definition of the subject in eighteenth and nineteenth-century English empiricist and liberal thought as an entity whose actions are always in the final analysis determined by self-interest. It has yet to be seen what impact these lectures will have, but they provide enlightening and substantial clarifications of Foucault's ideas on the State and of his notions of 'governmentality' which should prove invaluable to those interpreting and applying his work.

The History of Sexuality: Volumes 2 and 3 (1984)

In 1984, a month before Foucault's death, Volumes 2 and 3 of *The History of Sexuality* were published. These works are quite different from his other works as much in their style as in their choice of historical period. Volume 2, *The Use of Pleasure* (UP) opens by throwing into question the traditional notion of 'sexuality' as a historical constant with Foucault asking further, why sexuality has been the object of such intense moral preoccupation in history. In order to answer this question he looks to Antiquity as 'one of the first chapters' of a general history of the 'techniques of the self' (UP: 11). He then turns his attention to the practices and ethics surrounding sexuality in Ancient Greek thought in the fourth century B.C. examining prescriptive texts relating to sexuality and pleasure, diet and exercise, economics and the running of households, family structures and same-sex relationships. In the course of his discussion,

Foucault draws attention to both the differences and resonances between Ancient Greek and Christian thought and practices.

In the next volume *The Care of the Self* (CS), Foucault returns to his early interest in the history of dream analysis and the first section of the book is a detailed examination of a text by Artemidorus, *The Interpretation of Dreams*, written in the second century A.D. with a particular focus on its treatment of sexual dreams. The rest of Foucault's book deals with the first two centuries A.D. which marked the golden age of Roman thought and the beginnings of Christian thought. He notes the emphasis on sexual austerity which accompanied the growth of a culture of the 'cultivation of the self'. This culture included various sets of physical, mental and spiritual exercises which were intended to help individuals free themselves from enslaving desires, to allow them to become masters of themselves and to lead a beautiful life which would be an example to others. Foucault examines medical recommendations in relation to diet and exercise and the regulation of sexual practices and describes prescriptions concerning marriage, the male love of boys and notions of virginity.

Aside from various methodological statements in the introduction to Volume 2, these two last works have not been as readily taken up as most of Foucault's other major works. Indeed they tend to be somewhat bland and empirical in comparison with the other work he was publishing at the same time. It is the shorter works which appeared notably in such volumes as *The Foucault Reader* (FR) originally published in 1984, which have been the focus of critical attention.

Lectures: The 1980s

The monumental 500-page volume of Foucault's 1982 lectures *The Hermeneutics of the Subject* (HER) published in 2001 and translated into English in 2005, provides a very detailed history of practices and ideas concerning the cultivation of the self. These lectures examine the formation of the subject and ethical systems in Antiquity ranging from the Ancient Greeks to the thought of Imperial Rome in the first two centuries A.D. An additional volume of lectures delivered in 1983 at Berkeley, titled *Fearless Speech* (FS) was also published in 2001. These lectures focus on notions of speaking the truth and 'frank speech' and the relation between truth and power in Antiquity. They also include some useful general statements about Foucault's method concerning what he describes as 'the history of thought' and interesting discussion on historical notions of truth.

Apart from new publications of previously unpublished work, collections of already published work have also appeared since Foucault's death.

The most important of these, titled *Dits et ecrits* (DE), appeared in 1994 in French as an enormous four volume collection of his shorter writings. A number of these writings had never appeared in French before. This collection provided readers with a significant number of new perspectives on his work. They showed that Foucault's books were but the tip of the iceberg of intense empirical research and reflection and showed his gradual development of certain ideas. Foucault had often been accused by critics of being cavalier in his research. The French historian Jacques Léonard asks in relation to *Discipline and Punish* for example: 'When a philosopher engages with historians, they wonder ... if he is a sufficiently erudite scholar to dare to talk in this way: does he have enough index cards, are they comprehensive, well catalogued? Are his files as thick as our own? And his bibliography?' (Léonard, 1980: 10–11). *Dits et écrits* and the recent publications of Foucault's lectures go a long way towards showing that his files are sufficiently thick, perhaps even thick enough to satisfy the specialists.

Unfortunately in English, Foucault's shorter works are scattered widely across several collections. The three volumes of translated *Essential Works* (1997, 1998, 2000) as well as *Foucault Live* (1996) collate only a fraction of this work and not in the chronological order that makes the French collection so revelatory. Nonetheless, these volumes allow ready access to at least some of Foucault's shorter works in English and one can look forward perhaps to a more complete set of translations in years to come. Leaving aside now this chronological account of Foucault's work, the remaining chapters will embark on a more theoretical examination of a number of his ideas.

End Notes

[1] The three articles are 1966e; 1968b; and 1970a. The books are 1973n; 1986b; 1986c. *This is not a pipe* was expanded when published as a book and also appears as a book in English (1973o).

[2] The proceedings of this conference were published in the journal *Evolution psychiatrique* in 1971 under the title 'La conception idéologique de l'*Histoire de la folie* de Michel Foucault'.

[3] These opposing positions emerge for example in Colin Gordon's 1999 response to Ian Hunter's 1998 critique of Foucault's article 'Governmentality' (1978v).

[4] The English translation has rendered the French word 'police' by 'policy' in 1978zl: 70. The same word is translated by 'police' in Foucault's article 'Governmentality' (1978v: 222). Further, in the English translation of 'Governmentality' Foucault's dating of this formation of the concept of police in the seventeenth and eighteenth centuries is, in an error of translation, moved back to the twelfth and thirteenth centuries (1978u: 657; 1978v: 222).

FOUR   A Tool Box for Cultural Analysis

If merely reading Foucault's work, poses enormous problems, taking the next step and deciding how to actively use it poses a whole labyrinth of additional difficulties. Foucault often described his own work as a 'tool box', a description which has been eagerly seized upon by numerous commentators. He writes:

> I would like my books to be a kind of tool box which others can rummage through to find a tool which they can use however they wish in their own area ... I would like [my work] to be useful to an educator, a warden, a magistrate, a conscientious objector. I don't write for an audience, I write for users, not readers. (1974e: 523–4)

When it is a question of using merely one or two tools from Foucault's work the process remains relatively straightforward, but as soon as any attempt is made to carry off the whole tool box, the entire kit seems to fall apart at the seams.

Why does this happen? There are several reasons. First of all, Foucault continually changed and refined his concepts, not only on a major scale, but in very minute and subtle ways, something which makes his work extremely difficult to systematise for the purposes of a methodical and wholesale application. If this feature of his work makes it hard work for those interpreting his work in overall terms, it is also what makes it such a productive source of ideas for those applying quite specific tools piecemeal to particular domains. One is also struck by the strong, sometimes bitter, disagreements in the secondary literature over how Foucault's work should be interpreted and used. These debates are generated not just by the ambiguity produced by Foucault's constant remanipulations of his own ideas, but also by a profound uncertainty over just what sort of work he was producing.

Are Foucault's writings to be classified as academic works, political tracts or works of art?

Production in each of these separate domains is subject to different and sometimes mutually exclusive sets of rules. Within the academic field, there are those who wish to defend and promote the academic validity of Foucault's work either as a coherent philosophical and theoretical system in its own right, or as a series of empirical historical contributions to specialised areas. Foucault's work then becomes the object of standard academic commentary and research, an academic object in its own right. On the other hand, others are deeply suspicious of the academic credentials of Foucault's work and see both its subject matter and the widespread and sometimes eccentric and unschooled interest in his thought as an indication of its profound unsuitability for inclusion within the hallowed halls of academic rigour. The authors of one of the two *Foucault for Beginners* books observe for example: 'Foucault has left a great legacy – but a flawed one. His increasing cult status and political over-commitment overshadow his academic contribution' (Horrocks and Jevtic, 1997: 171). Those belonging to this school are at continual pains to point out the 'mistakes' in Foucault's empirical data, his unsound methodologies and his reckless disregard for 'objective truth'. At the more political end of the spectrum, there are those who admire Foucault as a radical subverter of all establishment status quos and wish to preserve his work at all costs from the slow and tortuous process of institutional and academic mummification at the hands of unread scholarly journals, sleep-inducing undergraduate lectures, and rigid scholarly orthodoxies.

Another view of Foucault's work holds that it operates more as a form of art to be experienced at a subjective level rather than as a form of rigorous intellectual endeavour where truth is empirically demonstrated. Depending on which side of the fence one is standing on, this can be a good or a bad thing. The commonly held view is that intellectual and artistic endeavour are vastly different, if not mutually exclusive, enterprises. The goal of art has been traditionally to generate a particular kind of 'experience' in the consumer, which has a transformative effect on how they see and experience the world. On the other hand, the aim of intellectual work is to demonstrate particular truths which are rigorously defined by means of various forms of logic and argument and supported by empirical data collection. At its pinnacle, this type of knowledge acquires the label of 'science'. The commonly held view is that the rules governing the production of art and the production of intellectual and scientific knowledge follow completely separate paths. [1] As we shall see later in this book, this opposition corresponds to what

Foucault characterises as a division between two forms of truth in Western history.

These debates not only draw attention to the difficulty of defining the status of Foucault's books, but also to the strictly enforced divisions between what qualifies as 'academic' work and other cultural expressions. The debates also raise questions about how these different kinds of work should be disseminated and used by people, as well as the status of these works in relation to truth claims. Foucault himself was deeply committed to the idea of breaking down the barriers that prevented people from accessing the full range of cultural production and knowledge. He was opposed, for instance, to the idea of setting up a '"cultural park" for delicate species of scholars threatened by the rapacious inroads of mass information, while the rest of the space would be a huge market for shoddy products' (1980i: 326–7).

Foucault's 'method'

Foucault described the work he did as 'an experiment much more than a system. No recipe, hardly any general method. But technical rules, documentation, research, verification' (1983e: 414). Elsewhere he goes even further and confirms what many of his worst critics have always suspected. After stating that he has no method which he is willing to apply across different areas, he declares:

> Personally, I conduct myself in an entirely unreasonable and pretentious manner, under the exterior trappings of modesty. But it is pretension, presumption, a mania of presumption almost in the Hegelian sense, of wanting to talk about an unknown object with a non-defined method. I can only cover my head with ashes, that's how I am. (1977zc: 405)

Those struggling to find a method in Foucault's work, wondering if they have somehow missed it along the way, or that perhaps there is just one more text out there that will make it all clear can, in the light of this statement, abandon their search and rest comforted in the bleak knowledge that they have free rein. Well, almost free rein. It is not enough to simply sprinkle all the right key words such as genealogy, power, discourse or panopticism at strategic intervals throughout one's text. If Foucault's work is often difficult to pin down, it is an immense monument to discipline and order in the historical analysis of ideas and thought. It is always possible to organise things differently, but even so, certain rules must still be observed. These rules involve processes of empirical and historical verification and the detailed and logical examination of existing categories.

Applying Foucault's work

One does not simply 'apply' Foucault's method in the same way that one applies ethnomethodology and other sociological methods, semiotic analysis, literary theory, or even various forms of Marxist theory or historical method. Most actual 'applications' of Foucault's method really amount to the transfer, via a process of analogy, of his concrete ideas about specific historical situations to other situations. So, for example, researchers in the area of postcolonial studies might borrow some of the ideas Foucault uses to discuss the way power operates in Western, more specifically French, history, extrapolating these to discuss development, humanitarian aid and local resistance in Third World nations (Escobar, 1999). Others might use Foucault's ideas on the disciplining of bodies to discuss institutional and training practices in sport (Smith Maguire, 2002) or dance performance (Burt, 2004). Alternately, they might transfer ideas from Foucault's historical discussions concerning the formation of the self in Antiquity to an examination of the formation of the nurse as professional (Goopy, 1997). Still others may use a combination of Foucault's discussions on the modern State (based on risk and insurance), the formation of the self, discipline and pastoral power, to discuss road safety and private transport (Packer, 2003). These kinds of applications do not involve the imposition of an abstract universal or scientific template, rather they involve argument by analogy and comparison. Unfortunately, in many instances, the importation of some of Foucault's more abstract terminology combined with bad translations do in fact tend to create the impression that a template is indeed at work.

Five basic principles

In an attempt to organise and bring some clarity into this situation I have distilled the philosophical assumptions underpinning Foucault's work into five closely interdependent principles which inform not only his choice of subject matter but also his methods and entire approach to his empirical material. The way in which these assumptions emerge varies considerably throughout his career but they all remain constant elements which permeate every aspect of his writings. Within these broad parameters, I will then outline a number of the concepts or tools associated with each these principles in Foucault's work. First of all, I shall briefly summarise all five principles before going on to discuss them in detail.

(1) The first assumption that Foucault makes is that it is possible to produce and describe all human knowledge and culture in an orderly manner, but at the same time, human attempts to create order are always limited and crumbling at the edges. All forms of order should be challenged at every opportunity, so that people can understand why current orders exist and reflect on whether or not they should be changed.

(2) The best tool to examine and dismantle existing orders is history. Every human action, idea and arrangement exists in time: everything has a beginning and an end. No aspect of human existence escapes from history.

(3) Foucault also consistently maintains that truth is a historical category. It is also a notion that has been of particular importance in Western history which has been marked, particularly since the Enlightenment, by a struggle between two mutually opposed methods of gaining access to the truth. On one side there is the 'intellectual' or 'scientific' method which has gained ascendency since Descartes and on the other hand an older method involving spiritual self-transformation and limit-experiences. Foucault deals with the opposition between these two approaches to truth in a variety of ways throughout his career, and consistently champions the non-Cartesian approach.

(4) Foucault also holds that knowledge is always shaped by political, social and historical factors – by 'power' – in human societies. It is absolutely essential to examine the relationship between knowledge and the factors that produce and constrain it.

(5) Finally, for Foucault, social justice is an essential ethical consideration that requires close and constant attention, examination, and action.

The presence of these five assumptions reinforces amongst those used to more pragmatic and mechanical methodologies, the impression of an impenetrable and mysterious methodological and philosophical grid at work in Foucault's writings and those of his followers. But perhaps rather than a methodology, it is the adoption of some, if not all of the assumptions that leads to something that vaguely resembles an 'application' of Foucault's work. It is the absence of one or more of these assumptions in specific applications which can make the latter appear, in some cases, so puzzlingly different from the original, in spite of claims to be derived (to greater or lesser extents) from Foucault's work.

For example, applications such as 'narrative therapy' (White, 2000) and some (but not all) forms of 'discourse analysis' (Fairclough, 2003) ignore the historical dimension of Foucault's approach and rely more heavily on phenomenological, ethnomethodological or linguistic research methods. These approaches focus on a notion of finding the truth of a subject situated wholly in the lived experience of the present. 'Narrative therapy', if posited on the idea of encouraging patients to construct a different story about themselves as subjects, in order to 'transform themselves' into something different, ignores the broad complex social and historical contexts within which general notions of subjectivity arise. Likewise, certain (but again by no means all) forms of analysis practised by those interested in 'governmentality', ignore the ethical emphasis in Foucault's work with its outrage at various forms of social injustice and limitations on people's freedoms. These analyses often have the opposite effect of drawing attention to loopholes in the system with a view to closing them up, ignoring the anarchic dynamic in Foucault's work, which means that order is always limited and crumbling at the edges. [2]

Traditional philosophers for their part, sometimes treat Foucault's work as though it exists in some kind of a temporal vacuum, with Foucault practising a very dubious and imprecise philosophy which remains unsure of its own foundations (Han, 2002). The intrusion of historical elements and the historicisation of truth in his work is something to be deeply regretted. As one philosopher remarks:

> Foucault's philosophical points are embedded in often tedious historical commentary. *Discipline and Punish* is full of wearisome discussion of legal procedures, the efforts of particular penal reformers, the French, English and American penal systems, and even the architectural plans for the construction of schools, prisons and other institutions. Foucault even provides illustrations of discipline-enhancing features of schools and prisons and of disciplinary devices such as spanking machines. (Prado, 2000: 58)

On the other hand, historians complain that it is the boring philosophical commentary that hijacks all the interesting historical material in Foucault.

Foucault himself sees both philosophy and history as essential and mutually interconnected elements in his project. [3] If ideas and thought are often supposed to exist independently of history, Foucault argues that this is far from being the case. Further, various historical practices, systems of ideas and social and cultural institutions all embody, as well as produce, particular ideas and ways of thinking which can be analysed.

These various comments on the applications of Foucault's work are by no means intended to suggest that they are invalid and that people have to adhere to a strict party line when using Foucault. As he says himself, 'I believe the freedom of the reader must be absolutely respected. Discourse is a reality which can be transformed infinitely. Thus, he who writes does not have the right to give orders as to the use of his writings.' (1978r: 111 mod.)

As suggested at the beginning of this chapter, and as Foucault often argues himself, his work functions best as a tool box, rather than as a coherent system. The examination of certain assumptions underlying this work can, however, reduce the perception that a secret methodology that can only be unlocked by a privileged few is at work. I will now go on to provide a detailed analysis of how these assumptions emerge and operate in Foucault's work. It is important to emphasise once again that this division into five separate principles is artificial and that in practice they are all inextricably entwined across all of Foucault's writings.

Principle 1: Order

Foucault begins with the principle that there are any number of different ways of ordering experience and knowledge. Every existing order in culture, society and knowledge is limited, and alternative orders are always possible. It is important to continually challenge these orders as they often fix and perpetuate forms of social injustice and ignorance. All of Foucault's work is about order, or more specifically about the co-existence of different forms of order and the continual historical transformation of those orders and their interrelations. These orders exist both within culture and within the physical world. Indeed such is Foucault's enthusiasm for order and systems that he went so far as to proclaim at the height of the structuralist era that 'the system is currently our major form of honesty' (1967c: 582). In another interview, he adds:

> In every age, the way in which people reflect, write, judge, speak (right down to the street and to the most everyday conversations and writing) and even the way people experience things and react with their feelings; all of their behaviour is governed by a theoretical structure, a system, which changes with ages and societies – but which is present in all ages and all societies. (1966d: 514)

Even if Foucault later nuanced some of these ideas in response to the misunderstandings they generated, the words 'system' and even 'structure' constantly recur throughout his work. He even included the word 'system' in the name of his chair at the Collège de France (the 'Chair of the History Systems of Thought'). But if he freely uses these terms, he is careful to explain that, unlike the structuralists, he is not interested in setting up formal systems or templates which can be universally applied. Instead he is interested in how the traces left behind by the past are organised. He is also interested in those boundaries, margins or limits where order breaks down and also in the processes whereby one order is transformed into another. An order is never fixed or universal and never exists beyond certain limitations of culture, time and space. Thus, Foucault's work does not have 'predictive' or 'scientific' value. The other factor that differentiates Foucault's work from many of the structuralists is his interest in those points where structure and order break down, he is interested in the *limits* of human order, culture, structure and experience. It is precisely this rejection of formalism and of a universally applicable method, that makes

Foucault's methodology so difficult to apply, yet paradoxically at the same time renders it so attractive through its sheer flexibility and adaptability to a range of quite specific locations, times and situations.

There are two principles which emerge clearly in all of Foucault's work in relation to order. Firstly, there is no system that is unproblematic and that can be taken for granted. Secondly, one must be careful not to reduce one structure of order to another. In short, the same system, structure or theory cannot be applied indiscriminately to everything. Different objects, structures or processes should always be distinguished.

Words and things

O ne of the most fundamental confusions in our culture is the tendency to assume that words and things have the same structure and that words transparently reflect and represent the structure of things. Or to put it another way, that our way of talking about the world reflects the world as it really is in itself. Foucault argues that there is no necessary neutral and fixed connection between words and things or between our knowledge and things. The order of words and the order of things can only exist in analogous relations. An order of words may appear the same as an order of things, but the order of words is using analogy or mimicry or some other process to produce this effect.

The non-transparent relation between words and things and the fact that somehow our knowledge never quite matches what is actually out there is, in Foucault's view, the logical consequence of the fact that humans are limited historical beings. Our inability to formulate a knowledge which is fixed and absolutely true is not the result of the loss of an original natural innocence or 'fall from grace'. Neither is knowledge a mark of a divorce from 'nature' and 'real life'. Foucault puts it in these terms, following the historian of science Georges Canguilhem:

> The fact that man lives in a conceptually structured environment does not prove that he has turned away from life, or that a historical drama has separated him from it – just that he lives in a certain way, that he has a relationship with his environment such that he has no set point of view toward it, that he is mobile on an undefined or a rather broadly defined territory, that he has to move around to gather information, that he has to move things relative to one another in order to make them useful. Forming concepts is a way of living not a way of killing life. (1978a: 475)

Foucault insists time and time again in his work that no existing order can be taken for granted. As he so often does, he takes an extreme example to help make his point. In the preface to *The Order of Things* he describes the difficulties of some aphasics when faced with the task of organising coloured skeins of wool on a table top. They will try endless combinations of similarity and difference, for instance, placing the lightest skeins in one corner, the red ones in another, soft ones somewhere else, others rolled in a ball yet elsewhere. But no sooner has this order been created than they create another set of orders 'and so' as Foucault says 'the sick mind continues to infinity, creating groups then dispersing them again' (OT: xviii).

This example allows Foucault to draw attention to the very space, the apparently neutral table top, which serves as a backdrop or support for this process of ordering. This level cannot be taken for granted. He says, 'the threshold above which there is a difference and below which there is similitude – is indispensable for the establishment of even the simplest form of order' (OT: xx). To put it more simply, for the aphasic, the white rectangle of the table top simply does not provide a sufficient threshold for the establishment of order. It is not merely a question of recognising that different orders are possible, but one must search for the very principles that give rise to particular ways of constructing order, one must search for those systems which make it possible to actually see that an order exists. Between our system of words and things there is another level which obscurely sets out what relations of order should exist between words and things and which allows for the establishment of systems of similarity and difference, and for divisions between the true and the false, and the agenda for common 'problems'.

Foucault argues in *The Birth of the Clinic*, that it is shifts in this level that account for changes in the field of medical knowledge at the end of the eighteenth century in France. Traditional accounts of this historical change argue that doctors finally discarded old imaginary and mythological schemas in favour of more rational systems and at last started 'looking' at things 'properly' by conducting solid empirical research. They finally 'discovered' what their ignorant forebears had been unable to see, blinded as they were by myth and superstition. It is indeed true that they did see something new, Foucault says, but it was because the relation between words and things had changed. New objects of knowledge could now be examined. There now exists a new table top that allows for a different arrangement of the skeins of wool.

In his much quoted analysis of a passage from Borges which cites a highly improbable system of animal classification found in a 'certain Chinese encyclopaedia', Foucault further draws attention to the difference between the order of words and the order of things. As he notes 'The animals "(i) frenzied, (j) innumerable, (k) drawn with a very fine camelhair brush" – where could they ever meet, except in the immaterial sound of the voice pronouncing their enumeration, or on the page transcribing it? Where else could they be juxtaposed except in the non-place of language?' (OT: xvi–xvii). This is an order that can only be imagined within language. It does not reflect objects in the world of 'things'. In short, words and things possess separate orders which cannot be reduced to each other. Words and concepts do not simply translate or represent things – they have a life and order of their own which in turn interrelates with the life and order of things. A complex series of exchanges: reflections, influences and mimicry is constantly taking place between these different systems of order.

Nothing is fundamental

It is not simply just a matter of emphasising the difference between the general order of words and the general order of things, these orders need to be broken down still further. Foucault's work runs deliberately counter to many of the philosophies and theories produced in the modern era, whose goal is to reduce all orders to one common principle. Instead he tries to discern as many different orders as possible and to examine the intersections and divergences amongst them. As he says:

> Nothing is fundamental. That is what is interesting in the analysis of society. That is why nothing irritates me as much as these enquiries – which are by definition metaphysical – on the foundations of power in a society or the self-institution of a society, and so on. These are not fundamental phenomena. There are only reciprocal relations, and the perpetual gaps between intentions in relation to one another. (1982f: 356)

A good example of this differential analysis can be found in Foucault's seminal article 'Governmentality'. Here he provides a detailed analysis of the historical distinctions, shifts, intersections and divergences between different orders of government in Western Europe: between the art of self-government (morality), the government of the family (economics) and the government of the state (politics) (1978v). Foucault's non-reductive analysis in this piece has provided a whole host of researchers with ideas for complex and layered examinations of how government and administrative mechanisms operate. A similarly detailed, if less polished account of the functioning of power at different levels of the social body can also be found in Foucault's 1973 lectures *Le pouvoir psychiatrique*.

At one end of the spectrum, Foucault's non-reductive approach makes it possible to argue that cultural production cannot be reduced to struggles for social distinction and domination or to the effects of other kinds of material conditions. (This kind of reductionism tends to operate in the work of Pierre Bourdieu and in the work of thinkers influenced by Marxist thought.) And at the other end of the spectrum, his work also makes it possible to argue that the physical world is not simply the reflection or embodiment of our ideas about it. It is possible, for example, to produce an analysis of architecture which examines at one and the same time the effects of ideas – architectural design, and things – actual buildings. As Foucault argues, an architect may well have had certain intentions and ideas in designing a building but the concrete physical space might produce a large range of quite different responses from those who frequent the buildings – this then reflects back on future design and so on it goes. He provides an illustration of this by referring to a building constructed for workers in 1859 which was designed with the intention of promoting freedom and autonomy. Unfortunately, the building only had one entrance which meant that comings and goings were visible to all, with the ensuing consequences of surveillance and intrusion of privacy. But again as Foucault notes 'it could only be oppressive if people were prepared to use their own presence to watch over others' (1982f: 355).

Stuart Hall noting that Foucault was 'deeply committed to the necessary non-correspondence of all practices to one another' (Hall, 1981: 36), complains that this means that Foucault can have no unifying 'theory' or ideological stance from which to criticise society and the State. But others, such as Tony Bennett (1998: 83–4) and the French historian Roger Chartier, argue that this is a plus for cultural analysts. Chartier notes in describing the impact of Foucault's work: 'cultural history has lost its ambition to be all-embracing, to be sure, but it has perhaps gained an unprecedented attention to the texts, henceforth freed from the reduction to ideology that had destroyed them as discursive practices' (1988: 111).

Quite apart from the historical orders Foucault describes himself, there are many ways in which his own work can be organised and interpreted, and Foucault himself frequently engages in different kinds of re-ordering of his past output. The fluidity of categories in his work makes it simultaneously exciting, frustrating and vastly unsettling and numbers of readers are reduced to the kind of frenzied aphasia described in *The Order of Things*, desperately arranging and rearranging Foucault's ideas into orders that seem to work for a while until other equally exciting possibilities present themselves. In the next chapter, we will examine Foucault's tool of choice for dispersing and reorganising orders, namely history.

End Notes

[1] For an extended exposition of these kinds of oppositions and debates in relation to Foucault's later works see O'Leary 2002: 69–104, 121–38.

[2] This tendency in some writings of the governmentality school is noted by Pat O'Malley (1998) who criticises the lack of sustained attention to 'resistance' in such writings.

[3] For an extended discussion of the debates over whether Foucault is a historian or philosopher see O'Farrell (1989).

Principle 2: History

For Foucault, 'history' is the tool par excellence for challenging and analysing existing orders and also for suggesting the possibility of new orders. History is about beginnings and ends and about change and freedom. As he remarks towards the end of his career:

> It is one of my targets to show people that a lot of things that are a part of their landscape – that people think are universal – are the result of some very precise historical changes. All my analyses are against the idea of universal necessities in human existence. They show the arbitrariness of institutions and show which space of freedom we still enjoy, and how many changes can still be made. (1988a: 11)

In short, history can be used as a tool to show the limits of every system of thought and institutional practice and to break down the oppressive claims to universal truth of any one system. In opposition to eternal, fixed and unchanging entities, Foucault proposes history, beginnings and ends and constant change.

He also suggests that perhaps the specific 'order' (or 'table top' to use the analogy from *The Order of Things*) underlying all modern knowledge and culture might in fact be history. In *The Birth of the Clinic* he declares, 'We are doomed historically to history, to the patient construction of discourses about discourses, and to the task of hearing what has already been said' (BC: xvi). He also adds that in Western culture, we perceive everything that has been said in the context of a historical process where things follow on from and influence each other and accumulate. This might seem obvious, but there are cultures which in fact arrange their knowledge in other ways (1967d: 292). But while admitting that history does indeed occupy a 'privileged place' in his analysis, Foucault hastens to add that he does not want to set up history as another kind of ideal metatheory which will explain everything (1967d: 292–3). History has the unique advantage of allowing any universal claims to be challenged as soon as they are made by demonstrating that they are not constants.

But, Foucault does not write just any history: the subject matter and objects he addresses and the tools he uses are very particular, and differ markedly from older styles of mainstream history. First of all, there is the kind of history he is writing. Foucault began his work in the late 1950s and continued into the 1960s in an area which could very generally be described as the 'history of science' and the 'history of ideas'. Then during the 1970s he widened his histories to include something that looked like the history of institutions, the history of the modern State and finally in the 1980s, the history of ethical systems. But there is one large problem with all of these descriptions – none of them quite work when applied to Foucault's writings. The reason for this is that he is using different tools of organisation from those employed by mainstream historians.

There are two main features that distinguish Foucault's approach. The first and most important of these relates to the level he is addressing, something which we alluded to in the last chapter using the analogy of the table top. As Foucault explains late in his career, he used the term 'archaeology' rather than 'history' to very precisely indicate his focus on this level, a level where certain objects (for example madness) are formed as possible objects of knowledge (1983g: 445). The second feature that distinguishes Foucault's work from older styles of history is his resolute adoption of a principle of discontinuity, which, as he explains, is also a notion used by other radical historians. We will examine this second feature in more detail in the next chapter.

The historical a priori

Let us begin by looking at the first feature – the cultural 'table top' which allows orders to emerge. The definition of this level is perhaps one of the most difficult and elusive things about Foucault's work. [1] Over the years he used a number of different technical terms to designate this level. Each time he introduced a major shift in the way he described it, he also renamed his methodology. Hence the terms historical a priori, 'implicit knowledge' and the 'unconscious of knowledge' are all associated with archaeology. 'Regimes of truth' or 'games of truth', are associated with genealogy, and 'problematisation' or 'thought' with something Foucault calls the 'history of thought'.

Perhaps the earliest term Foucault uses to characterise the cultural 'table top' is the historical a priori. The a priori is a notion usually associated with the work of German philosopher Immanuel Kant. What Kant means by this is that there are eternal 'ideal types' or templates of order which exist outside of time. Hence the idea of beauty, for example, is eternal and all works of art in some way refer back to that unchanging ideal. Foucault brings this philosophical ideal of order firmly into history. In his model, there are no ideal eternal orders existing outside of time which structure our existence and thought – these orders are all located in time. It is only possible to discover patterns once they have already occurred, and it is not possible to apply the orders discovered to future events. Foucault offers a definition in *The Order of Things*, where he explains:

> This *a priori* is what, in a given period, delimits in the totality of experience a field of knowledge, defines the mode of being of the objects that appear in that field, provides man's everyday perception with theoretical powers, and defines the conditions in which he can sustain a discourse about things that is recognised to be true (OT: 158).

It is 'a fundamental arrangement of knowledge' (OT: 157). What he means by this is that each historical period orders knowledge and constructs concepts according to certain rules. These rules can be deduced from a study of the traces of past knowledge and practices. It is far easier to see these in hindsight than deduce the rules that underlie our current practices. Foucault also uses the terms 'the unconscious of knowledge', the 'archive' and 'implicit knowledge' and 'conditions of possibility' to refer to the same ideas.

The episteme

In *The Order of Things*, Foucault also introduces a notion he famously labels the 'episteme'. Although his explanations are by no means clear in this book, the episteme or 'epistemological field' is in fact a subset of the historical a priori and describes the underlying orders, or 'conditions of possibility' which regulate the emergence of various scientific or pre-scientific forms of knowledge during specific periods of history. These 'epistemological fields' give rise to 'the diverse forms of empirical science' (OT: xxii). The episteme appears and disappears abruptly for reasons Foucault is not able to explain, much to the indignation of his critics as we have seen. He locates these abrupt and wholesale shifts in knowledge at the end of the Renaissance and at the end of the eighteenth century. They are also 'enigmatic': 'For an archaeology of knowledge, this profound breach in the expanse of continuities, though it must be analysed, and minutely so, cannot be "explained" or even summed up in a single word' (OT: 217). [2]

As we saw in our account of *The Order of Things* in Chapter 3, during the Renaissance all knowledge was based on the idea that one could 'read' the true nature of things by using a principle of resemblance. In the Classical Age which followed, knowledge was based on the idea that words and things could be arranged into orderly tables. In the nineteenth century, the search for historical origins formed the basis for the organisation of knowledge.

Archaeology

During the 1960s Foucault used the term 'archaeology' to describe his approach to the history of knowledge. The term appears briefly in *Mental Illness and Psychology* and in *Madness and Civilisation*, and his books *The Birth of the Clinic* and *The Order of Things* both include the word 'archaeology' in their subtitles. But it was not until 1966 that he began to offer sustained definitions. He explains that he originally borrowed the term from Kant to describe a historical practice of philosophy (1971o: 60) and that he liked the word because he could play with its meanings. He adds that in Greek, *arche* means beginning and that it also resonates with the word 'archive' meaning the traces left behind by cultures in history. To extrapolate further from Foucault's ideas, the word also allows us to think of our present as the top layer of a kind of archaeological dig. One digs down through history to understand the present, to understand what we are today. [3] As Foucault puts it: 'In a way we are nothing other than what has been said, centuries ago, months, weeks ago' (1978c: 469). In short, to employ a term he uses later in his career, archaeology is always very much aimed at producing a 'history of the present'.

Archaeology also has an ethical and political function, in that it is intended to throw into question 'certain relations of power' and to have a 'liberating function'. Foucault hopes that it can provide 'a model of what has happened that will allow us to free ourselves from what has happened' (1974h: 644). Foucault also noted in 1966 that his project was a political one, insofar as it involved a critique of the humanist philosophies which had provided an umbrella justification for so many questionable political regimes in both the East and the West (1966d: 516). What is interesting about these particular views is that that they run counter to received wisdom in the secondary literature (admittedly amply aided and abetted by other remarks offered by Foucault) that the principal difference between 'archaeology' and 'genealogy' is that archaeology deals with neutral theoretical systems of knowledge and genealogy deals with power and real practical struggles. Archaeology is usually characterised as the somewhat politically deficient method Foucault used before his 'enlightenment' at the beginning of the 1970s and his development of a far more adequate 'genealogy'.

But if the word 'power' does not appear in his work prior to 1970, the analysis of social institutions was amply present. As he said in response to criticisms, he certainly did not have a 'guilty conscience' in relation to his earlier work, given his extended analyses of the working of institutions and economic structures in both *Madness and Civilization* and *The Birth of the Clinic* (1969i). If his books were not considered to be relevant to any political agenda at the time they were written, by the late 1960s and early 1970s the plight of marginal groups and the operation of institutions had well and truly become the objects of general political activism. So much so, in fact, that Foucault was to remark in 1977:

> This reversal of values and of truths ... has been important to the extent that it does not stop with simple cheers (long live insanity, delinquency, sex), but it permits new strategies. You see, what often bothers me today, in fact, what really troubles me, is that all the work done in the last fifteen years or so, often under hardship and solitude, functions only for some as a sign of belonging on the 'good side' of insanity, children, delinquency, sex. (1977m: 222)

A number of those using Foucault's work even now still neglect these earlier books because of the absence of a theoretical terminology relating to power. Thus one comes across research in the area of health which cites liberally from *Discipline and Punish*, but fails to mention the much more pertinent *The Birth of the Clinic*. The latter is in fact a particularly good case study of instances of what Foucault later came to term 'governmentality', and shares a number of structural commonalities with his book *Discipline and Punish*, notably in the comparisons at the beginning of both books of two historically contrasting institutional regimes.

Regimes of truth

The publication of Foucault's inaugural speech at the Collège de France, 'The orders of discourse' in 1971, saw a shift away from the terminology he had developed for his archaeological project, to a new set of terms. In this and subsequent work, he introduced terms such as 'genealogy', 'power' and 'the will to truth' and a little later the 'apparatus' (dispositif). In the mid-1970s, he also added a notion which he described as equivalent to his earlier notion of the historical a priori (1984g: 460). This was the idea of 'regimes of truth' (or later 'games of truth') which he defined as 'the ensemble of rules according to which the true and the false are separated and specific effects of power attached to the true'

(1977e: 132). Again, these rules are quite specific to particular historical periods and societies. The 'apparatus' or 'dispositif', is another term Foucault uses to describe the same level during the 1970s. He defines the latter as a strategic relationship between diverse elements 'consisting of discourses, institutions, architectural forms, regulatory decisions, laws, administrative measures, scientific statements, philosophical, moral and philanthropic propositions' (1977s: 194). If 'archaeology' was the method which addressed the level Foucault describes as the historical a priori, genealogy is the method Foucault uses to analyse regimes or games of truth and the 'dispositif'. The structural similarity between the historical a priori and regimes of truth can be seen most clearly in Foucault's 1979 lectures at the Collège de France where he describes three successive regimes of truth in relation to the art of government in European history, echoing the analysis he conducts in *The Order of Things* in relation to the history of scientific knowledge (NBP: 20-2).

However it is more than just a question of a simple equivalence. Foucault actually modifies his views on how this level functions. In his archaeological work, knowledge, truth and systems of power exist and interact on an equal level, with a complex series of checks and balances between each of these three terms. Knowledge is primarily a way of organising and ordering the social and physical environment to make it manageable. But at the beginning of the 1970s, Foucault adopted a new model of order and argued, following Nietzsche, that knowledge itself at its very origin was the product of struggles for domination and power. As he puts it in the summary of his 1970 lectures at the Collège de France: 'interest is thus posited radically prior to the knowledge that it subordinates as a mere instrument' (1971s: 14). He also contends in 'Nietzsche, genealogy, history', that the will to know 'rests on injustice' and is 'malicious' (1971a: 387). A certain arrangement of power directly produces discourses and discursive practices. Foucault adopts, following the Ancient Greek Sophists, a 'strategic' notion of knowledge: 'we build discourses not in order to arrive at the truth, but to win' (1974h: 632). He further argues in 1973, that arrangements and strategies of power 'give rise to affirmations, negations, experiences, theories, in brief to a whole game of truth' (PP: 15).

He provides a detailed account of this argument in lectures delivered in Brazil in 1973 (1974i), based on reflections on an 1873 posthumous text by Nietzsche. In Foucault's account, Nietzsche argues that on a small planet, by complete accident, intelligent animals invented a thing called knowledge. Knowledge, rather than being an innate property which distinguished humans from animals, is in fact the result of a struggle and a compromise between basic warring animal instincts within humans. Neither does it reflect the external order of the world. This argument allows Foucault to adopt the extreme position that every relation we have with ourselves and the world is one of power, violence and domination. He describes Nietzsche's position in this way:

> Thus, between the instincts and knowledge one finds not a continuity but, rather, a relation of struggle, domination, servitude, settlement. In the same way, there can be no relation of natural continuity between knowledge and the things knowledge must know. There can only be a relation of violence, domination, power, and force, a relation of violation. Knowledge can only be a violation of the things to be known, and not a perception, a recognition, an identification of or with those things. (1974i: 9)

The instincts that give rise to knowledge are negative instincts – they are not instincts that help us exist in harmony with things, but instincts which put a distance of contempt, hatred and fear between ourselves and objects. Foucault notes further, 'There cannot be particular types of subjects of knowledge, orders of truth, or domains of knowledge except on the basis of political conditions that are the very ground on which the subject, the domains of knowledge, and the relations with truth are formed' (1974i: 15 mod.).

Here power and politics are absolutely primary. In the model Foucault proposes in his various writings in the early 1970s, the desire to create order is at its very origin an exercise of power. Ordering by its very nature is about exercising power over self, others and the physical environment. Foucault's Nietzschean characterisation of power and knowledge subsequently led to his adoption from 1975–7 of the idea that relations of power were strategic and war-like with his most extensive discussion of this position to be found in his 1976 lectures *Society Must Be Defended*. During this phase of his work Foucault describes relations of power as a form of war: peace, politics and the State as simply strategic configurations in a kind of permanent and generalised war, with the final decisions being made by force of arms. But Foucault was clearly uncomfortable with this extreme position and he generally prefers during this period to grant knowledge and power equal status in the form of his well-known notion of 'power-knowledge', where power and knowledge generate each other in endless cycles.

Genealogy

Foucault makes a reference to the term 'genealogy' as early as 1967 saying: 'my archaeology owes more to Nietzschean genealogy than to structuralism properly so called' (1967d: 294). This statement emphasises how close the archaeological and geneaological projects actually are. Foucault defines the latter in 1971 as a form of history which is systematically opposed to the search for ahistorical foundations and metaphysical essences. As Foucault writes in 'Nietzsche, genealogy, history', '"effective" history', or in other words, 'genealogy'

> differs from the history of historians in being without constants. Nothing in man – not even his body – is sufficiently stable to serve as a basis for self-recognition or for understanding other men. The traditional devices for constructing a comprehensive view of history and for retracing the past as a patient and continuous development must be systematically dismantled. (1971a: 380)

This is of course the same mission as that of archaeology. People have in fact puzzled at great length over how to describe the difference between 'archaeology' and 'genealogy' in Foucault's work, a problem not made any easier by Foucault's own brief and less than enlightening comparisons. Most people settle for the approximate idea that archaeology deals with discourses and genealogy deals with power. In one of his famous reinterpretations of his own earlier work, Foucault takes himself to task for what he perceives as its short-comings, saying that although he had a vague notion of the 'central problem of power', it was something that he had 'not yet properly isolated' (1977e: 15).

'Nietzsche, genealogy, history' (1971a) is often regarded as one of Foucault's most important text on the genealogical method. However it is a text that needs to be approached with caution, as it advances a number of ideas about genealogy that Foucault was to discard shortly afterwards. Like *The Archaeology of Knowledge*, it also proposes a whole series of rather confusing categories which are by no means easy to apply. Later in a lecture delivered in 1976 (1977f), Foucault describes genealogy as a form of research aimed at activating 'subjugated' historical knowledge, that is, knowledge which has been rejected by mainstream knowledge, or which is too local and specific to be deemed of any importance. In this account, he characterises archaeology as the process of unearthing and analysing subjugated knowledge and genealogy as the method of strategically disseminating such knowledge so that it can be effective for people's struggles. Unfortunately this description is far too general to be of much use at a concrete level.

If one is considering practicalities, the reality is that there is not really a great deal of difference between the tools Foucault uses to engage in either archaeology or genealogy. The distinction is to be found rather, in how Foucault characterises that level where the historical orders of knowledge and culture emerge, and where objects of knowledge are formed. Or as Foucault puts it succinctly in 'The order of discourse': 'The difference between the critical and the genealogical enterprise is not so much a difference of object or domain, but of point of attack, perspective and delimitation' (OD: 72). If archaeology addresses a level at which differences and similarities are determined, a level where things are organised simply to produce manageable forms of knowledge, the stakes are much higher for genealogy.

Genealogy deals with precisely the same substrata of knowledge and culture, but Foucault now describes it as a level where the grounds of the true and the false come to be distinguished via mechanisms of power. In the case of archaeology, patterns of differences and similarities form in close relation to something Foucault describes as 'ideology' or more generally as 'non-discursive practices'. But the latter were not primary. As for genealogy, the historical division between the true and the false is more directly the result of power. Further, in the early 1970s, Foucault argues that power is prior to and produces knowledge. The differences between the two approaches in Foucault's work can be seen in comparing two statements about the level underlying knowledge. In 1967, he said:

> Beneath what science knows about itself is something that it doesn't know; and its history, its becoming, its periods and accidents obey a certain number of laws and determinations. These laws and determinations are what I have tried to bring to light. I have tried to unearth an autonomous domain that would be the unconscious of knowledge, which would have its own rules, just as the individual human unconscious has its own rules and determinations. (1968d: 54 mod.)

These 'rules and determinations' underlie the historical organisation of similarities and differences in knowledge and culture. By 1971, Foucault had shifted his way of describing this 'unconscious' and it had become a matter of the division between the true and the false, between inclusion and exclusion; it was more clearly an exercise of power, rather than simple organisation. He explains: 'My problem is essentially the definition of the implicit systems in which we find ourselves prisoners; what I would like to grasp is the system of limits and exclusion which we practice without realising it; I would like to make the cultural unconscious apparent' (1971g: 73). In short, archaeology is about the 'conditions of possibility' which give rise to knowledge, whereas genealogy is about the 'constraints' that limit the orders of knowledge. In both instances, Foucault is dealing with the same level, he has simply changed his emphasis and way of viewing it.

Problematisations

But even the fortunes of genealogy are limited in Foucault's work, and if one still finds occasional references to this term later on, in the 1980s

Foucault is far more interested in describing what he calls 'the history of thought', which addresses a level he has now redefined as 'thought', 'problematizations' and 'regimes of practice'. Foucault gradually lost interest in explaining power as a general war-like situation in the late 1970s. A change took place in how he characterised the table top which underlay the historical orders of culture. In the 1980s, his focus shifted to the ordering of self – a self which exists as an integral part of the world and the social body. The self is ordered in relation to freedom, a freedom which has the capacity to refuse to co-operate in the exercise of power. Thus Foucault returns from a new angle to his pre-1970 position which holds that there is always something in human experience that escapes the exercise of power. Not every attempt to create and modify order involves the direct exercise of power.

One of the terms that emerges during this late period in Foucault's work is 'problematisation'. This is the level at which the agenda is set for common problems under discussion in a particular time and place. People actually create this level individually and collectively through quite specific actions and words which can be traced historically. Foucault says:

> We have to understand very clearly, I think, that a given problematisation is not an effect or consequence of a historical context or situation, but is an answer given by definite individuals (although you may find some answer given in a series of texts, and at a certain point the answer may become so general that it also becomes anonymous). (FS: 172)

Foucault first developed a notion of examining 'problems' in history in a paper originally delivered in 1978 (1980b) and refined this notion over the years to eventually come up with the idea of 'problematisation'. He offers a very useful definition of this concept and of 'the history of thought' in his book of lectures *Fearless Speech*. As he routinely does every time he renames his approach, he distinguishes what he is doing from the history of ideas and from social history. He says he is not trying to identify when a specific concept appears, or write the history of a period or institution. He describes the history of thought as 'the analysis of the way an unproblematic field of experience or set of practices which were accepted without question ... becomes a problem, raises discussion and debate, incites new reactions, and induces a crisis in the previously silent behaviour, habits, practices and, institutions' (FS: 74). But Foucault is also careful to forestall any charge of 'historical idealism' in relation to this notion: 'When I say that I am studying the "problematisation" of madness, crime, or sexuality, it is not a way of denying the reality of such phenomena ... The problematisation is an "answer" to a concrete situation which is real' (FS: 171–2). Foucault once again reinterprets his past work in the light of this new conception, listing madness, crime, sex, and the self; all as acute 'problems' that have emerged for debate at various periods in history.

The history of thought

As early as 1966, Foucault was already describing what he did as the history 'of all that "contains thought" in a culture, of all in which there is thought'. Thought, he argued could be found 'in philosophy, but also in a novel, in jurisprudence, in law, in an administrative system, in a prison' (1966a: 267). He reinforced these ideas later in his career, noting:

> We need to free ourselves of the sacralisation of the social as the only instance of the real and stop regarding that essential element in human life and human relations – I mean thought – as so much wind. Thought does exist, both beyond and before systems and edifices of discourse. It is something that is often hidden but always drives everyday behaviours. There is always a little thought occurring even in the most stupid institutions; there is always thought in silent habits. (1981g: 456)

From this is it clear that Foucault is opposed to the idea of 'thought' as something divorced from action and from real material existence. Every human institution and action activates some form of thought, even if the individual practising that action is not aware of the thought they are putting into play. In adopting this view, Foucault is deliberately challenging the 'theory/practice' divide. Theory is already a practice, something that occurs in a particular time and place and is generated by specific individuals. Thus in 1980 Foucault explains that he is interested not in 'institutions', 'theories' or ideologies, but in 'practices'. Hence, Foucault's history of the prison is not a history of a particular institution, but it is a history of 'the practice of imprisonment' (1980c: 225) of which the institution forms but one element. The notion of practice makes it possible to treat all cultural and human activities at the same level and to discern general patterns of order across categories that are usually hermetically divided from each other in terms of traditional analysis. So, for example, one can compare literature, cinema, scientific theory, social institutions, policy documents, economic trends and political movements all at the same level and come up with very interesting results.

The history of the present

Foucault often comments that he is examining the past in order to throw light on contemporary 'problems'. His notion of the 'history of the present' has lent its name to a well-known Foucauldian research network based in both Canada and the UK and also to a journal. This wide usage testifies to the fascination of this idea for many applying his work. Even in his earliest work on psychology, Foucault expressed an interest in the confrontation between past and present, and the heavy hand of the past weighing down every present moment. In 1967, he declared: 'I seek to diagnose, to carry out a diagnosis of the present. To say what we are today and what it means, today, to say what we do say.' (1967e: 91). Almost ten years later he also proclaimed famously in *Discipline and Punish* that he was writing 'the history of the present' (DP: 31), and in 1983 he continued this theme, explaining, 'the question I start off with is: what are we and what are we today? What is this instant that is ours? Therefore, if you like, it is a history that starts off from this present day actuality' (1988d: 411). This 'history of the present' is not simply a diagnosis, it is also an intervention. Foucault says that it is his aim to write in order to make the past no longer present. He wishes to relegate the past to the past, to show how strange it is – to force his readers to live in the present to discover the connections there, not with the past. It is only in the present that one can make changes. In order to be free, one needs to continually expose what remains alive of the past in the present and relegate it to the past. To be unaware of the past is to be trapped by it.

Conclusion

To summarise briefly, 'archaeology' examines the 'conditions of possibility' underlying the emergence of various systems of knowledge (of which scientific knowledge is a subset) and of the ways in which these systems of knowledge create the grounds for producing statements recognised to be valid. Genealogy, on the other hand, examines the constraints, the 'regimes of truth' that underlie the historically variable divisions between the true and the false in knowledge and culture. If Foucault used archaeology to focus mainly on scientific and pre-scientific knowledge and associated institutions, with genealogy he widens his focus to more general processes which define instances of social regulation such as the prison, and the modern state and the emergence of social institutions in general.

The 'history of thought' deals with how particular areas of human experience become problems at specific times in history, notably problems of sexual conduct and the formation of subjectivity and the self. It is important to emphasise, however, that the division between these three historical approaches is a highly artificial one, and there is in practice a great deal of overlap between all these categories. Foucault also characterises the different phases in his work in different ways. In the introduction to *The Use of Pleasure* (UP: 4–6), he notes that he originally began with an analysis of 'discursive practices' and the 'human sciences', and then moved on to examine manifestations of power, finally taking up an analysis of 'the subject'. He also recasts his work in overall terms as the way people first of all constitute themselves as subjects of knowledge, then as subjects who act on others exercising relations of power, and finally as ethical subjects in relation to morality (1983c: 262). If Foucault does indeed shift his points of view and angles of attack and subject matter during his career, structurally and philosophically his approach remains fairly constant. In the next chapter, we will look at some of the specific historical methodology that Foucault employs.

End Notes

[1] For a very detailed and somewhat controversial critique of this level in Foucault's work from a philosophical point of view see Han (2002).

[2] A few years later Foucault was to remark far less formally: 'This break is my problem, not my solution. If I keep going on about this break, it is because it is one hell of a puzzle and not at all a way of solving things' (2004c: 124).

[3] Foucault also uses the metaphor of geology to describe this method (2004c: 92).

SIX   Discontinuity and Discourse

Discontinuity and the event

The principle of discontinuity is one of the essential characteristics of Foucault's approach to history and while his most detailed discussions of this idea occur for the most part in his historiographical works of the late 1960s and early 1970s, it is a principle that he never abandons. Why is Foucault so insistent in his rejection of continuity as a tool for historical explanation? The problem is, he says, that it in fact implies a whole host of 'metaphysical' and unprovable assumptions about history and experience, assumptions which ultimately entrench existing systems of power and injustice. Thus he embarks on a quest to find every possible discontinuity, break and difference. Also crucial to Foucault's practice of history is that embodied form of discontinuity – the 'event'. Every human experience, activity, idea and cultural form can be analysed as an event or as series of events – something that has a beginning and an end. Foucault acknowledges his debt to particular historians in developing these ideas of discontinuity and the event: historians such as Fernand Braudel, François Furet, Emmanuel Le Roy Ladurie, the Cambridge historians, the Soviet historians and even Marxist philosopher Louis Althusser (1967d: 280–1).

These historians, the 'serial' historians in particular, were often criticised for favouring 'structure' over the event in their analyses of the effects of climate and long-term economic cycles. But Foucault argues that such practices of history actually expand the territory of the event, by demonstrating that change and discontinuity exist at every level, not just at the level of battles, dynasties and governments (AK: 7–8). Foucault (1972b: 428) refers to the work of French historians Huguette and Pierre Chaunu in this context. The ships entering and leaving the Port of Seville constitute one type of event. Underneath this layer we find another set of events occurring as fluctuations in market prices, then beneath this layer again we find economic growth and recession. Often such events are only perceived in a confused fashion by contemporaries, and it is up to historians to later uncover and analyse the long-term significance of these interrelated layers in their broader context. Foucault adds with a characteristic touch of irony: 'for it is quite clear to us now that the reversal of an economic trend is much more important than the death of a king' (1972b: 428) The orders or patterns of these different series of events can be described and their interaction examined.

Apart from proposing complex layers of events, Foucault also offers another alternative to the 'forms of order implied by the continuity of time' (OT: xxiii) and that is the orders of space and simultaneity. He argues, for example in *The Order of Things*, that if natural history can be related to anything other than itself, it is not to the subsequent development of Darwinian theories of evolution, but to other contemporary forms of knowledge, namely general grammar, and the analysis of money and wealth. In other words, similarities of order are not only to be tracked down in the sequences of time, but in events that were occurring at the same time as each other.

Continuity and its assumptions

Foucault argues that continuity is based on a number of assumptions which he sees it as his duty to challenge:

(1) First of all, in traditional history, notions such as tradition, cause, effect and influence, are all used as magical formulas to explain change. When major contradictions really can't be smoothed over in such a fashion, then concepts such as 'social conditions', 'mentality', 'world view', 'spirit of the age' and 'crisis' will all be wheeled out.

(2) The second assumption is that there is a constant human nature, an essence of 'man' that remains the same throughout history. In this model, the way humans experience the world is basically unchanging, the only difference being that people discover more and more 'truth' as history progresses.

(3) Further, continuity presupposes that certain 'objects' and 'categories' or classifications remain the same, unchanged throughout history, that they have their own eternal metaphysical essences. So, for example, there has always been something called 'mental illness' just waiting to be 'discovered' by science, to be rescued from the ignorance and superstition which classified it as an untreatable madness or 'demonic possession'. Likewise, disease was merely waiting for proper scientists to empirically observe what was actually going on in reality, to take over from the dubious quacks who insisted on applying superstitious remedies out of old books.

(4) Continuity also assumes that there is a particular end or goal to history, that all events and all change are tending towards an absolute point – this might be the

classless society of Marx, or the absolute rationality of Hegel ('the real is rational'), the progress of scientific truth or biological perfection as the result of evolution.

(5) Another feature of the continuist view is that history has progressed inevitably to the present, in a marvellous conquest of Reason and scientific truth over error and superstition. A succession of 'great men' and geniuses have fostered this advancement. The past merely exists as an imperfect and somewhat embarrassingly quaint prologue to the present.

(6) Finally, continuity also eliminates the possibility of chance events. Nothing ever happens without a reason. The rationality of progress, ideology, scientific truth or the working out of some political or religious destiny mean that history is determined in advance, and there is nothing anybody can do to alter the final outcomes: any changes made simply confirm the inevitable end result.

In short, for Foucault, the idea of continuity is one of the most important pillars propping up the existing status quo with all its injustices. It also makes the world a very boring and homogenous place and fosters a tendency to turn to the past to justify certain quite intolerable behaviours in the name of 'tradition'. History, Foucault argues, is not the result of intention, destiny and design, but the result of human error, illusion, accidents and struggles for power (1971a: 380–1) and many current social arrangements should be viewed in this light.

A new organisation of history

In order to challenge traditional ways of organising history, Foucault (1967d: 283) decided to resort to a kind of 'systematic game'. Instead of trying to explain away historical anomalies, he would focus on them and try to meticulously describe the events at all levels that marked the passage from one historical state to another. He begins by examining the way documents, texts or discourses are habitually divided up and classified by historians into categories which perpetuate the notion of continuity. Aside from criticising the author and the work, as we have seen in previous chapters, Foucault also criticises the notion of the scientific or academic 'discipline'. For example, we can't speak about the Ancient Greeks practising chemistry and biology without being anachronistic or without introducing a complex and rather questionable network of analogies and resemblances.

Foucault (1966a: 262) explained in 1966 that he mainly deals with the 'verbal traces' left behind by institutions and theories and other practices. The problem then is to organise these traces into 'what logicians call "classes", aestheticians call "forms", social scientists call "structures"'. One of the advantages, which is also a significant difficulty, with this approach is that the practitioner is obliged 'to read everything, to know all the institutions and all the practices ... which means that one will take up Don Quixote,

Descartes and a decree by Pomponne de Bellièvre about houses of internment in the same stroke' (1966a: 262). In short, no text, no institutional trace is too insignificant and by examining them all at the same level, the cultural historian is able to come up with some surprising results. The exponential amount of research this method requires did not appear to worry Foucault, but it is scarcely surprising that other scholars have baulked at the prospect. As Raymond Bellour asks Foucault in an interview in 1966, 'how do you read everything?' (1966a: 262). This practice of placing the most diverse of texts and practices at the same level always remained a feature of Foucault's approach and he constantly sought to refine his rejection of the idea of any differences and hierarchies in his source material.

However, faced with the real difficulty of an inexhaustible archive, Foucault later formulated the idea of a 'history of problems' in order to introduce some reasonable limitations into the selection of material, which would at the same time clearly spell out why some material was excluded. He uses the notion of a history of problems to distinguish what he is doing from general social history, arguing that he is not interested in studying a 'period' or the history of an institution during a given period. This, he says, would indeed require an exhaustive examination of all the available documentation and a fair division between the examination of different periods. But studying a 'problem' means a different choice and treatment of material. Foucault adds that he concentrates heavily on prescriptive and programmatic texts which tend to create the impression of a perfect order. These prescriptions were of course, not usually achieved. In *Discipline and Punish*, for example, Foucault looks at the texts of 'programs' for prisons, schools and a disciplinary society in generals (such as Jeremy Betham's Panopticon). In *The Use of Pleasures* and *The Care of the Self*, Foucault relies on 'prescriptive' texts – texts that describe how people ought to behave, how societies ought to be constructed – and not on texts describing 'what actually happened'. The examination of these 'programmatic' texts leads to a history that differs from history written with the more usual aim of 'grasping a "whole society" in its "living reality"' (1980c: 233). Foucault again later in his career made reference to his own personal experience and biography to explain his selection of subject matter. He also used the idea of the 'specific intellectual' located within a particular discipline, institution or social setting as another way of providing parameters for the choice of research matter.

Discourse

In the late 1960s Foucault generally focused on the historical 'traces' left in the form of 'discourses'. The notion of 'discourse' has now entered common theoretical parlance, as much through Foucault's work as the work of other theorists who modelled their work on linguistics in the 1960s. It has also found considerable fortune more recently through the methods of critical discourse analysis (CDA) (Fairclough, 2003). 'Discourse' itself was originally a technical term in linguistics and rhetoric, meaning a reasoned argument, but in some usages it has now come to mean something equivalent to 'world view'. Foucault readily admits in *The Archaeology of Knowledge* that his own use of the term was somewhat equivocal and that he had used and abused it in a multitude of ways (AK: 107). In the most general sense, he uses it to mean 'a certain "way of speaking"' (AK: 193). He also uses it to define 'the group of statements that belong to a single system of formation [of knowledge]', for example 'clinical discourse, economic discourse, the discourse of natural history, psychiatric discourse' (AK: 107–8).

The term has now become indissolubly linked with Foucault's work and has generated a number of misunderstandings, not least of which is the idea that for Foucault there is nothing outside 'discourse', and also that his analysis can be used as a kind of universal template. It is very important to emphasise here that Foucault argues that we can only examine a system of discourse, an archive, once it has already happened. We cannot extrapolate from one specific historical order and say that a particular rule will be valid tomorrow or next year. One can only describe the rules of a past system of discourse, we cannot make those rules prescriptive and apply them in the future. In short, as we have already mentioned, Foucault's historical method does not operate as a scientific methodology. One can only formulate the rules of already 'dead' discursive systems.

Interestingly, for all its close associations in the secondary literature with Foucault's work, 'discourse' scarcely appears in his work except rather infrequently in fairly commonplace contexts before *The Order of Things* and then only occasionally after 1972. It appears in the guise of 'historical event' in the new preface to the 1972 revised edition of his 1963 work *The Birth of the Clinic*, but not in the main body of the text. Foucault first starts to use the term in *The Order of Things* but only in a very limited and specialised historical context to describe a particular process of using words to represent the order of things during the eighteenth century. In his subsequent work, Foucault adopted the more familiar view of discourses as verbal traces left behind by history. In this model, discourses do not 'represent things'; they are not transparent windows onto the real world. Neither are they merely signposts to hidden meanings that have to be endlessly searched for. Instead, Foucault argues, discourses have their own materiality, density, thickness and consistency as objects in the world and just as economics has laws so does the arrangement of discourse. [1] These 'discourses' are both objects and events, historical traces left behind in words, and they form the building blocks of Foucault's archaeological method.

Discursive practices

In *The Archaeology of Knowledge*, Foucault develops a whole series of categories to organise both discourse and its relation to other practices, events and objects. The most widely-known and widely used of these terms is the discursive practice. Foucault notes in explaining his notion of 'discursive practice', that 'to speak is to do something' (AK: 209). Discursive practices operate according to rules which are quite specific to a particular time, space, and cultural setting. It is not a matter of external determinations being imposed on people's thought, rather it is a matter of rules which, a bit like the grammar of a language, allow certain statements to be made. To distinguish a discursive practice, one might ask a question similar to the one Foucault asks in *The Order of Things*: 'What conditions did Linnaeus (or Petty, or Arnauld) have to fulfil not to make his discourse coherent and true in general, but to give it at the time when it was written and accepted, value and practical application as scientific discourse – or, more exactly, as naturalist, economic, or grammatical discourse?' (OT: xiv). Even if Foucault has mentioned specific names and sciences here, the rules which define a discursive practice do not necessarily always coincide with the works of specific authors, or with specific disciplines or sciences. Thus, even if Foucault does not specifically use the term 'discursive practice' in his discussion of anti-Machiavellian literature in his famous lecture on 'Governmentality' (1978v), he is still clearly referring to the same notion. This literature criticising Machiavelli's political theories spans three centuries from the sixteenth century until the nineteenth century. Foucault observes that in spite of its negative critical function it operated as 'a positive genre, which had its object, its concepts, its strategy', adding further that it is 'in its positivity' that he wished to consider this literature (1978u: 638) [2]. It is worth noting here that when Foucault uses the word 'positivity' in his writings, he is usually referring to an organised field of knowledge. During the 1960s, he often uses the word to characterise pre-scientific knowledge.

Each discursive practice deals with a field of objects, which are things presented to thought and are the occasion or the matter on which thought is exercised. For example the objects of geometry are certain ideal solids and the objects of psychiatry are certain morbid mental states. These objects do not exist independently of knowledge, they are not 'discovered' but are constructed in relation to a whole set of physical, social and cultural occurrences. It is important to note that the definitions Foucault often provides for sciences or scientific practices are in fact identical with the definitions he provides for the discursive practice, emphasising that science is simply but one particular form of discursive practice. In the summary of his 1971 lectures at the Collège de France, Foucault offers a useful definition which applies as much to science as discursive practices. These practices he says: 'are characterised by the demarcation of a field of objects, by the definition of a legitimate perspective for a subject of knowledge, by the setting of norms for elaborating concepts and theories' (1971s: 11).

Non-discursive objects and practices

A number of critics have taken Foucault to task for reducing every-thing to discourse. Foucault refuted this characterisation of his position on several occasions. As he says in reply to a critic: 'You are attributing to me the idea that the only really analysable element, the only one which is available to us is discourse. And that, as a conse-quence, the rest doesn't exist. Only discourse exists ... In fact, it doesn't make any sense to say that only discourse exists' (1974h: 637). He offers the example of 'capitalist exploitation', which came into being without needing a theoretical discourse. Elsewhere he also makes a clear distinc-tion between discourse and other objects on several occasions, noting for example: 'there is nothing to be gained from describing this autonomous layer of discourses unless one can relate it to other layers, practices, insti-tutions, social relations, political relations, and so on. It is that relation-ship which has always intrigued me' (1967d: 284).

Neither are discourses the only way in which culture can be presented and interpreted. So for example, the visual arts (and by extension the per-formance arts such as dance) are not just another way of 'saying some-thing', of pronouncing a discourse. Foucault explains:

> Making a form appear, is not a roundabout way (whether it be more subtle or more naïve) of *saying* something. Everything that people do is not, in the final analysis, a decipherable murmur. Discourse and figuration each have their own mode of being; but they maintain complex and tangled relations: It is their reciprocal relation that needs to be described. (1967f: 622 original emphasis)

Just as Foucault was interested in the material and substantial existence of discourse, and in undermining notions of discourse as representation, he applied the same principles to art. He was fascinated in the late 1960s by the work of the late nineteenth century French painter, Manet. He saw the artist as having invented a 'painting-object', which subverted the whole notion of art as a simple representation or picture of an exterior reality (2004a: 47). Manet, says Foucault, draws attention in his work to the fact that his paintings are canvases in a frame, objects in their own right, not windows through which one can see reality. The same ideas also attracted Foucault to René Magritte's surrealist paintings (1968b).

In establishing the relations between elements of discourse and 'non-discursive' elements, such as political, social economic or institutional factors or the visual arts, Foucault is very careful to stress that these relations are not ones of influence or cause and effect. He is also at pains to avoid the traditional idealist/materialist division. An idea does not 'cause' a social or economic event, or vice-versa. Ideas do not 'influence' other ideas. Economics is not the material infrastructure and 'theory' or 'culture' the frivolous superstructure. Ideas, discourse and political, economic or social phenomena in Foucault's system are analysed at the same level for their common structures and common elements. It is not a matter of dividing history into two levels, the airy level of ideas (or discourses) and the earthy and 'real' level of 'material' occurrences. In the concluding pages of *The Archaeology of Knowledge*, Foucault mounts an impassioned case in favour of the materiality of discourse and words: 'Has not the practice of revolutionary discourse and scientific discourse in Europe over the past two hundred years freed you from this idea that words are wind, an external whisper, a beating of wings that one has difficulty in hearing in the serious matter of history?' (AK: 209).

Conclusion

A fter 1971, however, Foucault more or less abandons the notions of discourse and of the discursive practice and mentions the notion of discontinuity less and less. He explains in 1977, for example, that he is not interested in drawing distinctions between the discursive and non-discursive as his grid of analysis is not a linguistic one (1977s: 198). Discourse does resurface briefly in Volume 1 of *The History of Sexuality* however, where he describes discourse as the location where power and knowledge intersect. Foucault specifies here that it is not a question of the popular idea of an opposition between a dominant and an excluded discourse, but rather a matter of a complex and unstable network of strategic exercises of power and resistance operating across a large range of discourses (HS: 100–1). If he refers further to 'discursive practices' briefly in passing in his work in the early 1980s, it is simply to list them amongst other practices (1984b: 201). But if Foucault abandons the specific words relating to archaeology and discourse, he retains the same structural forms implied by the radical rejection of discontinuity and merely develops and refines the same concepts using different terminology. We will now leave aside the discussion of history to turn to the idea of truth in Foucault's work.

End Notes

[1] For a fascinating and detailed application of Foucault's ideas on the materiality of the document in the field of library and information science see Frohmann (2000).

[2] The English translation of this article (1978v: 203) appears to be referring to a slightly different version of the lecture from the one that appears in *Dits et écrits* (1978u: 638). The version which appears in STP is the same as the one in *Dits et écrits*.

Principle 3: Truth

Truth plays a major role in the way Foucault structures his writings. It could even be argued that his entire work is one long effort to reinstate a form of truth that has been consistently marginalised since Descartes – a form of truth that relies on history, on patient and constant work and 'exercise' by every individual in their daily lives in the world. It is a form of truth that is accessible to, and is indeed revealed by, the most marginalised of individuals – mad people, ill people, prisoners, those designated as 'abnormal'. It is a truth that does not have a fixed and unchanging content and is not the province of a privileged few, but can be acquired by anyone through exercises involving choices of action within their own specific historical, social and cultural settings.

There has been a great deal of discussion about Foucault's approach to truth. He is often accused of denying 'objective truth' and of introducing an amoral and highly dubious relativism. But he firmly insists that he is not engaged in a 'skeptical or relativistic refusal of all verified truth' (1982b: 330), noting further: 'all those who say that for me the truth doesn't exist are simple-minded'. (1984l: 456) This is not to say however, that Foucault's notion of truth is the same as his detractors. He argues that there are strict historically and culturally specific rules about how truth is both accessed and disseminated. One cannot make any claims about truth except from within quite specific cultural and historical settings. Further to this, any system of rules is also a finite system of constraints and limitations, therefore truth is of necessity the subject of struggles for power. In short 'truth', like every other category in Foucault's work, is a historical category. Foucault further specifies that the history of truth he is describing is specific to the West arguing that there has been an overwhelming obligation in Western history to search for the truth, to tell the truth and to honour certain people who are designated as having privileged access to the truth.

Foucault consistently maintains that he is not interested in spelling out for the reader what the concrete content of 'the truth' might actually be, instead he is interested in looking at the way rules are set up historically to grant or limit access to something called the truth. Foucault is only too willing to admit himself that his approach to these problems is constantly experimental:

> I am preoccupied by these relations of truth/power, knowledge/power. Now, this layer of objects, rather this layer of relations, is difficult to come to grips with; and as I don't have a general theory with which to apprehend these relations, I am, if you like, a blind empiricist, that is, in the worst of situations. I have no general theory, and neither do I have a reliable instrument. (1977zc: 404)

Foucault's 'fictions'

Foucault's experimental and non-definitive treatments of the complex interrelations between the categories of truth, knowledge and power have provided an absolute field day for philosophers, historians and outraged moralists alike. There is now virtually an entire philosophical sub-industry which deals with Foucault's notions of truth. Numbers of commentators have taken his refusal to define what truth is – his contention that there are strict but changing rules about how truth is produced and accessed and that those rules are often set in relation to political agendas – as a statement that Foucault does not believe in any kind of truth. Indeed as Foucault says himself: 'The problem of the truth of what I say is a very difficult one for me; in fact it's the central problem' (1980e: 242).

At an academic and purely technical level, he employs methods that are characterised by the use of positivist, critical and scholarly tools of archival research, meticulous documentation and historical methods of comparison, verification and citation. But at the same time, he calls into question the positivist foundation – that basic unit of incontrovertible empirical self-evident truth on which such critical edifices usually rest, namely 'the fact'. Foucault notes early on in his career, following Nietzsche, that the 'fact' is already an interpretation (1967b: 275). In other words, his writings are based on elements which are already 'fictions', things that have already been selected, fabricated and organised in certain ways. Given this situation, other interpretations and organisations of the same material remain a very real possibility at any time. There are no primary sources or even physical artefacts that one can accept without question. Everything is already a secondary source, an interpretation. As Vincent Descombes observes in his useful 1979 book *Le même et l'autre*, Foucault's approach makes things rather uncomfortable for other historians, as from a technical point of view their work presents all the same outward appearances as Foucault's. This can only mean that their own histories are also resting on a uneasy quagmire of uncertainty. The unsettling revelation produced by Foucault's approach goes a long way to explaining the relentless pursuit by a number of scholars in tracking down every possible empirical 'mistake' and 'error' of interpretation in Foucault's work. [1] It is a desperate attempt to redress the disturbing unbalance Foucault has produced in that comforting equilibrium of what everyone accepts as true and the status accorded to those qualified to pronounce such truths.

But Foucault's unbalancing of the scales has actually been extremely productive, forcing others to question their own certainties, to take a fresh look at old material and to unearth material previously ignored as being outside the canon of acceptable knowledge. It has also forced people to look at different ways of organising concepts and to find new ways of addressing unequal power relations and social injustice, at every level of the social body.

But again, one has to be very precise here. To say that Foucault's facts are all 'fictions' and that he is merely producing another 'fiction' is not to say by any means that he is just making it all up and that he can say whatever he likes. Foucault insists on this point on a number of occasions. For example he describes *The Order of Things* as 'a pure and simple fiction: it is a novel, but it is not I who invented it, it is the relationship of our age and its epistemological configuration with that whole mass of [historical] statements' (1967d: 286). Later when discussing the reception of *Madness and Civilization* and the kind of 'experience' it generated – indeed continues to generate amongst its readership – Foucault observes that in order for that particular experience to take place, his book needed 'to be true in terms of academic, historically verifiable truth. It can't exactly be a novel' (1980e: 243).

Although these points about the tension between 'fiction' and Foucault's historical material have been discussed endlessly in the secondary literature, confusion continues to reigns. One popular current interpretation is that it is the 'experience' that counts when one is reading Foucault's work, and whether or not his historical and empirical claims are accurate is of little consequence. But clearly for Foucault, issues of historical accuracy did in fact matter a great deal. At various points in his career, he was involved in detailed exchanges with other scholars on the subject of the accuracy or otherwise of his historical data. [2] In an exchange with the historian Lawrence Stone concerning *Madness and Civilization*, he refutes point by point a number of historical errors that Stone had accused him of committing. In the course of this polemic he makes reference to 'the probity essential to any scientific work' (1983h: 41).

What prevents the 'fictional' elements of Foucault's work from floating off into a kind of post-modern indeterminacy and a vague 'anything goes' stance is its attachment to history, to the practicalities of concrete existence and the material existence of things – even when those things such as words and ideas have traditionally been regarded as insubstantial. Foucault comments that he is

> intrigued by the existence of discourses, by the fact that words took place. These events functioned in relation to their original situation, they left traces behind them, they continue to exist, and they exercise in that very subsistence in history, a certain number of manifest or secret functions ... My object is ... The accumulated existence of discourses. (1967d: 289 mod.)

Ideas and words have a material and historical existence and they can be analysed alongside other historical artefacts and events. People's very lives and whole existences have been, and are, at stake in these words and these ideas.

In an interesting article titled 'Lives of infamous men' (1977k), Foucault explains that for years he had been making use of archival documents; brief reports on a variety of obscure, unfortunate and wretched people who had come to the notice of institutions such as the asylum or the legal system. He says: 'real lives were "played out" in these few sentences: by this I don't mean they were represented, but that their liberty, their misfortune, often their death, in any case their fate, were decided at least in part. These discourses really crossed lives; existences were actually risked and lost in these words' (1977k: 160 mod.). This passage also draws attention to another factor that limits Foucault's fictions: his commitment to exposing social injustice and intolerable exercises of power. Foucault's works may indeed be described as fictions, but they are fictions which are generated in relation to quite specific technical mechanisms of historical verification, with an aim of drawing attention to forgotten people and forgotten forms of knowledge or those otherwise deemed to be of no importance.

Idealism and empiricism

This odd and immensely complex balance in Foucault's work between the empirical and the 'fictional' is extraordinarily difficult to maintain and the secondary literature has used his work to support both idealist and materialist forms of reductionism in cultural studies. On the one hand, his work has been used, as we saw in Chapter 6, to support the idealist claim that discourse and representation is all, and that nothing exists outside of discourse. At the other end of the spectrum, his work has been used to undertake meticulous studies of institutions and practices which aim to demonstrate that ideas about the self, truth and ethics are merely the product of the material logic of institutions and struggles for power and distinction within the social body. This position is particularly favoured by those who apply notions of governmentality to the analysis of social institutions, bureaucracies and professional practices. Foucault, however, emphasises that engaging in such research is not a matter of joining, as he so elegantly puts it, 'the great warm and tender Freemasonry of useless erudition' (1977f: 79). It is not about countering the abstractions of theory with the everyday reality of 'facts', or opposing speculative knowledge with a spurious scientific rigour (1977f: 83). It is not about letting the 'facts' finally speak for themselves with their cumulative weight demonstrating a self-evident truth: this is the classic empiricist project. Foucault's collections of empirical data, rather than bolstering up existing systems actually undermine them. The knowledge he collects shows the limitations and arbitrariness of existing systems and disciplines of knowledge. The kind of knowledge gathered by institutions is often carefully and strategically selected and based on the elimination of other knowledges or even of its own history, as Foucault argues is the case with psychiatry. By unearthing all the knowledges rejected by these institutionalised disciplinary systems and examining the historical and sometimes quite scurrilous reasons for the rejection of some knowledge and inclusion of others, Foucault's work challenges the idea that knowledge proceeds by the mere systematic accumulation of self-evidently 'true' 'facts'. He aims to demonstrate that knowledge in fact accumulates and organises itself strategically and politically.

Foucault also adds the further qualification that he is not proposing a model of a direct experience of the world uncorrupted by knowledge. He is equally insistent that his approach is not about challenging 'the contents, methods or concepts of a science' (1977f: 84), but rather about challenging the 'centralising effects of power which are linked to the institution and functioning of an organised scientific discourse within a society such as ours' (1977f: 84 mod.). It is this attention to the way knowledge and truth are strategically shaped and organised by exercises of power, as well as the rejection of the idea that the truth is out there just waiting to be discovered, which distinguishes Foucault's work from the tenets of empiricist philosophy and method. This is a fine distinction that a number of Foucault's English-speaking imitators have ignored, seeing Foucault's work simply as an opportunity to give a modern, trendy and more acceptable face to entrenched practices of Anglo-Saxon empiricism.

The dual history of truth

Leaving aside the question of the truth status of Foucault's own work, let us look at how he characterises what he describes as the 'history of truth'. There is an interesting dual structure throughout all of Foucault's work in relation to the operation of truth in Western history. This structure emerges in a number of different ways in his work. During the 1960s, generally he refers to truth in two ways, firstly in relation to limit-experiences such as dreams, madness and death, and secondly in relation to Reason, rationality and science. In the 1970s he changes the way he structures this dual history. If there are still two terms – one he characterises as a universalising continuist model and the other which constructs truth as an event – he concentrates almost exclusively on an idea of truth as being the pure product of mechanisms of power. In the 1980s, he finally undertakes an extended historical examination of the model of truth which a post-Cartesian rationalist view of knowledge had tried so hard to discredit and a model that he had championed in one form or another throughout his career. In all his work, Foucault takes the position that the Classical Age saw the boundaries between these two approaches to truth acquisition become more rigidly defined. The Enlightenment also saw the rise to dominance of one of these systems – namely a model of Reason, science and rationality with pretensions to universality. This way of ordering concepts arrogated to itself the privileged position of having sole access to the truth and relegated all other approaches to the status of superstition, mythology, entertainment (popular culture) or means of maintaining social order (religion). It also relied on a number of institutions (asylums, hospitals, schools, prisons, factories and so on) to both promote and further generate this version of truth.

Science

During the 1960s Foucault took a particular interest in the way science organised itself as a form of knowledge and the mechanisms it used to exclude particular people and experiences. Foucault was interested in science for a number of reasons. One of these was that 'science' had set itself up as the ultimate form of rational thought since the Enlightenment, with scientific reason becoming the privileged way of accessing truth. The idea was that for knowledge to acquire value as 'truth', it had to constantly strive to become 'scientific', to construct and organise concepts according to certain rigorous criteria of scientificity. This was the model which produced dreams of a 'scientific' Marxism in the 1960s. There was also a movement across the social sciences to set themselves up with the same prestige and the same epistemological rigour as the hard sciences. The method used by the hard and the pure sciences, such as physics and mathematics, was generally regarded as the best and indeed the only way to discover the truth about the world, human society and every other aspect of human existence in post-war society. It seemed that there was nothing that science could not do.

If one still finds many vestiges of this view of the world based on a belief in the superiority of science in the contemporary setting, it no longer exerts the overwhelming force that it did during the three decades following World War II. Foucault's interest in science in this context was therefore hardly surprising, but what was surprising to his readers was his thorough and meticulous undermining of the notion of the universality of science and scientific method. Far from seeking a way of applying his own method to all forms of knowledge, as was the general practice with theorists seeking to emulate scientific method or set up grand philosophies, he also wished to demonstrate how specific and how restricted his own methods were. As he says in *The Archaeology of Knowledge*, 'I not only admit that my analysis is limited, I want it so; I have made it so' (AK: 158). This is not to say that he did not hanker after developing some 'theory' of his own especially in his earlier work before eventually coming to adopt the position in the late 1970s that this was not essential or even desirable.

Further to this, as Foucault points out in *The Order of Things*, the assumption made by traditional history of ideas was that non-scientific or pre-scientific knowledge was not organised but simply provided 'evidence of a state of mind, an intellectual fashion, a mixture of archaism and bold conjecture, of intuition and blindness' (OT: ix). Foucault wanted to demonstrate that it was not a question of past ignorance, and the non-scientific and superstitious versus the triumphal march of Reason and progress embodied in such noble and rigorous sciences as mathematics and physics. Science is only a particular configuration of knowledge amongst others, so, for example, he argues that 'archaeological territories' can include literary and philosophical texts, institutional regulations and political decisions, police regulations, legal as well as scientific texts (AK: 183–4). Science emerges from this archaeological background as a particular way of ordering propositions but it does not supersede all other knowledge practices.

All forms of knowledge do not need to be 'scientific' in order to be valid and the methods and procedures of science, although suitable for some bodies of knowledge are not universally applicable. Scientific knowledge is not inherently 'superior' or more 'true' than other forms of knowledge. A 'scientific practice' in Foucault's account is a particular set of codified relations between a precisely constructed knower and a precisely constructed object, with strict rules which govern the formation of concepts. Foucault is interested in the historical emergence of this particular form of knowledge while criticising the view expressed by traditional histories of science, that science signals the discovery of truth. Scientific disciplines do not mark the emergence of a pure disembodied truth conquering the errors of myth, superstition and political intrigue.

89

Rather they are produced in conjunction with a variety of political, social and historical factors, which all form an essential part of their makeup. Foucault's approach is aimed at breaking down the power that 'science' exerts, showing that it is not the only means of accessing the truth. The belief in 'science' exercises considerable power in terms of excluding and invalidating other forms of knowledge and propping up particular social relations and hierarchies and forms of exclusion and inclusion, not least of which is the division between the so-called First World and Third World. Once again we see here Foucault's project of the disassociation of orders in action: the insistence that one order should not be reduced to another, in this case that the orders of knowledge and truth should not all be reduced to one order – namely the order of science. On the other hand, all of this is not to make the claim that the propositions of science are merely social constructions which are unconnected to the physical world. We will examine this broader history in the next chapter, but for the moment let us now turn to that second pole in Foucault's 'history of the truth', a truth that in his view has been consistently sidelined and gagged since the Enlightenment.

The limits

In his examination of culture and knowledge, Foucault always starts with limitations, exclusions and restraints, and marginal experience. He notes: 'There is not one culture in the world where everything is allowed. And we have known for a long time that man does not begin with freedom, but with the limit and the line not to be crossed' (1964g: 100 mod.). Looking back on his work 15 years later Foucault comments: 'I made an effort, in particular, to understand how man had transformed certain of these limit-experiences into objects of knowledge – madness, death, crime. It's always a question of limit-experiences and the history of truth. I'm imprisoned, enmeshed in that tangle of problems' (1980e: 257).

During the 1960s he characterised this excluded experience in different ways: as dreams (1954), madness (MC), death (BC), the fantastic imagination (1964b), and sexuality (1963b) and finally a certain form of experience related to language (OT). It is a question of an entire poetic, spiritual and tragic appreciation of humans' limits and their relation to the 'Other' (the unknown, the different, what lies beyond). Dreams, madness, death, sexuality, literature all point to this silenced truth in Foucault's work. Try as they might, Reason and the processes of scientific rationalisation are not able to silence these experiences and the latter always re-emerge to resist and undermine the monotonous empires of conformity and the 'normal'. Throughout his entire career, Foucault saw it as his task to re-activate these experiences and to continually draw attention to the limitations of rational forms of order in knowledge and culture. In the original preface to *Madness and Civilization* which unfortunately only ever appeared in complete form in the original 1961 edition of the book, Foucault notes:

> One can do a history of the limits – of those obscure gestures, necessarily forgotten as soon as they are performed, through which a culture rejects something which for it becomes the Exterior ... Interrogating a culture on its limit-experiences, is to question it within the confines of history on a rupture which forms the very birth of its history. (1961a: 161)

A culture forms its identity in relation to what it rejects. In his preface to *Madness and Civilization*, apart from designating madness as something that has been excluded and silenced in Western history, Foucault names other divisions and 'exteriors', for example the 'Orient'. The Orient represents in Western history the mystical and magical elements of a past that has been rejected. This idea was taken up by Edward Said, in what was to be the first extended 'application' in English of Foucault's ideas to new research, his influential book *Orientalism* (1978). Another silenced and disqualified exterior includes the realm of dreams where, as Foucault lyrically puts it, 'man cannot prevent questioning himself on his own truth – whether it concerns his destiny or his heart' (1961a: 162). Foucault had of course already written a lengthy discussion on the history of dream interpretation in 1954. Yet another 'exterior' was formed by sexual prohibitions and sexual repression – a division which rendered a 'happy world of desire' impossible (1961a: 162). Foucault was of course later to reject such a simplistic notion of sexual repression and desire. In short, defining the limits of a culture throws into relief the identity of that culture, the values and systems of order it chooses to adopt. The experience of the exterior, the outside, the limits, the absence of any universal human subject is a theme that Foucault shared in common with a number of literary figures operating in post-war France. Foucault explains, 'The idea of a limit-experience that wrenches the subject from itself is what was important to me in my reading of Nietzsche, Bataille, and Blanchot' (1980e: 241).

Apart from his discussions on madness, death and sexuality, there is also an interesting discussion in Foucault's work during the 1960s relating to art and the imagination. Reason, in setting itself up as the sole means of access to the truth, also silenced a certain type of imaginative experience which was not only to be found in literature but also in early scientific writings. Imagination, like other areas of experience, also had to be subordinated to the new rules which came into being during the

91

Classical Age about what was true in relation to material, social and political existence. Only 'applied' imagination was of interest: scientifically plausible, socially and politically 'useful' works – these were the 'serious' works of art. In 'The order of discourse', Foucault, in discussing the constraints produced by a particular 'will to truth', notes: 'I am thinking of the way in which for centuries Western literature sought to ground itself on the natural, the plausible, on sincerity, on science as well – in short on true discourse' (OD: 55 mod.). All the rest became merely popular 'entertainments' and diversions for the masses. [3]

Older forms of imagination were not merely the pale and docile servants of rationality. It was also an imagination, which as the historian Jacques Le Goff suggests in his fascinating book *The Medieval Imagination* (1988) was not simply limited to the world of books and literature. It insinuated itself into the very fabric of the everyday. Medieval scientists were quite happy to include strange and imagined or semi-imagined plants, animals and places in their scientific classifications. Such things were regarded as marginal and exceptional phenomena but not untrue for all that.

For example, the sixteenth century naturalist Aldrovandi, in his description of snakes includes a list of the different meanings of the word snake, the history of the word and its synonyms, a description of the snake's anatomy, habits and habitat, citations relating to snakes, legends, myths and dreams about snakes, its medical and magical uses, its heraldic uses, historical facts about snakes, hieroglyphics, snake gods, the way snakes can be eaten and so on (OT: 39). To our modern eyes this would scarcely constitute a scientific (therefore 'true') description of a snake, but as Foucault notes all these things are things that can be 'read'. The reason why Aldrovandi's description seems so foreign to us, so outrageously 'unscientific', is that during the Renaissance there was no distinction between what one observed or 'read' in nature and what one read in books (OT: 39). Knowledge was governed by a different division between the true and the false. As Foucault says 'The division, so evident to us, between what we see, what others have observed and handed down, and what others imagine or naïvely believe, the great tripartition, apparently so simple and so immediate, into *Observation, Document*, and *Fable*, did not exist' (OT: 129).

Once language is defined as inherently rational and Reason becomes the only means of access to truth, then madness and the fantastic imagination can only be error and non-being. In silencing madness, the fantastic imagination, and other limit-experiences, a whole avenue of access to the truth has been repressed and as Foucault argues, a whole area of human experience. There is no longer any way of 'representing' this experience. Nonetheless, there is still something that persistently resists. Foucault refers to the works of famously mad authors, Artaud, Nerval and Nietzsche:

That [these experiences] can hardly receive any formulation except a lyrical one does not prove that they are dying out, nor that they are prolonging in spite of everything an existence that knowledge rejected a long time ago, but maintained in the shadows, they are vitalised in the most free and most originary forms of language. And their power of contestation is only all the more vigorous for that (HF: 223).

The 1970s

In the 1960s, Foucault dealt with the experiences of the limits at a general social and historical scale, and at the end of his career he particularised this experience to an individual and subjective – if still firmly historical – level. But during the 1970s, this anarchic exterior all but disappeared in his work. He abandoned the characterisation of an all-conquering Reason opposed by an almost silenced but still courageously resisting other of '"spiritual experiences" … such as dreams, madness, folly' (1964d: 72). It is no longer a question of an opposition between the Same and the Other, and the Interior and Exterior, instead it is a question of two 'positions' (PP: 236) or two 'histories' (1974i: 4) of the truth in Western history.

In his lectures at the Collège de France in 1973 and 1974 (PP: 237) Foucault argues that a continuist and all pervasive universal view of truth, replaced an older and more archaic view which saw truth as something rare and discontinuous that had to be carefully sought out. The modern view represented by science saw truth as inhabiting the entire world. All one needed was the right scientific instruments and methods to discover what was around in abundant evidence. In opposition to this there was the idea of truth as an event, a truth which appeared in rare locations such as at Delphi which housed the oracle, or on rare occasions such as during the 'crisis' of an illness in pre-eighteenth-century medicine. It was also a truth that could only be accessed by a chosen few such as prophets, the wise and the mad, who had performed the right exercises and rituals. Foucault characterises the opposition between these two positions as an opposition between the demonstrative truth of scientific knowledge, versus something he calls 'truth-event'.

Needless to say, Foucault enthusiastically takes the party of 'truth-event' and characterises his latest incarnation of the 'archaeology of knowledge', as being aimed at showing that 'scientific demonstration is basically no more than a ritual, that the supposedly universal subject of knowledge is in reality only an individual who has been historically qualified according to a certain number of modalities, that the discovery of truth is in reality a certain modality of the production of truth' (PP: 238).

He describes 'the dominant and tyrannical power' that the new 'technology of demonstrative truth' has exercised in order to gain ascendency since the Renaissance (PP: 238). It is a technology of truth which has used all the instruments of disciplinary power to enforce its reign. This general schema is as we have seen a familiar one in Foucault's work and runs in various forms even through his earliest work, for example in 'Dream, imagination and existence' (1954), where the truth event of the dream is reduced to a universal scientific pathology by Freud. In other lectures also delivered in 1973, Foucault takes another angle, on this dual mani-festation, this time in the form of 'two histories of the truth' (1974i: 4). One history involves an internal history of the sciences where truth con-cerns the regulation of scientific propositions; the second history and the one that Foucault is interested in, concerns what he describes as 'exter-nal' history of truth. This history describes how people's relation to truth is defined via means of certain forms of subjectivity, types of knowledge and fields of objects (1974i: 4). These categories are all formed by particu-lar relations of power in this account, resulting in what Foucault describes as a 'politics of truth' (1974i: 13).

Foucault continues his discussion of the close links between truth and power in an interview in 1977 where he develops in detail his famous notion of 'regimes of truth'. Truth in Western society, he argues, is defined by scientific forms of knowledge and associated institutions. Economic and political mechanisms demand its constant production, it is circulated, consumed and regulated via educational institutions and the media, and it also forms the object of political debate and social struggle (1977e: 131).

The 1980s

Foucault's final characterisation of the dual history of truth in Western society is characterised by his opposition between 'intellectual knowl-edge' (savoir de connaissance) and the 'knowledge of spirituality'. [4] Each type of knowledge has its own separate historical system of rules in rela-tion to the acquisition of truth. Intellectual knowledge, which encompasses scientific knowledge, presumes a universal subject who 'discovers' the truth. Spiritual knowledge sets up rules about how to acquire truth via a process of self-transformation. This latter form of knowledge also relates directly to art – including literature, the visual and performance arts. Indeed one might argue that the process of self-transformation is a funda-mentally artistic one. We will, however, leave a more extensive discussion on this front until the last chapter. In the next chapter we will turn our attention to Foucault's discussion on power.

End Notes

[1] For a somewhat ambiguous catalogue of this kind of industry in relation to Foucault's later work, see O'Leary (2002).

[2] See 1971o; 1971r; 1980b; 1983h.

[3] A perfect illustration of this ascendency of a particular way of organising truth as it affects imaginative artistic work can be found in C. Wright Mills' famous 1959 book *The Sociological Imagination* (Mills, 1959). See in particular pp.14–18.

[4] There is a tricky problem of translation here in that the English translates both 'connaissance' and 'savoir' as 'knowledge'.

EIGHT   Power and Culture

Principle 4: Power

Foucault's name is linked most famously with the notion of power and also with the idea that knowledge and truth exist in an essential relation with social, economic and political factors. It is well known that Foucault addresses the question of power in his writings subsequent to 1970, but similar themes can also be found in his earlier work even if such themes are not couched in the same terms. Foucault (1971b: 159) explains that in the early 1960s he was impressed by the attempts of certain Marxist historians of science to link geometry and calculus to social structures. But the problem with Marxist attempts to link the actual disciplinary content of science with economic, social and historical factors was that they made the links too simple. In Foucault's view, the relation between social and economic structures and the actual content of science was in fact far more complex than one simply being the expression of the other. He therefore embarked on his studies of psychiatry and medicine with a view to examining these complexities. In *The Archaeology of Knowledge*, Foucault briefly adopted the term 'ideology' to refer to these social, economic and political structures, using the term in much the same way as he subsequently used power.

But whatever the terminology, he remains firm in his rejection of a long-standing assumption in Western philosophy that there is a fundamental opposition between knowledge and power, that the purity of knowledge can only exist in stark opposition to the machinations of power. As he puts it, the accepted view is that 'If there is knowledge, it must renounce power. Where knowledge and science are found in their pure truth, there can no longer be any political power. This great myth needs to be dispelled' (1974i: 32).

In *The Archaeology of Knowledge* Foucault criticises the idea that 'ideology' and science are mutually exclusive. If the proposition that science does not exist in isolation from power or ideology is now a fairly familiar one, it is usually assumed as a result, that such a relation immediately undermines the truth claims and validity of science. This conclusion is, however, still premised on the notion that knowledge and power can never be mixed. Foucault, for his part, insists that exposing the 'ideological' functioning of a science and treating it as merely one practice of knowledge amongst many is not to attack its legitimacy or the validity of its propositions as a science. Within science there are internal 'thresholds' which mark how that knowledge is systematised, how propositions are constructed, formalised and validated (AK: 186). Thus Foucault is able to make a distinction between the 'archaeological' level where 'objects are constituted, subjects are posed and concepts are formed' (1971b: 162) and the 'epistemological' level of science. This second level operates as a coherent and strictly regulated system of propositions. Hence in relation to medicine:

> It is obvious for example, that the notion of tissue or the notion of organic lesion have nothing to do – if the problem is posed in terms of expression – with the unemployment situation in France at the end of the eighteenth century. And yet, it is nonetheless obvious that it is these economic conditions, such as unemployment which led to the appearance of a certain type of hospitalisation, which then made possible a certain number of hypotheses ... and finally the idea of tissue lesions came up, a fundamental notion in the history of the clinic. (1971b: 161)

The 'objects' of Clinical Medicine were constructed rather than 'discovered' in the context of the particular political and social conjuncture of revolutionary France. Quite workable propositions were then constructed in relation to those objects. It is certainly not a matter of the purity of a rational scientific thought beating down all obstacles in its 'progress' towards the 'truth' through the inexorable exercise of reason, versus the evil political machinations and imperfections of the outside world and the unenlightened. As Foucault shows in *Madness and Civilization, The Birth of the Clinic* and *Le pouvoir psychiatrique*, the sciences of psychology and clinical medicine are indissolubly linked to certain forms of institutional practice, historical events and governmental policy and political intrigue, not to mention sheer accident. But this does not mean, for all that, that at the epistemological level of their propositions, these forms of knowledge have no therapeutic value and are not operative in relation to the physical world. As Foucault is careful to point out, the division between the true and the false at the level of scientific propositions 'is neither arbitrary nor modifiable nor institutional nor violent' (OD: 54). [1]

Ideology

Foucault very quickly became dissatisfied with the notion of 'ideology' and after a brief Marxist style flirtation with the term in the wake of

1968, he rejected it out of hand. The first problem, he says, is that the concept presumes the existence of an unchanging universal subject whose access to the truth has been obscured by the mythological ways of thinking perpetuated by political and social institutions. As he explains:

> In traditional Marxist analyses, ideology is a sort of negative element through which is conveyed the fact that the subject's relation to truth, or simply the knowledge relation, is disturbed, obscured, veiled by the conditions of existence, social relations, or the political forms imposed on the subject from the outside. Ideology is the mark, the stigma of these political or economic conditions of existence on a subject of knowledge who rightfully should be open to truth (1974i: 15 mod).

Further to this, ideology makes the assumption that there are unchanging objects in the world just waiting to be 'discovered' by these universal knowing subjects, in other words that there is a 'superstructure' of ideas and beliefs which exist in opposition to a material 'infrastructure' of economic relations. Finally the notion of ideology implies that the passage of time (history) is marked by a continual 'progress' towards the 'truth'. In the process, the pettiness of political intrigue, and struggles for domination and power somehow fade into the background as all subjects discover their true and eternal niche in the order of the cosmos, and are overwhelmed by the blinding evidence of 'truth'.

The transition to power

At the end of *The Archaeology of Knowledge*, Foucault asks 'Must archaeology be – exclusively – a certain way of questioning the history of the sciences?' (AK: 192). His answer to that is, of course, no, and the book he published next, 'The orders of discourse', marks the beginning of his move away from a specific focus on science to broader forms of knowledge relating to social organisation. It also marks the introduction of his notion of power.

What exactly is power? As is the case with archaeology, Foucault uses the term for a while without offering any definitions. Early on, he adopts the classic view of power as repressive, noting for example: 'for medicine, I tried ... to detect relations of power, that is necessarily the types of repression which were linked to the appearance of a knowledge' (1973d: 410). But he quickly discarded this idea and took another tack. If Foucault's ideas on power are notoriously changeable there are certain principles which remain constant throughout his discussions. He uses these principles to distinguish his own views on power from more traditional – particularly Marxist – models.

Power and resistance

The most important feature of Foucault's theories on power is that for him power is *not* a 'thing' or a 'capacity' which can be owned either by State, social class or particular individuals. Instead it is a *relation* between different individuals and groups and only exists when it is being exercised. According to this scenario a king is only a king if he has subjects. Thus, the term power refers to sets of relations that exist between individuals, or that are strategically deployed by groups of individuals. Institutions and governments are simply the ossification of highly complex sets of power relations which exist at every level of the social body. How Foucault characterises the operations and limits of these exercises of power varies considerably. He initially put forward the hypothesis that power was co-extensive with the social body (HS). There were no pockets of freedom which escaped power relations, but instead resistance existed wherever power was exercised (1977ze: 142). This resistance was everywhere and at every level, right down, as Foucault says, to the child who picked his nose at the table in order to annoy his parents (1977zc: 407). Although Foucault insisted on several occasions that resistance was not doomed to inevitable failure in the face of the omnipresence of power, numbers of his readers still found it difficult to understand how such resistance could not be compromised, since in effect it could only ever be the mirror of the power being exercised. Foucault tried to get around this problem by briefly proposing something he called the 'plebs', which was a certain 'something' which existed in individuals and groups that escaped relations of power and which limited the exercise of power (1977ze: 137–8). He also toyed briefly with the notion of 'counter-conduct' which existed in opposition to the forms of conduct which were imposed by the exercise of pastoral and subsequently governmental power (STP: 195–232). [2]

But it was not until his 1979 Tanner lectures and subsequently, that Foucault was able to offer a more refined and usable version of the same ideas. In this model, power still pervades the social body at all levels, but it does not encompass every social relation and its exercise if extensive, is limited. He distinguishes power from relationships of exchange and production and also from relationships of communication (1981b: 324), thus distancing himself respectively from both Marx and Habermas. Power becomes a way of changing people's conduct, or as he defines it, 'a mode of action upon the actions of others' (1982b: 341).

In addition to this, Foucault argues that power can only be exercised over free subjects. By freedom, Foucault means the possibility of reacting and behaving in different ways. If these possibilities are closed down through violence or slavery, then it is no longer a question of a relationship of power but of its limits. Of course, those exercising power can threaten and indeed exercise violence but those who are being confronted can refuse to modify their actions. It is at this point that the relationship of power breaks down and becomes something else. Foucault provides a useful example of what he means in the Tanner lectures:

> A man who is chained up and beaten is subject to force being exerted over him, but if he can be induced to speak, when his ultimate recourse could have been to hold his tongue preferring death, then he has been caused to behave in a certain way. His freedom has been subjected to power ... There is no power without potential refusal or revolt. (1981b: 324)

Power is not owned by the State

A second way in which Foucault distinguishes his ideas on power is by criticising models which see power as being purely located in the State or the administrative and executive bodies which govern the nation State. The very existence of the State in fact depends on the operation of thousands of complex micro-relations of power at every level of the social body. Foucault offers the example of military service which can only be enforced because every individual is tied in to a whole network of relations which include family, employers, teachers and other agents of social education. The grand strategies of State rely on the co-operation of a whole network of local and individualised tactics of power in which everybody is involved. Foucault (1977zc: 406–7) observes that if the police certainly have their methods ('we know what those are' he adds ironically) so do fathers in relation to their children, men in relation to women, children in relation to parents, women in relation to men and so on. All these relations of power at different levels work together and against each other in constantly shifting combinations. The State is merely a particular, and ultimately precarious, configuration of these multiple power relations. It is not a 'thing' or a universal essence (NBP: 5, 79).

Power is productive

The third point Foucault makes about power, again a criticism of more traditional models, is that power is not about simply saying no and oppressing individuals, social classes or natural instincts. Instead, argues Foucault, power is productive. By this he means that it generates particular types of knowledge and cultural order. Power and oppression should not be reduced to the same thing for a number of reasons in Foucault's view. Firstly, there are multiple and very different relations of power extending throughout the entire social body and to identify power with oppression is to assume that power is exercised from one source and that it is one thing. Secondly, some people *want* to exercise power and find pleasure in doing so, others find pleasure in resisting power (HS: 45). Thirdly, power produces particular types of behaviours, by regulating people's everyday activities, right down to the way school children hold a pen or sit at a desk. This is something that Foucault also describes as the 'microphysics of power' and 'capillary power': 'where power reaches into the very grain of individuals, touches their bodies and inserts itself into their actions and attitudes, their discourses, learning processes and everyday lives' (1975m: 39). Foucault develops this view of power as 'productive' rather than 'repressive' to well-known effect in Volume 1 of *The History of Sexuality*. Here he argues that sexuality, far from being reduced to silence by the Victorians, became the object of proliferating knowledge which worked in conjunction with administrative mechanisms of social organisation from the end of the eighteenth century onwards.

Power and knowledge

One of the most important features of Foucault's view is that mechanisms of power produce different types of knowledge aimed at investigating and collecting information on people's activities and existence. The knowledge gathered in this way further reinforces exercises of power. As Foucault puts it in 1972: 'There is not knowledge [connaissance] on one side and society on the other, or science and the State, but the basic forms of "power-knowledge"' (1972n: 17). In short, knowledge and power operate almost interchangeably. On most occasions, however, Foucault discusses the relation between power and knowledge without using the hyphenated term, thus creating more of a distinction between the two categories. In actual fact, the hyphenated term which has also been translated in English as power/knowledge, appears relatively infrequently in Foucault's work, with notable but brief appearances in *Discipline and Punish* and also in Volume 1 of *The History of Sexuality*. He explains in these books that no form of knowledge emerges independently of complex networks of power and that the exercise of power produces certain types of knowledge.

Foucault proposes a series of different historical configurations of this general nexus of power-knowledge and these are respectively: disciplinary power (which historically replaces older forms of sovereign power), biopower and then governmentality. The final term mutates in his work into a discussion of freedom, truth and the subject, and ways of guiding one's own and others' conduct, leaving discussions of power behind. Let us now turn to an examination of these configurations of power and knowledge in Foucault's work.

Disciplinary power

Disciplinary power and its associated 'disciplinary society' are amongst the most popular and widely disseminated ideas derived from Foucault's opus. As such it is worth taking a little time to explain these notions. They first appeared in Foucault's work in relation to the birth of psychiatry in his 1973 lectures *Le pouvoir psychiatrique*, but it is in *Discipline and Punish* that his most extended and well-known discussions concerning the development of a modern 'disciplinary society' are to be found.

In Foucault's account, disciplinary power first began to develop in earnest at the end of the eighteenth century and onwards. It both replaced and worked in tandem with an older form of power which Foucault designates ('without really being delighted with the word' (PP: 44)) as 'sovereign power'. In this system, which operated in feudal societies, there are highly individualised authority figures such as the king, the priest and the father who are designated as the holders of power and to whom allegiance is owed. It is a power which operates via divine right, public ceremony and by making examples of those who transgress authority. Sovereign power operates as a 'macrophysics' in opposition to the 'microphysics' of disciplinary power which seeks to individualise every element of the social body even the most lowly (PP: 28). Foucault argues that forms of sovereign power began to become less and less efficient as a way of regulating the behaviour of populations in Europe towards the end of the eighteenth century leading to the development of new techniques of social control.

Discipline, Foucault says, is a 'technology' aimed at: 'how to keep someone under surveillance, how to control his conduct, his behaviour, his aptitudes, how to improve his performance, multiply his capacities, how to put him where he is most useful: that is discipline in my sense' (1981h: 191). Disciplinary techniques were first developed in the army and the school, and then were very quickly applied to hospitals, factories and prisons. If the 'disciplinary society' started to emerge in full force in the eighteenth and nineteenth centuries, it didn't come out of nowhere. Isolated disciplinary techniques already existed in Ancient and Medieval times and Foucault cites the Roman legions and monasteries as being cases in point (1978k: 515). He also draws attention to a major transformation which took place in the army at the end of the seventeenth century with the introduction of the rifle, which meant that soldiers had to be trained how to use them. As a result it was no longer simply enough to be strong, soldiers had to be taught how to co-ordinate their movements as a group and to respond instantly on command (1978k: 514–15; 1981h: 191). Foucault describes these new mass forms of training bodies, gestures and behaviours as a 'political anatomy' aimed at producing 'docile bodies' whose economic and social usefulness could be maximised (DP: 138).

The organisation of space

Foucault lists a number of techniques or principles which facilitated the operation of these mechanisms of power. First of all, space was organised in a particular way, starting with a principle of 'enclosure' which meant that people were locked away into institutional spaces: criminals into prisons, children into schools and workers into factories. Within these broad 'enclosures', smaller partitions, such as cells and classrooms, dormitories and hospital wards were created. People in these enclosures were also 'ranked', thus children were divided into 'classes' according to their age and soldiers according to a chain of command. All of these divisions required specially designed architecture to physically maintain these organised social spaces.

The organisation of activity and behaviour

The second set of disciplinary techniques Foucault describes relates to the organisation of activity. Firstly, the development of timetables meant that groups of people could all be engaged in the same task at the same time in schools, factories and workshops. Secondly, forms of group activity were organised: people were trained to perform the same set of movements at the same time, for instance army drills or marching, or reciting lessons together. Thirdly, methods of training the body and its gestures were perfected. In schools children were taught to hold a pen correctly and to sit at their school desks in a particular way. All of this was aimed at making the body a much more efficient unit which would waste minimal time in performing useful activities. The success of disciplinary power, Foucault argues, was guaranteed by additional technologies of generalised surveillance.

The Panopticon

Surveillance in modern societies is guaranteed via a mechanism Foucault describes as 'panopticism'. The Panopticon was a prison designed by the

103

English philosopher Jeremy Bentham in the 1790s. It was based on the architectural principle of a ring shaped building with cells grouped around a central tower. An observer in the tower could see into each of the cells, but because of a system of louvres, the occupants of the cells could not see into the central tower. This meant that people in the cells, whether they were mad, prisoners, workers or school children eventually modified their behaviour to act as though they were being watched all the time. The idea was widely adopted at the beginning of the nineteenth century as a highly efficient model of social regulation and control. Foucault (1977h: 154 mod.) elaborates: 'There is no need for weapons, physical violence, material constraints. Just a gaze. An inspecting gaze, a gaze which each person feeling its weight will end up by interiorising to the point of observing himself; thus each person will exercise this surveillance over and against himself'. It is about preventing people from doing wrong and indeed taking away their very will to do wrong. This is the principle on which modern society operates according to Foucault, and a host of other researchers have enthusiastically taken him at his word finding panoptic mechanisms at work in schools, hospitals, prisons, shopping malls, airports and indeed in almost any other contemporary public or institutional space.

Normalisation

Up until the end of the eighteenth century, crimes were regarded as offences against the king who would take his revenge by making examples of selected offenders. At the end of the eighteenth century, any crime became a crime against the whole social body, and the criminal, as a result, became the enemy of society. This led to the idea of a 'dangerous' and 'monstrous' individual. Only someone who was 'sick' or who was not quite rational, or indeed human, could offend against the entire social body. The legal system began to call on a whole array of experts including psychiatrists, social workers and educators whose function it was to determine the normality or otherwise of individuals and to define their very identity in terms of their deviation from the 'norm'. A society which punished infractions against the law was replaced by a society which sought to cure and rehabilitate 'diseased' and 'abnormal' individuals. As Foucault puts it 'we thus enter the age of what I would call social orthopedics. I'm talking about a form of power, a type of society that I term "disciplinary society", in contrast to the penal societies known hitherto. This is the age of social control' (1974i: 57). In contemporary society, in Foucault's view, there is an insoluble conflict between these two models in our judiciary system: between whether to judge wrong-doing in accordance with the law, or to diagnose abnormality within the framework of a medical model.

The examination

One particularly effective technique in the exercise of disciplinary power is the examination (at school, at work, in hospitals and asylums). Foucault argues that the examination is able to combine both surveillance and normalisation and turn people simultaneously into objects of knowledge and power. Through the examination, individuals are required to reproduce certain types of knowledge and behaviour. Their performance can then be measured, and entered into a data bank which compares them with others. The examination allows people to be 'individualised', to become 'cases' which are measured against other cases and are then filed and used by the social sciences (psychology, sociology, psychiatry) to generate further knowledge. All this data can be generalised and statistical 'norms' can be established with the resultant knowledge being used to tighten control over both populations and individuals. 'Solutions' can then be found to the ways in which particular individuals or classes of individuals deviate from the established norms.

Foucault describes a whole dream of a disciplinary society which arose at the end of the eighteenth century. This dream envisaged a vast social machine with meticulously co-ordinated cogs developing ever more finely adjusted forms of training aimed at 'the individual and collective coercion of bodies', leading eventually to 'automatic docility' (DP: 169). But it is a Utopia of a perfect social order which has cost millions of lives and has met with considerable and often successful opposition. As Foucault points out, a disciplinary society is by no means the same as a *disciplined* society (1980b: 15). Both the dream of a perfectly disciplined society and resistance to it are still very much the order of the day in present times – even more so perhaps than when Foucault was writing during the 1970s.

Biopower

But if 'discipline' was the major configuration of power in Foucault's work from 1973–75, Volume 1 of *The History of Sexuality* marked a shift in his ideas. Discipline becomes merely a 'pole' (HS: 139) or 'a family' (1981h: 193) in a whole range of technologies of power that arose in the modern age. If discipline was developed first historically, techniques of managing the life and death of populations were not far behind. Populations in this instance are not just large groups of people but are collections of living organisms with birth and death rates, different demographics and various states of health. Foucault describes the technologies used to manage populations as 'biopolitics' or 'biopower'.

If the focus of disciplinary power was the creation and control of the individual via methods of training the body and behaviour, the focus of bio-power was the life, death and health of entire populations. Thus forms of knowledge and practices relating to hygiene, public health, the control of reproduction and sexuality became the subject of administrative interest, with very detailed forms of knowledge being put in place to gather knowledge and manage populations. Sexuality was a key factor in this process and became the means by which populations could be disciplined medically, morally and also the means by which, of course, the population could be reproduced. Various structures to ensure the healthy and disciplined reproduction of that population had to be introduced to this end. Sexuality allowed access to both the life of the body and of the species and was, Foucault argued, 'employed as a standard for the disciplines and as a basis for regulations' (HS: 146). Thus, in Volume 1 of *The History of Sexuality*, and also his lectures *Society Must be Defended*, discipline becomes merely a subset of 'biopower'. The other side of the coin of this control over the life of populations was the control over their death and Foucault argues that never before in history had such bloody wars or such systematic practices of genocide occurred as under the regimes which adopted a strategy of 'biopolitics'.

Governmentality

Again, like discipline, biopower only occupied a primary position in Foucault's work for a short period. In his 1978 lectures at the Collège de France, he declared that he had been wrong about the disciplinary society, hastening to add however, 'but I am never completely wrong, of course' (STP: 50). The new idea he proposed was 'governmentality' which he says, instead of restricting freedoms as did discipline, allowed for the incorporation of these freedoms into the mechanisms which guide people's behaviour in the social body. He also notes that in his analysis of the problem of population and biopower he kept on coming back to the notion of government. In the sixteenth century, there were a whole series of problems centred around 'how to govern oneself, how to be governed, how to govern others, by whom the people will accept being governed, how to become the best possible governor' (1978v: 202). By 'government', Foucault means the techniques and procedures which govern and guide people's conduct. He offers the examples of the 'government of children, government of souls and consciences, government of a household, of a state, or of oneself' (1980m: 81). When he first introduced the term however, his focus was exclusively on government in the restricted sense of the 'exercise of political sovereignty' (NBP: 3). He explains in his original definition that by the word 'governmentality' he means three things: firstly, the institutions and knowledge which manage the population; secondly the pre-eminence of certain exercises of power based on administrative practices of governance; and thirdly, the process by which a State, based on a system of law in the Middle Ages in Europe, was replaced by a way of administering a population (1978v: 219–20). In short, 'governmentality' is the rationalisation and systematisation of a particular way of exercising political sovereignty through the government of people's conduct. The idea of governing a population, rather than simply ruling over a territory, Foucault says, is something that only started to appear in Europe in the sixteenth century, adapting aspects of the pastoral forms of governance aimed at saving people's souls which already existed in the Church (STP: 130–4).

Like both discipline and biopower, governmentality exists in opposition to sovereign forms of power. This is not to say that sovereign power is entirely superseded. Sovereign power involves obedience to the law of the sovereign who is the representative of God on earth and is also concerned with ruling over a territory. Government, on the other hand, concerns the tactical means of attaining a number of goals, including the wealth and health of the population of the State and the increase of that population which would then make up the strength of the State, rather than it being a simple matter of owning territory. Later, Foucault argued that contemporary society is actually undergoing a 'crisis of governmentality' (1980e: 296 mod.). People in the contemporary era, he says, have become dissatisfied with the various institutions, practices and procedures which 'ensure the government of some people by others' and which guide people's conduct' (1980e: 295).

Increasingly, however, Foucault began to move away from an analysis of the government of the general social body and of 'populations' towards notions of how individual subjects were governed and governed themselves. He gradually broadened the term 'governmentality' to include all forms and techniques of the government of both individuals and groups. If some indications of this broader interest are already visible in Foucault's 1978 lectures (STP: 124–243), this theme was not developed until a couple of years later in his work. The transition from his interest in power as it operates at a general level in the social body, to a closer focus on the relation between the subject and truth can be clearly seen in this passage from the summary of his 1980 lectures at the Collège de France:

> How is it that in Western Christian culture the government of men demands on the part of those who are led, not only acts of obedience and submission but also 'acts of truth,' which have the particular requirement not just that the subject tell the truth but he tell the truth about himself, his faults, his desires, the state of his soul and so on. (1980m: 81 mod.)

Foucault's final work concentrates on how the subject governs itself and is governed by others, in short on notions such as ethics, freedom and truth and in the next chapter we will turn to a discussion of the ethical underpinnings of Foucault's work.

End Notes

[1] For similar comments see Gordon, 2000: xvii–iii.

[2] As for the notion of 'dissidence', Foucault observes, 'I would rather have my tongue ripped out than use it' (STP: 204).

NINE Ethics and Subjectivity

Principle 5: Ethics

Foucault is frequently criticised for attacking a variety of social practices and institutions without proposing anything in their place. As he says: 'I am not at all the sort of philosopher who conducts or wants to conduct a discourse of truth on some science or other. Wanting to lay down the law for each and every science is the project of positivism ... Now this role of referee, judge and universal witness is one I absolutely refuse to adopt' (1976d: 64–5). Underlying all Foucault's discussions is his rejection of the idea that anything is fixed or self-evident in any domain of human culture or production, but this is coupled at the same time with a very strong commitment to the idea of social justice.

In all of his work, Foucault makes a number of assumptions about the way human beings modify both their own and other people's behaviour. This happens through a complex interplay of choice, action and constraint. Foucault assumes that people will always seek to modify the actions of others, in short to exercise power, but he also assumes that people will at the same time resist such attempts. Although there are always multiple social and historical constraints, there is always a way of modifying those constraints, namely a margin of freedom. In addition to this, people also seek to modify their own behaviour and the way they experience the world with particular goals in mind about the kind of persons they want to become, within their given social and historical setting. This is, as Foucault insists himself, an extremely optimistic philosophy. No matter how bad the situation is, there are still different options for action and change even if these are very limited in some cases. Some critics have nonetheless read Foucault's focus on the limitations, injustices and the dark side of human existence as pessimistic, but Foucault's view is that to ignore unjust practices within the social body is to tolerate them and perpetuate their existence thus condemning a whole section of the population to despair.

At different points in his career, Foucault places different emphasis on these various elements. Detailed discussions of how people actively modify their own individual behaviour and interior experience of the world are generally to be found mostly in Foucault's post-1982 work. Sustained analyses of how people modify their behaviour at a more collective level are to be found in his work of the 1960s, and in the 1970s, where Foucault provides detailed accounts of how institutional and other social structures shape people's lives.

In his later work, Foucault suggested that all his earlier work had in fact been about how people exist as subjects in the world, even if he hadn't articulated this sufficiently. Thus, he argues in a discarded preface to Volume II of *The History of Sexuality* that one of the three axes of *Madness and Civilization* was 'the definition of a relation to oneself and to others as possible subjects of madness' (1984b: 202). One could debate whether this was what Foucault was actually doing in *Madness and Civilization* (in the mid-1970s he also redefined this work as a study of power). The book is perhaps not so much about the construction of a mad subject as about the 'objectification' of madness, or the way a society has created institutional and scientific structures (sets of meanings or order) around a number of behaviours and biological states. One could even go so far as to say that *Madness and Civilization* is about the annihilation of a particular subject.

The subject

The subject in one form or another occupies a key position in Foucault's work. But what exactly does this term mean? It is a term that people have had considerable difficulty in pinning down. To define it at the most general level, the 'subject' is a philosophical category which describes an entity which is able to choose courses of action. One must also distinguish between the subject and the individual, for example Foucault (1982b: 331) notes that he is interested in a form of power that 'transforms individuals into subjects'. Here he is using the word subject in two senses: in the sense of being controlled by others, and also in the sense of being attached to an identity through awareness and knowledge of self. As we have already mentioned on several occasions, Foucault was consistently opposed to nineteenth century and phenomenological notions of a universal and timeless subject which was at the source of how one made sense of the world, and which was the foundation of all thought and action. The problem with this conception of the subject according to Foucault and other thinkers in the 1960s, was that it fixed the status quo and attached people to specific identities that could never be changed. Later in his career Foucault admits that early on he perhaps identified the subject too closely with a certain humanist conception of man. In his revised opinion the 'death of man' did not mark the death of the subject as well but was really more a question of a historical shift in the way people formed their subjectivity and constructed themselves 'in an infinite, multiple series of different subjectivities that will never have an end' (1980e: 276).

But if Foucault to some extent identified humanism and the general category of the subject in his earlier work, the idea of a historical subject – which was changed by outside events, which modified itself and was not attached to a fixed identity – is not something that just suddenly appears without warning in Foucault's work in the late 1970s and early 1980s. The common critical view, now less prevalent with the more extensive publication of Foucault's writings, was that his focus on the subject in his later work was a sudden and mysterious occurrence and marked a rejection of an earlier radical stance. A careful examination of his work, however, reveals this is far from being the case. Even in his earliest publication, 'Dream, imagination and existence' (1954), Foucault plays (albeit more than a little obscurely) with the idea of multiple and fragmented subjectivities, notably in relation to a 'dream-subject' which is not a reflection of a fixed past or future identity but only exists during the process of dreaming (1954: 57).

Foucault's rejection of the subject during the 1960s reflected his wish to dissolve identities, to organise knowledge in a different way. His critique of humanism in the 1960s attracted an avalanche of accusations of nihilism and political disengagement, but as he explains, the rejection of humanism does not imply a rejection of 'human rights' and 'freedom'. On the contrary, he argues, it is humanism with its notion of an unchanging essence of human nature that has restricted these values. He offers the example of 'feminine virtue', pointing out that at the turn of the twentieth century, people would have unhesitatingly agreed that it was a part of universal humanism. Such a view is certainly no longer adhered to in contemporary Western society (1988a: 15).

During the 1960s, in place of the subject, Foucault proposed anonymous structures and networks of knowledge which did not originate in individual consciousnesses. Thus, in the case of a work of literature or a scientific theory, it is not a matter of analysing the motivations, creativity and discoveries of an individual who is the originator of that work, but in looking at what structures and patterns that work shares, and also does not share, with others. As Foucault put it in 1967: 'the formal relations that one discovers in this way were not present in anyone's mind ... contemporary criticism is abandoning the great myth of interiority' (1967d: 287). He also provided another example in a television interview in 1971 (1974a). At the end of the eighteenth century, he says, medical practice came up with the idea that dissecting corpses was the best way to search for the causes of illness and death. Traditional histories of medicine have explained this idea as the result of the genius and personality of one man, Bichat. It is far more interesting, Foucault argues, to look at ideas of illness and death in the general historical context of the late eighteenth century which saw the emergence of new concerns about large and healthy populations as a means of increasing the wealth of new industrial societies.

In 1972, while still opposing unchanging philosophical 'interiority' with the anarchic 'exteriority' of historical events (1972c: 284), Foucault raised the possibility of a subject which could be modified through the practice of discourse. In a discussion concerning Jacques Derrida's interpretation of Descartes' text *Meditations* (1993), Foucault draws a distinction between a didactic model of discourse, where an unchanging and fixed subject demonstrates and 'teaches' an already acquired truth, and between a 'meditation' which allows the subject to change him or herself via a practice of discourse. Both the writer and the reader undertake an exercise which leads them towards the truth, from 'darkness to light, from impurity to purity' from doubt to certainty. Foucault concludes, 'in short, meditation implies a mobile subject modifiable through the discursive events that take place' (1972a: 406). This is clearly a model of a changing subject firmly located within a historical process, a subject who is engaging in a sequence of exercises of self-modification. Foucault later returns to this idea in proposing the idea of a transformative 'book experience' in relation to his own work, as opposed to the 'truth book' or 'demonstration book', namely books which teach something and instruct people on what to think (1980e: 246). He returns to Descartes' *Meditations* again in his lectures in 1982 on the hermeneutics of the subject (HER: 340–1).

Foucault argues in his later writings, that Descartes' work actually represents a transition between two forms of the construction of the subject in relation to truth in Western history. Descartes undertakes his meditations in order to arrive at an idea of a universal knowledge and subject (the so-called 'cogito' – I think therefore I am) which will lead to the rejection of these very methods of finding the truth through a process of self-transformation. In the post-Cartesian model, truth is just waiting in nature to be 'discovered'. Anybody can 'discover' this knowledge if they have the right scientific 'method' and tools and can come up with 'clear and distinct ideas'. The subject does not need to be 'pure' or ethical in order to be able to access truth about the world as was the case in older spiritual systems. The scientific 'method' Descartes proposes operates regardless of the moral or ethical status of the subject using that method. Foucault designates this intellectual method introduced by Descartes as representing a break in the way truth operated in Western history. Older systems of spiritual knowledge, which required work on the self in order to access the truth, were displaced in favour of new forms of scientific and intellectual rationality.

Very early in his work in 1961, Foucault is already referring to this idea of a historically constituted truth and a subject who arrives painstakingly at truth through a long exercise on himself. In discussing the ideas of the seventeenth-century mathematician and astronomer Johannes Kepler, Foucault contrasts him with Descartes who impatiently discarded 'error', relegating it to an oblivion to be forgotten in the clear light of science. Kepler for his part, according to Foucault, 'did not state a new truth without indicating by which path of error he had just travelled; thus it was *his* truth' (1961c: 171). This opposition was also something that Foucault was later to examine at great length in relation to Ancient Greek and Roman notions of the subject.

In proposing a 'history of the subject', Foucault once again emphasises that, like 'truth', the subject is not prior to history. Rather, it is constantly dissolved and recreated in different configurations, along with other forms of knowledge and social practices (1977e: 118). The subject is a form, not a thing and this form is not constant even when attached to the same individual. Foucault notes differences for example, between the political subject who votes and the sexual subject of desire. In both cases, he says, one has a different (even if overlapping) relationship to oneself. And neither is the self an isolated entity. The individual in constituting him or herself as the subject of his or her own actions uses 'models that he finds in his culture and are proposed, suggested, imposed upon him by his culture, his society and his social group' (1984q: 291). Thus the self that is created is a form that relies very much for its existence on its interaction with other people, history and culture. This is opposed to the notion of a true self that needs to be 'discovered' in introspective isolation and can only be revealed once cultural and historical veils have been swept aside. Foucault in fact describes three forms of the 'exercise of thought' in Western history which relate to the acquisition of truth and knowledge and to self-formation. These forms include: firstly, remembering or recognising one's original truth (self-discovery); secondly, self transformation; and thirdly discovering an external point of certainty and truth on which all else rests (science) (HER: 441–2). Foucault strongly favours the second process.

Ethics and Antiquity

After 1982 Foucault abandoned his favourite period, the Classical Age, and turned his attention to Ancient Greece, Rome and the early Christian period, and to their ideas about ethics, notably in relation to sexuality and self-formation. If, as we have seen, there is a strong ethical focus in all of Foucault's work, it is not until after 1980 that he starts to provide a specific and detailed historical analysis of ethical systems, although one can already see the beginnings of such an analysis in his 1978 lectures.

The tone of Foucault's last two books differs markedly from his previous work. Except for the introduction to *The Use of Pleasures*, the sense of a strong critical presence behind the historical analysis that underlies his other work is missing. However if one examines the text more closely, particularly in the context of Foucault's remarks in interviews, an interesting picture emerges. It might appear that Foucault is quite favourably disposed towards Greek ethics but if one looks more closely, the latter is based on a whole range of things that Foucault had criticised heavily in his earlier work and continued to criticise in interviews. The Greek ethics he is examining is based on the exercise of power by a small elite and completely excludes people such as women, slaves and the working classes. Likewise, the specifically sexual ethics is centred on male virility and penetration with an active subject and a passive object. It is also obsessed with fears of the violence of the act and the loss of vital force. As Foucault says quite categorically: 'All that is quite disgusting!' (1983c: 258).

Foucault is very clear that he is not proposing Ancient Greek and Roman ethics as a model for today. If there is a certain similarity in some of the problems faced by the Ancients and by people today, the similarities lie in the fact that it is a question in both cases of determining how best people should relate to themselves and others in the absence of strong political and religious systems of authority based on the rule of law. He is suggesting, rather, that we plunder the 'cultural inventions of mankind', for 'devices, techniques, ideas, procedures, and so on', that can be helpful as tools for analysing and attempting to change the current situation (1983c: 261).

Ethics and morals: Definitions

In general, Foucault describes ethics as the kind of relation an individual has with him or herself. The essential condition for the practice of ethics is freedom, the ability to choose one action, not another. Foucault specifies that 'ethics is the considered form that freedom takes when it is informed by reflection' (1984q: 284). He makes a distinction between moral codes (which are simply collections of rules and precepts) and ethics. Any moral action, Foucault argues, means that one has to work on oneself in some way. As he says, 'there is no moral conduct that does not call for oneself as an ethical subject' (UP: 28). In some systems of morals the emphasis is placed on obedience to a moral law with systems of penalties for non-compliance, whereas in others the emphasis is placed on the kind of relationship the individual develops with him or herself through different actions, thoughts and feelings. Foucault is far more interested in this latter kind of system and argues that our contemporary society is in fact oriented in this direction.

He suggests that there are four aspects to the way an individual constitutes him or herself as the moral subject of their actions. The contents of these aspects vary according to culture and historical period.

(1) The first aspect relates to the part of the individual which acts as the focus of moral conduct. Foucault uses the terms 'ontology' and 'ethical substance' to describe this level (UP: 37, 26). This is the part of the self that needs to be worked on in order to achieve moral conduct. Foucault argues that for contemporary people in Western society, it is feelings, for early Christians it was desire, and for the Ancient Greeks it was acts (1983c: 263). So, for example, for Ancient Greeks, it was the action of not sleeping with boys that was the moral target, for the Christians it was not desiring the boy at all, even in one's innermost secret self, and for contemporary people it is recognising one's true feelings and having healthy desires.

(2) The second aspect concerns what makes an individual recognise their moral obligations. Foucault describes this as 'deontology' or the 'mode of subjection' (UP: 37, 27). Depending on the historical period or culture, it might be divine law revealed in a holy text such as the Bible, or it could be social customs or the harmonious order of the cosmos. It might even be the attempt to make one's life an example to others (for the Ancient Greeks), or rationality (for post-Enlightenment atheists and agnostics).

(3) The third aspect relates to the means by which individuals transform and work on themselves. Foucault also employs the terms 'ascetics' and 'ethical work' in this instance (UP: 37, 27). A whole variety of physical and mental techniques can be employed to this end, for example, self-discipline in the areas of food such as fasting or eating only particular types of food. Other methods might include meditation techniques to control how one uses one's mind and the sort of thoughts that enter into one's head, intellectual techniques of writing and keeping journals, or the way one trains one's body – to move in particular ways, to withstand extreme conditions.

(4) Finally there is the question of what sort of person an individual might want to be: pure, immortal, free, or master of the self. Here Foucault employs the Greek word 'telos' and also 'teleology' as a description of this level (UP: 37, 27). Thus the aim might be eternal salvation or to be somebody who is in control of themselves and not at the whim of every earthly desire.

This four-part scheme appears in the Introduction to *The Use of Pleasures* and also in a 1983 interview (1983c) and has been particularly popular in the secondary literature. This is how Foucault classifies ethical systems in general, but what of his own personal morality as an intellectual?

Foucault's morals

In an interview conducted in San Francisco in 1980, Foucault somewhat surprisingly describes himself as a 'moralist' and lists 'three elements in his "morals"' namely 'refusal, curiosity, innovation' (1988e: 1). By 'refusal', Foucault means that nothing in our culture, social arrangements or experience should be accepted as self-evident, fixed or definitive. Foucault's whole ethical project is centred on trying to make people aware of the limits of the systems in which they are operating and to lower their threshold of acceptance in relation to entrenched forms of injustice and exercises of power. Far from adopting a wishy-washy model of liberal tolerance of the 'anything goes' variety, Foucault argues that we must be absolutely intolerant of the 'intolerable'. As he says, his aim is to show people they are much freer than they think (1988a: 10).

There are two tools that are helpful in undermining and exposing supposedly self-evident fixtures: curiosity and innovation. 'I dream of a new age of curiosity' (1980i: 325) he says, defining curiosity as an acute interest in and concern for everything that exists, an eagerness to look at one's familiar surroundings and find them strange, a disregard for traditional divisions between what is regarded as important knowledge and what is regarded as trivial knowledge. 'Innovation' follows on naturally from curiosity. By this, Foucault means continually seeking out new things to think about and imagine, and never being satisfied with one's acquired knowledge and world views. Of crucial importance in the formulation of these three principles is Foucault's rejection of all forms of social injustice, and of what he terms a crystallisation or freezing of power relations 'to the profit of some and the detriment of others' (1988e: 11). Foucault's extensive militant activity in support of various oppressed and marginal groups after 1970 also attests to his intense concern for social justice. The intensity of his outrage at various forms of social injustice is evident not only in his choice of subject matter, but also in his shorter political writings on issues such as the abolition of the death penalty, the treatment of prisoners, and on political and legal oppression both in France and in other countries. There is also a certain tone which permeates much of his work, drawing very direct attention to the injustices perpetuated against certain groups, both in the past and today.

Foucault notes that if, in his books, he used documents about marginal and rejected people in history, 'it was doubtless because of the resonance I still experience today when I happen to encounter these lowly lives reduced to ashes in the few sentences that struck them down'. He explains he tried to understand:

why it had suddenly been so important in a society like ours to 'stifle' (as one stifles a cry, smothers a fire, or strangles an animal) a scandalous monk or a peculiar and inconsequential usurer. I looked for a reason why people were so zealous to prevent the feebleminded from walking down unknown paths. (1977k: 158)

In a polemic with Jacques Derrida over the latter's critiques of *Madness and Civilization*, Foucault takes him to task for his platonic assumptions of the superiority of a philosophy which exists somehow suspended outside of time and events. For Derrida, he says, his own work on madness must seem 'naïve indeed ... in wanting to undertake this history on the basis of these derisory events which are the enclosure of some tens of thousands of people or the organisation of an extra-judiciary State police' (1972c: 283).

Foucault, proposes an ethics which is not based on adherence to the law or recognition of authority, such as the authority of the Church, a political party or the State (1978t: 262). Instead he suggests that it is the responsibility of each individual to reflect upon and choose how they wish to exist in the historically and culturally specific situation they find themselves in. Indeed, one might argue that Foucault's work both contributes to and participates in a general cultural shift in the wake of the 1960s from an ethics based on obedience to the law and a system of the forbidden and the permitted, to an ethics based on the division between the possible and the impossible (Ehrenberg, 1998: 15). In Foucault's view, if nothing is ever ideal in history, there is always something that can be done, even if it is not easy (1984f: 612). The possibility of redressing certain injustices always exists even if changes bring new dangers and new problems in their turn. For example, Foucault points out that the closure of mental hospitals in the wake of anti-psychiatry movement has led to new dangers, which is not to say that criticisms of these institutions should not have been made in the first place. What it means is simply that the 'ethico-political' work people must engage in is ongoing and never ending (1983c: 256).

The arts of existence

Amongst the tools that can be used as a means of accomplishing this 'ethico-political' work are devices which Foucault describes as 'techniques of the self' or the 'arts of existence' which he defines as 'those intentional and voluntary practices by which men not only set themselves rules of conduct, but seek to transform themselves, to change themselves in their singular being, and to make their life into an *oeuvre* that carries certain aesthetic values and meets certain stylistic criteria' (UP: 10–11). Foucault had long wanted to be able to describe his own work as art and to break down traditional divisions between art and intellectual knowledge. He made comments to this effect during the 1970s (1976r: 122) and is quite happy to allow his archaeological project to be described as a poetic one (1974h: 644). In a discussion with the Japanese avant-garde theatre director Shugi Terayama, he expresses his willingness to promote this blurring of the artistic and the intellectual, and says that he wished that the kind of academic political and historical theory he produced could be disseminated at a wider cultural level in the same way as art:

> [L]ike painting, music and theatre, I would like historical theories and knowledge to go beyond the traditional forms and deeply impregnate daily life. I would like to proceed in a fashion so that people could freely use these theories and knowledge for their pleasure, for the needs in their life, to deal with problems they face and for their struggles. (1976i: 84)

By the 1980s Foucault had found a way of achieving this goal in relation to his own work, in describing his writings as 'experiences' which not only transformed himself as he produced them, but which were also offered as open invitations to the public to have their own experience while reading them. By 'experience', Foucault means a subjective event that transforms the way people relate to themselves and to each other and to their surroundings. It is something that is 'neither true nor false' (1980e: 243), he says, but for all that is still firmly tied to a particular cultural and historical situation (UP: 4).

Foucault has been extensively criticised for identifying ethics and aesthetics. He is accused of advocating an elitist pursuit for dilettantes with time and money on their hands, but it is a criticism which is based on a misunderstanding of his notion of 'art' and also of 'experience'. In using the word 'art', Foucault is referring to a work that is realised over time, which employs a number of techniques which are designed to create a particular kind of order. 'Experiences' also arise within the context of particular concrete historical constraints. His focus is, as always, on an idea of historical practice, rather than an ideal form (for example 'beauty') existing in a heavenly realm outside of history. The art Foucault is talking about involves a difficult and ongoing work, or craft, which can be practised by any member of the social body. It is also a work that is undertaken within a specific cultural and historical context, never in isolation. People are born already belonging to a particular context and they use the tools provided by that context to modify the way they belong and the kind of choices they make.

Conclusion

Foucault's recognition that there is no culture in the world which allows everything and his persistent attacks on established systems of order in every domain, do not mean that he is arguing, as some have suggested, that all constraints should be done away with. It is worth quoting Foucault here as much for the clarity of his formulation as for the colourful example he uses:

> The important question here, it seems to me, is not whether a culture without restraints is possible or even desirable but whether the system of constraints in which a society functions leaves individuals the liberty to transform the system. Obviously, constraints of any kind are going to be intolerable to certain segments of society. The necrophiliac finds it intolerable that graves are not accessible to him. But a system of constraint becomes truly intolerable when the individuals who are affected by it don't have the means of modifying it. (1982l: 147–8)

Elsewhere, Foucault re-iterates the same point providing an even more entertaining example. According to the accepted model of power as repressive, Foucault declares, 'preventing a child from scribbling on the walls would be an unbearable tyranny'. Instead he prefers to regard power as

> a relation in which one guides the behaviour of others. And there's no reason why this manner of guiding the behaviour of others should not ultimately have results which are positive, valuable, interesting and so on. If I had a kid, I assure you he would not write on the walls – or if he did, it would be against my will. The very idea! (1988e: 12)

If I have quoted Foucault at some length here, it is to emphasise that contrary to a common critical perception, Foucault was not operating as an amoral nihilist whose only aim was to wreak as much social havoc as possible. Foucault was not intent on reducing every order to chaos and leaving it at that, rather he was interested in showing that one cannot simply assume that certain institutions, disciplines or objects of knowledge are truths that go without saying. They are all orderly constructions that have emerged over time and one can ask questions about how those orders have been built. As he notes in *The Archaeology of Knowledge* he only accepts existing historical categories in order to question them, take them apart, see whether they are worth putting back together again or whether in fact new categories should be formed (AK: 26). He argues further that it is not a question of saying that every relation of power and every category is bad, but rather that everything is dangerous. One must be ever alert for current dangers and be aware that today's solution is tomorrow's problem.

Foucault's work, rather than providing a rigid philosophical system or methodological template, works best as a tool box giving people ideas they can apply to the most diverse of areas. For all the best efforts of some of his critics to declare his thought superseded, 20 years after his death its impact continues to grow as people in various applied and professional areas discover his ideas. Previously unpublished books of lectures and interviews are still appearing, with more to come, contributing new and unexpected material for specialists to consider and in English, numerous items remain as yet to be translated. Foucault insisted on numerous occasions that he wanted people to read his books and take away whatever ideas they found interesting for their own purposes, not apply them as a system. The extraordinary number of locations, both geographical and disciplinary, in which references to his ideas can be found – even if only in fleeting – testifies to the fact that this is precisely how people do in fact use his work. It is a work that has global appeal with not only a large English-speaking, European and South American contingent of scholars using his writings, but also small reading groups convening in Bengal to struggle with the English editions, and researchers and translators in China and Russia working in semi-isolation. Foucault said that he would like to imagine his books 'as rolling marbles. You can catch them, pick them up then send them off again. And if that works so much the better' (2004c: 107). It is a vision of his work that has now well and truly become a reality.

APPENDIX 1   Chronology of Foucault's Life and Times

Introduction

For a more detailed chronology of Foucault's life, times and works see DE I: 13–64. See also, on the net, Alt (2000). There are three biographies of Foucault by Didier Eribon (1991); David Macey (1993) and James Miller (1993). Eribon has also written a sequel (1994) to his 1991 work. For additional treatments of Foucault's general intellectual and social background see O'Farrell (1989: 1–19) and Châtelet (1979). Foucault himself also provides various accounts of the personal, historical and intellectual setting of his own work. See DE items 37; 50; 54; 55; 56; 141; 160; 161; 163; 192; 212; 216; 219; 234; 330; 242; 272; 281; 336; 343; 349; 362 and 2004b. (For an explanation of this numbering system see the bibliography.)

Chronology

1926   15 October Paul-Michel Foucault is born in Poitiers, France.

1945   Attends the lycée Henri-IV in Paris. End of World War II. Existentialist thought and the Communist Party 'the Party of the Resistance' are held in much esteem by intellectuals.

1946   Enrols in the Ecole Normale Supérieure (ENS) in Paris.

1949   Simone de Beauvoir, the founder of post-World War II feminism, publishes *The Second Sex*.

1950–3   Foucault briefly joins the French Communist Party. His decision to join is influenced by the war in Indo-china. Leaves when a number of Jewish doctors are arrested in the USSR for alleged treason.

1948–53   Obtains qualifications in philosophy, psychology, psycho-pathology and experimental psychology.

1952–4   Teaches psychology at the University of Lille and philosophy at the Ecole Normale Supérieure (ENS) in Paris.

1954   Publication of *Maladie Mentale et Personnalité* and introduction to Ludwig Binswanger's *Dream and Existence.* Beginning of the Algerian uprising. This war polarises French intellectuals and militants, particularly in the existentialist, Marxist and Gaullist camps.

1955   Foucault takes up a post as the Director of the Maison de France in Uppsala Sweden.

1956   The Khrushchev Report is released in the USSR condemning the 'personality cult of Stalin'. An uprising in Hungary is violently suppressed by Soviet troops. The centre-left government in France, including the Communist deputies, votes for special powers to aid in the 'pacification' of Algeria. These events provoke a mass exodus of intellectuals from the ranks of the Communist Party whom they perceive as changing tune to suit its own purposes rather than supporting the just causes of the oppressed. A general disillusion amongst intellectuals concerning party politics sets in.

1957   Publication of the collection of essays *Mythologies* by Roland Barthes, one of the key figures of the newly developing structuralist movement of thought.

1958   Foucault takes up a post in Poland as head of a new Centre for French Civilisation at the University of Warsaw. De Gaulle's right-wing government comes to power in France further alienating intellectuals from party politics and humanist and literary philosophy. Many young researchers turn their attention instead to apparently less ideological domains such as the human sciences and areas such as epistemology, ethnology and linguistics. The so-called 'father of structuralism', Claude Lévi-Strauss publishes *Structural Anthropology.*

1959   Foucault appointed director of the French Institute of Hamburg in Germany.

1960   Takes up a post at the University of Clermont-Ferrand in France.

1961   Foucault obtains his doctorate and his major thesis for this degree, *Madness and Civilization,* is published.

1962   Revised and retitled edition of *Mental Illness and Psychology* is published. The Algerian War ends. Publication of *Nietzsche and Philosophy* by Gilles Deleuze. Thomas Kuhn publishes *The Structure of Scientific Revolutions* which introduces the famous notion of paradigm to which Foucault's idea of the episteme is often compared.

1963   Publication of *The Birth of the Clinic* and *Raymond Roussel*.

1964   Claude Lévi-Strauss publishes *The Raw and the Cooked*.

1965   Foucault lectures in Brazil. Publication of one of the classic texts of anti-humanist structuralist Marxism, Louis Althusser's *For Marx*.

1966   Publication of *The Order of Things*, which provokes controversy in the press because of its anti-Marxist and anti-humanist stance and also its perceived affiliation with a new structuralist movement of thought which was beginning to pose a serious threat to the previously reigning philosophies of existentialism and phenomenology. The book is an instant best seller. Foucault also lectures in Hungary and moves to Tunisia to take up a Chair in Philosophy. Publication of *Ecrits* by psychoanalyst Jacques Lacan, who employs structuralist methods in his analysis of the unconscious. Publication of *Reading Capital* another classic of structuralist Marxism by Althusser, Balibar, Macherey and Rancière.

1967   Publication of *On the Normal and the Pathological* by historian and philosopher of science, Georges Canguilhem. Foucault was to write an introduction for the English translation of this book published in 1978. Publication of *Writing and Difference,* and *Of Grammatology* by the instigator of 'deconstructionism' Jacques Derrida.

1968   The 'events of May' take place with student and worker uprisings and a general strike in France. Student unrest also occurs in other countries: Japan, the USA, Poland, Germany and Mexico. In Tunisia Foucault puts himself at some personal and physical risk to support the cause of Tunisian student activists. Publication of sociologist/philosopher Jean Baudrillard's *The System of Objects*. Baudrillard was to become well known for his 'postmodern' ideas on the contemporary breakdown of the divisions between 'reality' and 'representation' as well as a short book provocatively titled *Forget Foucault*, published in 1977.

1969   Foucault is appointed to the Chair in Philosophy at the new experimental University in the Parisian suburb of Vincennes, the University of Paris VIII. Publishes *The Archaeology of Knowledge* and lectures in England for the first and last time.

1970–3   Foucault makes regular trips to the USA, Canada, Japan and Brazil and two trips to Germany to deliver lectures, seminars and set up networks with intellectuals and others.

1970   Appointed Professor of the History of Systems of Thought at the prestigious research institution of the Collège de France in Paris where he gives a course of public lectures and seminars almost every year until his death. Roland Barthes publishes *S/Z* which develops and applies methods of linguistic structuralism to literature. In December Foucault launches his inaugural series of lectures titled 'The will to knowledge'.

1971   Publication of Foucault's inaugural speech at the Collège de France, 'The order of discourse'. Foucault announces the creation of the Groupe d'informations sur les prisons (GIP), a collective of intellectuals, prisoners, ex-prisoners and their families, aimed at providing prisoners themselves with a public forum to help them activate to improve conditions in prisons. Foucault gives a lecture in Tunisia on the painting of Manet which was finally published in complete form in 2004. In November, Foucault begins his second series of lectures at the Collège de France titled 'Penal theories and institutions'.

1972   Continues activities with the GIP and participates in other groups organised along the same lines, namely the Groupe d'information – santé aimed at assisting health workers, and the Groupe d'information et de soutien des travailleurs immigrés, a support group for immigrant workers. A second edition of *Madness and Civilization* is published with a new preface. A discussion between Foucault and Deleuze titled 'Intellectuals and Power' is also published. Gilles Deleuze and Félix Guattari publish their celebrated work *Anti-Oedipus.* The course at the Collège de France is titled 'The punitive society'.

1973   Publication of *I, Pierre Rivière* ... In November Foucault starts his course for the year. These lectures were eventually published in 2003 under the title *Le pouvoir psychiatrique.*

1975   Publication of *Discipline and Punish.* Travels to Spain with six other intellectuals, film-makers and journalists to protest unsuccessfully against the execution of eleven Spanish activists opposed to the Franco regime. Foucault's course for this year was published in 1999 and translated into English under the title of *Abnormal* in 2003.

1976   Publication of the first volume of *The History of Sexuality*. Course titled *'Society Must Be Defended'*, subsequently published in 1997, and in English translation in 2003.

1977   Reviews a book by André Glucksmann, *The Master Thinkers*. Glucksmann is one of a group of young ex-Maoists dubbed the 'New Philosophers', who appeared on the scene in the late 1970s and created a media furore both in France and in the USA with their strong critiques of Marxism and the repressive regimes in Communist countries as embodied and symbolised by the gulag.

1978   Publication of the influential article 'Governmentality' in Italian. Foucault travels to Iran and writes a highly controversial series of articles on the political situation there. His annual course was subsequently published under the title of *Sécurité, Territoire, Population* in 2004. A book titled *La nouvelle histoire* (*The New History*) (LeGoff, 1978) is published. This book which provides a key to work by the famous school of 'Annales historians' makes a number of references to Foucault's work.

1979   Continuing attacks on Foucault's writings on Iran. His course for this year was published under the title of *Naissance de la biopolitique* in 2004. Jean-François Lyotard publishes *The Postmodern Condition*, which introduces the term 'postmodernism' into the humanities and social sciences. Sociologist Pierre Bourdieu publishes *Distinction*.

1980   The annual course is titled 'The government of the living' with a seminar series on Liberalism. Noted existentialist philosopher and novelist Jean-Paul Sartre dies. Foucault joins the huge funeral procession.

1981   Foucault's course is titled 'Subjectivity and truth'. A state of emergency is declared in Poland. Foucault is active on a committee of support for Poland working alongside exiled members of the dissident trade union Solidarity.

1982   The title of the course this year is *The Hermeneutics of the Subject* subsequently published in 2001 and appearing in English translation in 2005. Foucault travels to Poland in a truck with medications and other supplies in the company of the actor Simone Signoret and members of the humanitarian organisation Médecins du monde.

1983   Course at the Collège de France titled 'The government of self and others'. A version of these lectures which he delivered in Berkeley was published under the title of *Fearless Speech* in 2001.

1984   Foucault's annual lectures are titled 'The government of self and others: the courage of truth'. Volumes 2 and 3 of *The History of Sexuality: The Use of Pleasure* and *The Concern for Self* are published. Foucault dies on 25 June at the Saltpêtrière Hospital in Paris from a condition subsequently identified as AIDS.

APPENDIX 2　Key Concepts in Foucault's Work

Introduction

Foucault's terminology has always posed a significant challenge for critics and admirers alike. His readers are constantly confronted with terms he has invented himself, such as 'governmentality' (which he willingly describes himelf as a 'nasty word' (STP: 19)), or words which he has completely redefined for his own purposes, such as 'archaeology', 'genealogy', 'discourse', 'technology' or 'apparatus'. Then there are the words he has borrowed from Ancient Greek such as 'episteme' or 'techne'. Added to this are phrases such as 'discursive practice', 'pastoral power', 'regimes of truth' or such colourful creations as 'pangraphic panopticism' (PP: 57) and so on. Many readers have asked, and continue to ask, why not just use plain language, why this complex and baroque edifice of language? Foucault happily admits, understating the case a little perhaps, that he belongs to 'that category of people, who when they write spontaneously, write in a slightly convoluted manner' (1984e: 406).

In Foucault's earlier work, this complexity is perhaps partially the result of a new writer out to prove himself philosophically, but even at this early stage it is also an attempt to invite people to think about the ideas they usually take for granted. By playing with the meanings of words and inventing new ones, Foucault is inviting the reader to refuse to accept commonplaces at face value. His aim is to demonstrate that words do not transparently mirror things and that the connection between words and their meanings is not automatic, but instead the result of often byzantine historical, social and cultural processes. The firm grounding of Foucault's work in historical analysis, allows him to attach rigorous definitions and concrete examples to his terminology which he deploys in a highly logical and organised manner – even if following it initially demands a degree of patience from the reader. As he comments himself in relation to one of his well-known inventions, namely 'problematisation':

words are only barbarous when they do not clearly say what they mean; we know that many familiar words are barbarous because they say many things at once or say nothing at all, but, on the other hand, certain technical words which are bizarre in their construction are not barbarous because they say fairly clearly what they mean. (1988d: 413–4)

This guide to Foucault's terms and concepts – his 'tool box' – has been constructed with a view to assisting users of his work in the process of the clarification and definition of his terminology.

Instructions for use

- A key to all abbreviations can be found at the beginning of this book.
- Given the enormous scope and sheer quantity of Foucault's work, this list does not claim to be comprehensive. It can be used in conjunction with the indexes found at the end of Volume IV of the French collection of his shorter works, *Dits et écrits*, and the indexes of his books of lectures, as well as those found at the end of some of the English editions of Foucault's books.
- Only very brief definitions of each of the terms are provided here. Instead, this list is more intended to indicate where the best definitions and examples of concepts might be found in Foucault's own work. This is to aid those wishing to apply Foucault's ideas to gain first hand and accurate clarification on terminology and reduce some of the inevitable (if productive) confusions and distortions produced by multiple second-hand interpretations.
- To simplify matters, as there are quite a few editions of Foucault's various shorter works (not to mention translations into various languages), items have been listed in this guide according to the numbers allocated to them in *Dits et écrits*. These numbers can be found at the end of each item in the bibliography and have increasingly come to serve as points of reference for scholars working around the globe with multiple versions and different translations. Also for reasons of simplicity, and because of the existence of multiple editions, page numbers have been omitted.
- Where the item does not appear in *Dits et écrits* it is listed according to conventional date format.
- When referring to Foucault's books, I have used abbreviations for the titles and have referred to chapters. This is to facilitate consultation across various editions and translations.
- As the only edition available of *Histoire de la folie* in English is a heavily abridged version, I have referred to the French original (HF) as well as the English translation (MC). A translation is due out in late 2005.
- The books of Foucault's lectures do not include chapter numbers, so I have referred to the dates of individual lectures. The lectures in *L'hermeneutique du sujet* are each divided into two chapters representing the first and second hours. I have referred to these as (a) and (b).

KEY CONCEPTS

ANTIPSYCHIATRY   While Foucault emphasises that his own work cannot be described as antipsychiatry, he makes a number of sympathetic references to the movement in interviews and articles. See 95; 98; 143; 160; 173; 281; 336; 342; PP 21 Nov 1973.

APPARATUS (DISPOSITIF)   Foucault generally uses this term to indicate the various institutional, physical and administrative mechanisms and knowledge structures, which enhance and maintain the exercise of power within the social body. It first appears in his work in the mid-1970s (see 151). He also uses it in PP. 7, 28 Nov 1973. He finally offers an extended definition in 206. For examples see, 193; 195; 197; 198; 200; 239; 278; 306; HS pts. 4, 5; PP 28 Nov 1973. On apparatuses of security see STP 11, 18, 25 Jan 1978.

ARCHAEOLOGY   'Archaeology' is the term Foucault used during the 1960s to describe his approach to writing history. Foucault first refers to the 'archaeology of knowledge' in his work without explaining what he means. See, for example, MC ch. IV; HF pt. 1 ch. III. On the origins of the term and for a discussion of why Foucault chose the term 'archaeology', see 97; 221. For a complete, some might argue, excessively detailed exposition of Foucault's archaeological method, see AK. For an excellent brief definition of the term 'archaeology', see 34 (this article also provides a useful brief summary of OT). See also 48; 58; 59 (this is a good summary of AK); 66; 68; 330; OT preface, ch. 3; AK pt. III ch. 5, pt. IV ch. 1, pt. IV chs. 4, 5, pt. V. After 1970, Foucault uses the term archaeology only occasionally. See 221; 330. For an interesting definition of archaeology in the context of the analysis of power, see 139 (discussion) and on archaeology as an 'approach' rather than a comprehensive theory, see 169 and 281.

ARCHAEOLOGY VERSUS GENEALOGY   Foucault's remarks on the difference between archaeology and genealogy are generally rather vague and confusing. For distinctions between a 'critical' project and a 'genealogical' project, see OD. For an early distinction between the 'archaeology of knowledge' and the 'dynastic of knowledge', see 119. For the most complete discussion on the difference between archaeology and genealogy, see 193. See also STP 18 Jan; 1978 UP intro. ch. 1 for brief comments. On 'criticism' as archaeological in its methodology and genealogical in its goal, see 339. For another oblique discussion of the difference between the two, in terms of a distinction between the history of sciences and the genealogy of knowledges, see SMD 25 Feb 1976. Later, Foucault makes a distinction between the history of sciences and a genealogy of the subject (1993).

ARCHITECTURE   On the historical role of institutional and domestic architecture, and its role in social control, organisation and government, see 195 and 310. On institutional architecture (prisons, schools, factories, asylums, army barracks etc.)

and its role in the exercise of disciplinary power, see DP pt. 3. On architecture and the regulation of sexuality, see HS pt. 2 ch. 1. On town planning see STP 11 Jan 1978.

ART (PAINTING)   Foucault comments on his tastes in painting in 149. On Fromanger, see 150. On Manet, see 20; 149; 2004a. On Magritte, see 53; 307. For a very detailed description of Valasquez' painting Las Meninas and a discussion of representation, see OT ch. 1. On African art, see 12. On Klee, see 39; 43; 50; 53. On pop and op art, see 50. On Panofsky, see 51. On Rebeyrolle, see 118. On Byzantios, see 135. For comments on how an archaeology of painting might be conducted, see AK pt. IV ch. 6. On Renaissance art and madness, see MC ch. 1; HF pt: 1 ch. I. On Goya, see MC conclusion; HF pt. 3 ch. V.

THE ART OF EXISTENCE (LIFE AS A WORK OF ART)   On creating oneself as a work of art as opposed to discovering the truth about oneself see 308; 326; 329; 339; 344; 357; UP intro. ch. 1, pt. 1 ch. 4. For definitions of the 'arts of existence' in Ancient Greek philosophy see 338; 344; 350; CS pt. 2, conclusion; HER 3 Feb (a), 17 Mar (a) 1982. On the relation between art and intellectual knowledge see 139 (discussion); 174; 185; 272.

AUTHOR/ARTIST   Foucault challenged traditional notions of the author as being restrictive. For definitions, history and criticisms of the notion of the author, the artist and the 'work', see 8; 48; 54; 59; 69; 85; 2004c; OD. On the relation between the author (specifically Foucault) and his readers, see 236. He notes in 328 that a work should say, and show, how it is undertaken as a mark of respect to the reader.

BIOPOWER   Foucault argues that biopower is a technology which appeared in the late eighteenth century for managing populations. It incorporates certain aspects of disciplinary power. If disciplinary power is about training the actions of bodies, biopower is about managing the births, deaths, reproduction and illnesses of a population. See 197; HS pt. 5; SMD 17 Mar 1976; STP 11 Jan 1978. On 'biopolitics', see 274; 297; 364; HS pt. 5. In spite of its title, Foucault's series of lectures titled Naissance de la biopolitique barely mentions biopolitics.

BODY   For comments on the relation between political power and the body, and on ways of training the body to make it socially productive, see 131; 136; 138; 139; 157; 197; 221; 234; 297; 2004c; DP pt. 1 ch. 1, pt. 2 ch. 1, pt. 3 chs. 1, 2; PP 16 Jan 1974; SMD 17 Mar 1976. On the health of the body in relation to strategies of the economic and social management of populations, see 168; 170; 194; 257; DP pt. 3 ch. 3; HS pt. 4 ch. 4. On the body as prison of the 'soul', namely using the body as a means of controlling people's behaviour and existence, see DP pt. 1 ch. 1, pt. 2 ch. 1. On the disposal of dead bodies in Western culture, see 360. On the body as a way of experiencing man's finitude, see OT ch. 9.

CAPITALISM   For a critique of the notion of capitalism see NBP 21 Feb 1979. On the enterprise society see NBP 21 Mar 1979. On human capital see NBP 14, 21 Mar 1979.

COLONIALISM AND THE WEST   For comments on European colonial power and colonial ways of thinking, see 12; 108; 234; SMD 4 Feb, 17 Mar 1976; PP 28 Nov, 5 Dec 1973. On the notion of the West, and the impact of the West on the rest of the world, see 50; 119; 212. When delivering lectures and interviews in Japan, Foucault was always careful to emphasise the Western context of his work, and that he had developed his ideas within a Western, more specifically, a French setting. See 231; 232; 233. On Vietnam, refugees, boat people and the legacy of colonialism, see 271. On Western 'orientalism', see 4; 50; MC preface. On the impact of Western knowledge and Marxism as an instrument of struggle against the West in non-Western countries, see 119. On Tunisia, see 163. For a discussion of the origins of ideas concerning a global economy in eighteenth and nineteenth-century Europe see NBP 24 Jan 1979.

CONDUCT (RULES OF)   For definitions and the history of conduct and the 'conduct of conduct', see 306; 340; STP 22 Feb, 1, 8 Mar 1978. On rules of conduct versus actual conduct, see UP intro. ch. 3. On power and the determination of the conduct of others, see 356. See 'resistance' for 'counter-conduct'.

CONFESSION   For a brief history of confession and its change from a religious to a secular practice, see 198; 289; HS pt. 3. For some brief early remarks on confession and sexuality, see OD. For comments on Eastern practices of confession, see 216. On confession in the Western legal system, see 163; 349; 363. On the differences between confession and the ritual of penitence in the history of Christianity, see 1993; AN 19 Feb 1975. On confession as a form of knowledge-power, see HS pt. 3. On confession in relation to sexuality, see 181; 363; HS pts. 2, 3; AN 19, 26 Feb 1975. On practices of confession in Antiquity see HER 3 Mar (b), 10 Mar (a) 1982. On confession and psychiatry see PP 30 Jan 1974.

CONFINEMENT   On the 'Great Confinement' of mad and other marginal people in 1657, see MIP ch. V; MC chs. II, III, VIII; HF pt. 1 chs. II, III, IV. On the confinement of 'unreasonable' people in the eighteenth century, see HF pt. 3 chs. II, III. On confinement as it appears in the form of the gulag in the USSR and other socialist States, see 204; 209; 218. For suggestions regarding the historical reasons for a change from practices of exile to those of confinement, see 234. For brief comments on the history of confinement, see 83; 105; 143; 161; DP pt. 3 ch. 3; AN 15 Jan. 1975.

CRIME AND THE CRIMINAL   For an analysis of changes in the definition of crime and the criminal, see 139; 144; 220; HF pt. 3 ch. III; DP pt. 2 ch. 1; AN 29 Jan

1975; NBP 21 Mar 1979. On the social and economic usefulness of delinquency, see 297; 2004b; DP pt. 4; NBP 21 Mar 1979. On the criminal as the enemy of the Prince, see DP pt. 1 ch.1. On the criminal as hero, see DP pt. 1 ch. 2. On the criminal as a monster and enemy of society, see DP pt. 2 ch. 1, pt. 4 ch. 1. On crime and madness, see HF pt. 3 chs. III, V; AN 8 Jan 1975.

CULTURE   Foucault describes culture as 'a hierarchical organisation of values, accessible to everybody, but at the same time the occasion of a mechanism of selection and exclusion' (HER: 173). For general statements about culture and cultural analysis, see 23; 34; 46; 50; 83; 89; 285; HER 3 Feb (a) 1982. On the orders underlying culture, see OT preface.

CURIOSITY   For Foucault's comments on curiosity as a motivation for engaging in research and ethical projects see 338; 1988e. For a definition of curiosity and its ethical benefits see 285. On curiosity in more abstract terms see 20 and MC ch. I; HF pt. 1 ch. I.

DANGEROUS INDIVIDUALS   On how certain individuals come to be defined as 'dangerous' both to themselves and the rest of the social body, see 108; 142; 144; 165; 170; 205; 209; DP pt. 4 ch. 1; AN 15 Jan, 12 Feb 1975; PP 16 Jan, 23 Jan 1974. For an extensive and detailed discussion, see 220.

DEATH   On dreams, limits and death, see 1. On death and the life sciences, see 3. On the Renaissance view of death, see MC ch. I; HF pt. 1 ch. I. On medicine and death see BC chs. 8, 9. On death and the being of language, see 14; 38. On death as an event, see 80. On the decline in the ritualisation of death in the Western world, see SMD 17 Mar 1976. On modern techniques of mass destruction, see SMD 17 Mar 1976; HS pt. 5. For comments on suicide, see 308; 325.

DEATH PENALTY   Foucault was opposed to the death penalty and expressed his views on this issue in the public media. See 114; 161; 240; 246; 260; 300.

DERRIDA   Foucault responded to Derrida's critiques (1978) of his treatment of Descartes in MC at some length in two articles: 102 and 104. In both these texts he mounts what is, in effect, a critique of the whole deconstructionist project. (See also 119.) It is perhaps not surprising that the exchange effectively ended Foucault and Derrida's friendship until the early 1980s. See Macey 1993: 144–5, 237–8. Foucault also made a distinction between his own approach and deconstruction in 342 and 1994. For Foucault's own critique of binary oppositions (following Deleuze), see 80.

DESIRE   For brief and interesting comments on desire (following on from some of Deleuze's ideas), see 139 (discussion). For a brief and rather mysterious discussion on desire and discourse, see AK pt. II ch. 6. See also HS pt. 2 ch. 1. On the notion of the 'desiring subject' in Western thought, see UP intro. ch. 1. On Ancient Greek and on Christian notions of desire, see UP pt. 1 ch. 1. Also on desire see 1989c; OT ch. 10.

DISCIPLINE   Discipline is a mechanism of power which regulates the behaviour of individuals in the social body. Foucault emphasises that power is not discipline, rather discipline is simply one way in which power can be exercised, 341. See also AN 29 Jan 1975. Foucault introduces the term 'disciplinary society' in 139, discussing its history and the origins and disciplinary institutions. This piece also provides a good summary and expansion of some of the ideas in DP. See also 152; 297. For other early efforts to define disciplinary power, see PP 14, 21, 28 Nov 1973, 16 Jan 1974. For an extended discussion on what Foucault means by disciplinary power, its historical origins and for detailed examples, see DP pt. 3, pt. 4 ch. 3. See also 152; 194; 229; 297; 306; STP 11, 18 Jan 1978. Foucault also specifies that when he speaks of a 'disciplinary society' he does not mean a 'disciplined society': 277; 306. See also NBP 21 Mar 1979. Earlier in Foucault's work, one finds similar notions, for example, concerning the training of mad people in 'self restraint' and on the operation of surveillance in relation to madness in the nineteenth century, see HF pt. 3 ch. IV. On reigns of terror as the failure of discipline, see 172. On schools as disciplinary institutions, see 139; DP pt. 3 ch. 2. On four ways in which knowledge was organised by disciplinary power in the eighteenth century, see SMD 25 Feb 1976. On the history of the incorrigible individual who needs to be disciplined, see 165. After 1976, Foucault replaced 'discipline' with the notion of 'biopower'. On the contrast between disciplinary power and biopower, see SMD 17 Mar 1976. In 239, and STP biopower is in its turn replaced by Foucault's new notion of 'governmentality'.

DISCONTINUITY   Foucault uses a principle of discontinuity in his analyses, in order to undermine philosophical notions of unchanging essences in history. For definitions and discussion, see 47; 48; 58; 59; 66; 77; 84; 103; 192; 216; 219; 278; OT chs. 3, 7; AK pt. I, pt. II ch. 1, pt. IV ch. 5; OD.

DISCOURSE   Discourse is a rather slippery notion in Foucault's work but at its most basic he uses the term to refer to the material verbal traces left by history. It makes its first extended appearance in OT but mainly in the context of a description of eighteenth-century forms of representation. See OT chs. 2, 4, 7, 9. See also 34; 38. Foucault subsequently developed a broader definition of discourse as both a concrete object and event, and uses it as a building block for 'archaeology'. See 48; 58; 59; 139 (discussion); 221; 281; 343; OD. See also AK, in particular pt. II chs. 1, 3, 4, pt. III ch. 3, pt. V. Foucault shifts his emphasis once again in the early 1970s and defines discourse in relation to power in OD. It makes a brief reappearance in HS pt. 4 ch. 2, where discourse is the location where power and knowledge intersect. For a 'political' definition of discourse, see 186; AK pt. V.

DISCURSIVE FORMATION   The discursive formation is roughly equivalent to a scientific discipline. For definitions see AK pt. II chs. 2, 7. See also 58; 59; 60.

DISCURSIVE PRACTICE   This term refers to a historically and culturally specific set of rules for organising and producing different forms of knowledge. For definitions see AK pt. III ch. 3, pt. IV ch. 6. See also 66; 101; 340. On using the notion of discursive practice as a way of avoiding the dilemma of an opposition between science and ideology, see 338.

DREAMS   For a history of Western dream interpretation, see 1. On truth, dreams and limits, see 1; 4; 12; 20. On dreams, madness and Descartes, see 102; 104. On dreams and madness in the Classical age, see MC ch. IV; HF pt. 2 ch. II. On dreams and psychiatry in the nineteenth century see PP 30 Jan 1974. On Ancient Greek dream interpretation in relation to sexuality, see CS pt. 1. On Ancient Greek dream interpretation, see 295; 304; 332; 344, 363. On early Christian discussions of dreams, see 312.

ECONOMICS   For an extensive analysis of nineteenth and twentieth-century economic liberalism and the primacy of economics see STP 5 Apr 1978 and NBP. For an enlightening history and critique of notions of economic rationalism see NBP 28 Mar 1979. On the history and prehistory of economics see OT ch. 6ff.

EDUCATION   On a number of occasions, particularly after the student unrest of May 1968, Foucault discusses teaching methods and the role of the teaching academic in higher education, as well as the relation between universities and the State. See 78; 82; 89; 98; 119; 285. For an incisive critique of institutional mechanisms in relation to the university and the dissemination of research and critical writing in the early 1980s, see 1985. For interesting discussions on the relationship between teaching and power, see 161. See also 160; 341; 356. For comments by Foucault on his public lectures at the Collège de France as reports on his research rather than teaching, see SMD 7 Jan 1976. On education as a way of regulating access to discourse, knowledge and power, see OD. On education and the Ancient Greeks see FS ch. 4; HER 27 Jan (a), 17 Mar. (b) 1982. On the architectural and disciplinary arrangements in schools in the nineteenth century see DP pt. 3; PP 28 Nov 1973. On the history of special education see PP 9, 16 Jan 1974.

THE ENLIGHTENMENT (AUFKLÄRUNG)   On the legacy of the Age of Reason and the eighteenth-century enlightenment period, see 219; 279; 291; 306; 330; 353. For definitions, see 339; 351.

EPISTEME   This term refers to the orderly 'unconscious' structures or 'epistemological field' underlying the production of scientific knowledge in a particular time and place. Foucault remarks 'in any given culture and at any given moment, there is always only one episteme that defines the conditions of possibility of all knowledge'

(OT: 168). The original definitions appear in OT, where it only ever appears in the singular as either the 'episteme of Western culture', OT preface, chs. 3, 6, or as a specific historical configuration of the Western 'episteme', for example, the Renaissance, the Classical or the Modern episteme. See OT chs. 2, 3, 6, 7, 10. An early version of this idea emerges in Foucault's discussion of the isomorphisms or structures of order in language in a given age in 17. Epistemes subsequently appear very briefly in a plural form in his work. For a revised definition, see 58; AK pt. IV ch. 6. See also 109, where Foucault defines it as the relation between different sciences in a given period. In 206, Foucault describes the episteme as something purely discursive, a particular case of what he terms a 'dispositif' (apparatus).

ETHICAL AND POLITICAL RECOMMENDATIONS   Foucault, in spite of accusations of political and ethical nihilism, had firm views on the kind of ethical approach that he wanted to take in his work. He argued that he wanted to render certain taken-for-granted exercises of power 'intolerable', by exposing them to scrutiny. He argues that the exercise of power only remains tolerable by covering up its tracks. See HS pt. 4 ch. 1. He saw it as part of his task, to make people aware of how intolerable some previously taken-for-granted exercises of power actually were and show them that things could be different. See 91; 95; 120; 151; 160; 161; 204; 215; 238; 278; 279; 281; 285; 296; 326; 345; 346; 353; 359; 1988e. He argues in 339 that projects which propose radical universal solutions should be abandoned in favour of experimental work on the limits we face in our own daily lives and social situations. See also 351. Foucault notes that it is impossible not to think in terms of good and evil and of the true and false, but one must always question, in every situation, the content of these categories and where the line between them is drawn. See 161.

ETHICS   Ethics concerns the kind of relation one has to oneself. For definitions, see 336; 341; 342; 356; UP intro. ch. 3. On ethos see 339; 356; HER 10 Feb (b) 1982. For a distinction between ethics and ethos see 341 where Foucault suggests that 'ethics is a practice; ethos is a manner of being' (p. 377). On the four aspects of how the individual constitutes him/herself as the moral subject of his or her own actions, see 326; 344; UP intro. ch. 3. On the difference between moral systems which emphasise codes or sets of laws and those that emphasise individual self-transformation, see UP intro. ch. 3, pt. 1 ch. 4. For an account of a change in ethical structures in the Classical Age, see HF pt. 1 chs. III, V. For a rather obscure discussion on ethical forms in Western history, see OT ch. 9. On the links and differences between Ancient Greek and Roman and Christian sexual ethics, see UP intro. ch. 2; pt. 2 ch. 4 CS conclusion. On classical Greek ethics as a power relation over oneself and others see, UP pt. 1 chs. 3, 4.

EVENTS   An event is something that has a beginning and an end. For a lengthy philosophical definition of what constitutes an 'event', see 80. See also 10; 59; 84; OD. For early discussions where Foucault uses the term 'expression' or 'expressive act' instead of 'event', see 1. For a detailed discussion of the work of the Annales school of historians in establishing different layers of events, see AK pt. I, pt. IV ch. 5; 103, and for a critique of the way philosophy completely ignores events, see 104; 234. For an excellent discussion on the historiographical value of the notion of event, see 278. See also 192; 221. On knowledge as an event, see 101; 139. On truth as an event, see 146. On thought as an event, see 340. Foucault describes himself as a philosopher of the event in 234. On the image (photograph) as event, see 150.

EXCLUSION (OF INDIVIDUALS AND GROUPS)   The examination of the situation of people existing on the margins of society is one of the mainstays of Foucault's work. For some general descriptions of the processes by which societies exclude certain groups and individuals, see 83; 132; 137; 139; DP pt. 3 ch. 3. For comments on an analysis which focuses on the 'negative structures' or excluded groups, as opposed to more traditional approaches which focus on the mainstream, see 222. Here, Foucault also describes four general systems of exclusion which can be found across all societies. On the history of 'abnormal' individuals, see 165; AN. On the confinement of mad and other 'unreasonable' people as both a gesture of exclusion and of social organisation in the seventeenth and eighteenth centuries, see MIP ch. V, HF pt. 1 ch. III; OD and AN 15 Jan 1975. On the exclusions practised by discourse and language, see 25; OD.

EXPERIENCE   Foucault defines an experience as an interrelation between knowledge, 'types of normativity' and subjectivity in a particular culture at a particular time in UP intro. ch. 1. See also 43; 281; 338; 340. These ideas echo Foucault's earlier references to different types of 'experience' in HF, notably madness and also implicitly criticise phenomenological approaches. See also 4; 23. Foucault draws a distinction between scientific or conceptual knowledge (connaissance) and experience in HF pt. 2 ch. I. On sexuality as a historical 'experience', see UP intro. ch. 1.

FAMILY   For an extended discussion on the family as a model of sovereign power and its pivotal interaction with mechanisms of disciplinary power see PP 28 Nov, 5 Dec, 12 Dec 1973. On the history of the family and sexual regulation, see 336. On sexuality and the family in the nineteenth century, see HS pt. 4 ch. 3; AN 5, 12, 19 Mar 1975; 1989c. On the nineteenth-century origins of the modern family in relation to the crusade against masturbation, see 1989c; AN 5, 12 Mar, 1975. On the history of the administration of childhood, see 168; 257.

FICTION   On a number of occasions Foucault describes his work as 'fictions'. By this he does not mean that what he is saying is not true, rather that his writings are particular accounts or 'stories' about reality, not transparent representations of what is really out there. See 48; 197; 272; 280; 281; 328. For some poetic and rather obscure definitions of fiction and the 'fictive', see 38.

FILM   Foucault's comments on film are not very extensive. For comments on Marguerite Duras' films, see 159. For reviews and remarks on various films, see 140; 162; 164; 230; 284; 308. On the body in contemporary film and Sade, see 164.

FINITUDE   Foucault throughout his career emphasises in various ways the notion of the finite and limited condition of human existence and culture. On the 'finitude of man', see 8; 30; BC conclusion; OT chs. 8, 9, 10. For various definitions of finitude as it appears in a historical context, see OT ch. 9. On finitude and madness, see HF pt. 1 chs. I, V.

FOOD   On the place of food in early Christian techniques of self-formation and regulations and restriction surrounding food, see 312; 326; 344. On food and exercise in Classical antiquity, see UP pt. 2.

FOUNDATIONS/NON-REDUCTIONISM   Foucault often argues against the idea that there is a single foundation for knowledge or a single explanation for all human activity and social organisation. There is no *one* principle which explains everything else. See 221; 310. Instead it is a question of the interrelation of a complex and multi-layered range of elements. See also 281; 306; 1994; AK pt. II ch. 7.

FREEDOM   In 353, (cf. 362) Foucault notes that he believes 'solidly in human freedom'. Against nineteenth-century and existentialist views of an abstract freedom and a 'free' subject, and on freedom as a practice rather than a goal to be achieved, see 84; 310; 356. On Foucault's views about respecting the freedom of the consumers of his work to interpret his work as they wished without being instructed by him on how to act politically and socially, see 236; 238; 328; 357; 364; 1988e; SMD 7 Jan 1976. On the idea that knowledge starts with rules and constraints, not freedom, see 132. For earlier ideas along these lines, see 1; 25; 58; 84; AK pt. V. On the idea that real liberation lies in knowing oneself rather than through liberation movements, see 242. On freedom as a condition for the exercise of power, see 306; 356. On freedom as the possibility of transformation, see 330; 339. On thought as freedom in relation to action, see 342. On freedom and ethics, see 356; 357. On freedom, reason and madness in the Classical Age and nineteenth century, see HF pt. 1 ch. V, pt. 3 chs. I, V. For definitions of freedom in relation to governmentality, see STP 5 Apr 1978; NBP 17, 24 Jan 1979.

FREUD   For criticisms of Freud's approach, see 1; 2; 25; HF pt. 3 ch. IV; OT ch. 9.

FRIENDSHIP   For some interesting, but rather obscure comments on how Foucault saw personal friendship, see 234. On friendship and homosexuality, see 293; 311, 358. On friendship and the Ancient Greeks, see 313; 326; 344; HER 20 Jan (b), 27 Jan (a) (b), 3 Feb (b) 1982.

THE GAZE (LE REGARD)   Foucault's most extended treatment of 'the act of see-ing, the gaze' and its role in knowledge and the 'medical gaze' is to be found in BC. See also 195. On the primacy of vision and sight in the discipline of natural history in the Classical Age, see OT ch. 5. On the gaze in the new novel, see 17.

GENEALOGY   Genealogy is the term Foucault uses to describe his historical method during the 1970s. For an early mention of genealogy in relation to Foucault's method, see 48. See 84 for a discussion by Foucault of Nietzsche and genealogy. See also 139 for an extended and extremely interesting analysis of Nietzsche's historical approach to philosophy. At this stage Foucault was using the term 'dynastic researches' to describe what he was doing, rather than 'genealogy'. For further definitions of geneal-ogy, see OD. For a detailed set of definitions of genealogy as a method which opposes particular ways of linking power and knowledge, see 192; 193. For brief comments on the material Foucault uses for his archaeological/genealogical method, see 151. He also mentions genealogy in passing in STP 8 Feb 1978.

GEOGRAPHY   For Foucault's most extended discussion on this topic, see 169. For other references to geography and space, see 195.

GOVERNMENTALITY   Foucault originally used the term 'governmentality' to describe a particular way of administering populations in modern European his-tory within the context of the rise of the idea of the State. He later expanded his definition to encompass the techniques and procedures which are designed to govern the conduct of both individuals and populations at every level, not just the administrative or political level. For an early reference to 'governmental knowl-edge' in Foucault's work, see 126. See also 139, in relation to the 'inquiry' as a juridical form which takes hold during the fourteenth and fifteenth centuries. See 239 for Foucault's best-known (to date) exposition on this subject. This lecture is, however, only one of a more extensive series of lectures on the topic delivered in 1978 and 1979 – only published in their entirety in 2004. See STP and NBP. For various definitions of the notion of government and governmentality, see 274; 281; 289; 306; 345; 356; 359; 1988d; STP 1, 8, 22 Feb; NBP 10 Jan 1979. On the art of government, see 291; AN 15 Jan 1975; NBP. On technologies of govern-ment, see 364. For a definition of governmentality as the encounter between tech-niques of domination over others and techniques of the self, see 363. See also HER 17 Feb (a) 1982. On the links between the care of the self, 'telling the truth' (dire-vrai) and the government of others, see UP pt. 1 chs. 3, 4; HER 6 Jan (b), 13 Jan (a) (b), 20 Jan (a), 27 Jan (a), 3 Feb (a) (b), 10 Feb (b) 1982.

HETEROTOPIA   'Heterotopia' is a word coined by Foucault to mean a space which is outside everyday social and institutional spaces, for example trains, motels and cemeteries. For an extensive discussion, see 360. See also 310; OT preface.

HISTORICAL A PRIORI   This is the order underlying any given culture at any given period of history. It first appears in 3. See also OT preface, ch. 5; AK pt. III ch. 5; 345. Foucault also uses the phrase the 'positive unconscious of knowledge' (OT foreword), to refer to the same idea.

HISTORY AND HISTORIOGRAPHY   Foucault's entire philosophy is based on the assumption that human knowledge and existence are profoundly historical. He argues in 2 that what is most human about man is his history. He discusses the notions of history, change and historical method at some length at various points in his career. See 1; 48; 50; 58; 59; 68; 66; 84; 139; 132; 156; 221; 277; 278; HF pt. 1 chs. IV, V; BC preface; OT foreword, ch. 5; AK pt. I; OD; FS ch. 2, conclusion. On historical intelligibility see 281; STP 8 Mar 1978. For an attack on certain styles of Marxist history, see 119. On the structuralist movement and the political uses of history, see 103. For interesting comments by Foucault on how he sets the boundaries of investigation for his various studies, see 34; 156; 277; 278; 338. For an analysis of the historical methodology Foucault employs in DP, see 277. For a reply to critics who say that he denies history, see 281; 2004c. Against nostalgia for the 'good old days', see 310; 325; 344. For an argument that the solutions provided by past societies are not the answer to current problems, see 326. On the ethical obligations of the practitioner of historical research and writing, see 326; 1985. On history as a means of demonstrating that there is no such thing as historical necessity, that things could have been and could be otherwise, see 84; 330; 2004c. For brief comments on the history of history as a discipline, see OT ch. 5 and on history as a way of thinking, see OT chs. 8, 9, 10; SMD 28 Jan, 11, 25 Feb. 1976. On historicism, see SMD 25 Feb 1976; NBP 10 Jan 1979. For a general discussion of what constitutes a historical document, see 1989a.

HISTORY OF THE PRESENT   Foucault describes his work on a number of occasions as the history or the diagnosis of the present, as the analysis of 'what today is'. See 47; 50; 126; 200; 219; 221; 306; 330; 339; 351; 364; 1988d; DP pt. 1 ch. 1; FS conclusion. He notes that our own times and lives are not the beginning or end of some 'historical' process but a period like, but at the same time unlike, any other. The question should simply be 'how is today different from yesterday?'.

HOMOSEXUALITY   For historical discussions on the marginal status of homosexuals and for comments on the construction of homosexual identity, see 82; 200; 293; 336; HF pt. 1 ch. III; HS pt. 2 ch. 2, pt. 4 ch. 2. For a brief history of homosexual practices and on the existence and creation of forms of homosexual and gay culture, see 293; 311; 313; 317; 358. On homosexual practices and the Ancient Greeks, see 304; 311; 314; 326; 344; UP intro. ch. 2, pt. 1 ch. 4, pt. 4, pt. 5; CS pt. 6. On female homosexuality, see 293; 311, 358. On repressive measures against homosexuals, see 318; 349; 1989c.

HUMANISM AND THE DEATH OF MAN   During the 1960s, Foucault was noted for his critiques of humanist philosophy, which is founded on the belief that something called 'human nature' or 'man' is at the centre of all knowledge and morality, see 34; 37; 39; 50; 55; 69. For a definition of humanism, see 77. For a critique of the notion of human nature (following Nietzsche), see 132; 139. Foucault makes some modifications to what he means by the death of man in 281. On the differing definitions of humanism in Western history, see 339; 349; 362. For comments on the dangers of using humanism to justify struggles on the behalf of minorities, see 163. During the 1960s, Foucault also linked the death of man to the death of God, see 8; 13; 38; 50; OT chs. 8, 9, 10. For another definition of 'man' as he appeared historically in the nineteenth and twentieth centuries, see PP 21 Nov 1973. On the demise of humanism, see 54; 59.

HUMAN SCIENCES   Over the course of his career, Foucault changed his perspective on the history and role of the human sciences several times. For 'archaeological' definitions relating to the demise of a form of thought based on 'humanism' and on the dubious scientific status of the human sciences, see 2; 3; 30; 34; 50; 54; 59; 85; OT ch. 10. On the conflict between the human science and the 'hard sciences', see 59; 70; OT ch. 10. For an extended analysis on the historical and philosophical origins of the human sciences, see OT chs. 9, 10. On the human sciences and medicine, see BC Ch. 2. On the human sciences as forms of power-knowledge and on their role in the constitution of a disciplinary society, see 139; DP pt. 4 ch. 3; PP 21 Nov 1973. On the human sciences and the constitution of the subject, see 363. On the human sciences and new forms of political rationality, see 364.

IDEOLOGY   Generally, Foucault did not find the notion of ideology to be a particularly useful one and when he does refer to it, it is usually to criticise it, arguing that the notion (1) presupposes a 'truth' to which ideology stands in opposition, (2) implies that it is secondary to a material 'infrastructure' and (3) that it proposes a universal subject. See 139; 157; 192; 200; 238; OT ch. 10; AK pt. IV ch. 6; UP intro. ch. 1. For a brief period in the wake of May 1968, Foucault adopted a quasi-Marxist and untheorised use of the term. See 105; 106; 107; 108. On the author as an 'ideological product', see 69.

IDENTITY   Although Foucault's work is often hailed as one of the inspirations for various identity movements, Foucault himself favours the dissolution of identity, rather than its creation or maintenance. He sees identity as a form of subjugation and a way of exercising power over people and preventing them from moving outside fixed boundaries. See 80; 242; 266; 272; 280; 293; 358; 2004c. For a discussion of how genealogy or history can be used to dissolve identities, see 84. See also 339. For a discussion of resistance to an individualising power which ties people down to a particular identity, see 306; 349. For remarks on early Christian penitence as a method of rejecting identity and the self, see 363. For a rather obscure philosophical critique of modern Western thought as a thought of identity or the Same, see OT ch. 9.

IMAGINATION, THE FANTASTIC AND THE FABULOUS   The theme of the fantastic imagination emerged strongly in Foucault's earlier work but only made occasional appearances later on. For later references, see 198. For comments on an 'anthropology of the imagination' and the idea that the imaginary world has its own specific laws and structures. See 1; 6. For an extended discussion on the fantastic imagination, see 20. Also on the imagination, see 28; 36; 80. On imagination and discourse, see 43. On imagination and the devil in the sixteenth century, see 52. On the historical relation between imagination and madness, see MC ch. IV; HF pt. 1 ch. I, pt. 2 chs. I, II.

INDIVIDUALS AND INDIVIDUALISATION   On the individual as a nexus of relations between power and knowledge and as the product of power, see 139; 141; 169; 232; DP, pt. 3 chs. 1, 3; PP 7, 21 Nov 1973. On the role of prisons in creating individuals, see 156. On the role of schools, see 297; DP pt. 3 ch. 2. On resistance to 'government by individualisation', see 306. On the 'political technology of individuals', see 364. On the relation between individuality and death, see BC chs. 1, 9, conclusion. On the individual and the State, see 364. On 'individualism', see CS pt. 2. Foucault makes a distinction between the notions of the individual and the subject in HER 27 Jan (a) 1982. On individualisation in relation to pastoral power, see STP 22 Feb, 8 Mar 1978.

INSTITUTIONS   Foucault notes that institutions are a way of freezing particular relations of power so that a certain number of people are advantaged. See 1988e. For another definition, see 206. On the problems associated with using institutions as the starting point for the analysis of power, see 306; PP 7 Nov 1973. Foucault talks about analysing 'regimes of practice' or 'rationalities', rather than institutions per se. See 278; 322; 340. See also 139.

INTELLECTUALS   For definitions and discussions relating to the role of the intellectual, see 106; 123; 160; 234; 238; 269; 281; 285; 296; 310; 321; 330; 350. Foucault sometimes uses the terms 'philosopher' and 'intellectual' interchangeably. In the late 1970s and early 1980s there was much public discussion in France about the role of the intellectual. During this period Foucault tends to use the term 'intellectual' rather than 'philosopher'. On the 'specific' versus the 'universal' intellectual, see 192; 346; See also 157. On the relation between intellectuals and non-intellectuals, see 281. For critiques of the notion of intellectual as 'prophet' and purveyor of truth to the masses, see 163; 169; 192; 200; 336; 346; 350; 359; 362; 364; 1988d; 1988e; UP intro. ch. 1. On the political 'silence' of intellectuals in the early 1980s, see 353; 350. On the task of the intellectual as being to show people they are freer than they think, see 362.

INTERPRETATION, COMMENTARY AND HERMENEUTICS   Foucault, on a number of occasions, draws attention to and criticises the practice of 'interpretation' which endlessly searches for the 'hidden meaning' and 'truth' behind texts and what they 'really mean'. Rather than looking for 'hidden depths', Foucault advocates the treatment of texts as flat surfaces across which one can discern patterns of order. See 37; 46; 48; 58; 221; BC preface; OT ch. 10; OD. On the opposition between commentary and criticism and for useful definitions of both these terms, see OT ch. 4. See also OT ch. 8; AK pt. II ch. 1, pt. III ch. 4. See also 339 for definitions of an analytical framework Foucault describes as 'criticism' which subsumes both archaeology and genealogy. On the history of the hermeneutics of the self, see HER.

IRAN   In 1978, Foucault wrote a controversial series of reports on the Iranian revolution. For a chronology of events, see DE III: 663. Foucault was particularly interested in the notion of a 'political spirituality' which he saw emerging in relation to events in Iran. He defines 'political spirituality' as the will to create a new division of the true and the false via a new government of self and others (278: 233). See also 245. Also on Iran, see 241; 243; 244; 246; 248; 249; 251; 252; 253; 259; 261; 262; 269.

JUSTICE   See 132. For a discussion outlining notions of 'counter-justice' and 'popular justice', see 108.

KNOWLEDGE (SAVOIR AND CONNAISSANCE)   On knowledge as an event and historical rather than an innate human attribute, see 101; 139. See also 39; 55; 59. On 'subjected knowledges', see 193. On scientific knowledge and conceptual knowledge, see 219. On knowledge as a violence done to things, see 139. On knowledge as a weapon, see 161. On the difference between the two French terms for knowledge: 'savoir' and 'connaissance', see 71; 281; AK pt. I (English trans.). See also HER 24 Feb (a) 1982. On the relation between knowledge and language in the Classical Age, see OT ch. 4. On the way Renaissance knowledge was ordered and organised, see OT chs. 2, 3. (For brief overviews of OT see 34; 59; 281.) For an interesting distinction between knowledge and research, see 3. On the organisation of different 'knowledges' into disciplines in the eighteenth century, see SMD 25 Feb 1976, and in general, see OD. On the relation between Greek classical ethics, knowledge and truth, see HER 10 Feb (b) 1982. For a fascinating discussion on the difference between spiritual knowledge ('savoir spirituel') and 'intellectual knowledge' ('savoir de connaissance'), see HER 24 Feb (a) 1982.

LACAN   Foucault generally did not have a great deal to say about psychoanalyst Jacques Lacan, beyond mentioning his name on a number of occasions in connection with the structuralist movement and psychoanalysis, and making a couple of comments about the difficulty of his work. For brief comments on Lacan and language see 1; 37. See also HER 6 Jan (b) 1982 for remarks on Lacan's treatment of the links between the subject and truth. For responses to questions on the relation between his own work and that of Lacan, see 281; HER 3 Feb (b) 1982. Foucault politely says in both instances that Lacan had not had any significant impact on his own work. For a very brief interview on Lacan, and notions of the subject, power and psychoanalysis, see 299.

LANGUAGE   On the relation between language and things, and language as a thing in itself rather than something that simply points to 'reality', see 1; 4; 8; 10; 13; 14; 28; 38; 48; 139 (discussion); RR chs. 2, 7, 8; OT chs. 2, 4, 7, 8, 9, 10. On the history of language and linguistics, see OT chs. 2, 4, 7, 8, 9, 10; AK pt. II ch. 5, pt. III.

LAW   For a history of the Western legal system and the interaction between law, other sectors of society and general ways of structuring knowledge, see 139. On the clash since the nineteenth century between systems of law and punishment and medical/psychiatric or normalising systems, see 107; 142; 161; 205; 220; 297; 301; 356; 353; 1989c; HF pt. 3 chs. III, IV; AK pt. II ch. 3; DP pt. 1 ch. 1; AN 15 Jan 19 Mar 1975; On the difficulty of judging and punishing people in contemporary society, see 161; 353. On the history of law in relation to the constitution of sovereign power and the State in Europe, see HS pt. 4 ch. 1; SMD; STP. On ideas of law and order in twentieth-century thought, see NBP 21 Feb 1979.

LIBERALISM   For a very detailed history, analysis and definitions of liberal and neo-liberal ideas in relation to government and economics see NBP. See NBP 10 Jan 1979 for a summary of definitions. See also 274; 310; STP 18 Jan 1978. On post-World War II neo-liberalism in Germany and France, see NBP 31 Jan 1979ff. On American neo-liberalism see NBP 14, 21 Mar 1979.

LIFE   On the concept of biological life and the introduction of the notion of life as an organising principle into nineteenth-century knowledge, see 219; BC ch. 9. On the history of biology, the life sciences and the notion of life, see 77; 81; 132 and OT chs. 2, 5, 8; AK pt. II ch. 5, pt. IV ch. 3. On a modern 'technology of power centred on life' (HS: 190) see HS pt. 5; SMD 17 Mar 1976.

LIMITS   For useful discussions of the way cultures define acceptable behaviour and the way they also challenge the limits of such behaviour, see 23; 52; 83; 222. For a similar but more oblique discussion, see 25 and for a poetic discussion, see 38. On the limits of discourse, see 58. On 'limit-experiences' in Western knowledge, see 281. On a philosophical ethos of adopting a 'limit attitude', see 339. For comments on analysing the limits rather than the identity of a culture, see 4; 89; 1988d. On limits, sexuality and God, see 13. On the transgression of limits, see 13; 38; 52. On limits, death and language, see 14; 38; 43; BC conclusion. On writing as a transgressive act, see 69; 82. On madness as an absolute limit in the Middle Ages and Renaissance, see HF pt. 1 ch. I.

LITERATURE   In his earlier work, Foucault, draws attention to close links between the categories of literature, truth and madness in modern Western culture. See 25; 82; 83; 221; 222; OT ch. 3. For a definition of literature, see OT ch. 8; 1986a. On literary criticsim and the cultural role of literature, see 28; 1986a. Foucault comments on his tastes in literature in 154. For a distinction between imagination and madness, see 1; 20. On madness as the 'absence of work' and where the line between art and madness lies, see 4; 7; 8; 25; 30; 50; 82; 221; MC conclusion; HF pt. 1 ch. I, pt. 3 ch. V; RR ch. 8. On literature and madness in the Middle Ages and Renaissance, see HF pt. 1 ch. I; MC ch. I. On Racine, see MC ch. IV; HF pt. 2 ch. II; SMD 25 Feb 1976. On Don Quixote see 85; MC ch. I; HF pt. 1 ch. I; OT ch. 3. On eighteenth-century gothic and horror novels, see 11; 14; 18; 69; AN 29 Jan 1975. On Rousseau, see 7. On Sade, see 13; 14; 50; 82; 109; 164; MC ch. VII, conclusion; HF pt. 3 chs. I, V; OT ch. 6; HS pt. 2 ch. 1 pt. 5; AN 29 Jan 1975. On Diderot, see HF pt. 3 intro. On literature and the being of language, see 39; OT ch. 2. On Classical and Romantic literature, see OT ch. 4. On *Oedipus Rex* see 139. On Flaubert, see 20. On Mallarmé, see 28; 85; OT ch. 9. On Jules Verne and science fiction, see 36; RR ch. 5. On Raymond Roussel, see 10; 26; 50; 343; RR. On André Breton, see 43. On Blanchot, see 38; 48; 82; 85; 1985; 1986a. On Marguerite Duras, see 159. On Robbe Grillet, Sollers and other new novelists, see 17; 23; 28; 343. On crime fiction, see 116; 156; DP pt. 1 ch. 2. On Genet 82; 119. On literature and transgression, see 82.

MADNESS   Foucault returns to the theme of madness constantly throughout his entire career. His most detailed discussions can of course be found in MC and MIP. There is also an extended treatment in PP where he criticises some of his own earlier ideas. For useful brief summaries of MC, see 71; 83; 143 (the latter to some extent reworks Foucault's earlier ideas with reference to the anti-psychiatry movement and power). On the relation between madness and European society since the end of the seventeenth century, see 222. On his reasons for being interested in madness, see 161; 281; 2004c. On madness and (illegal) drug use, see 50. Cf. 80. For a detailed response to historian Lawrence Stone's criticisms of HF, see 331. On madness as something one encounters in all societies see MIP pt. 2, intro; 1989a. On madness and water, see 16. On madness and limits, see 23; 25. On madness, Descartes and dreams, see 102; 104; HF pt. 1 chs. II, V, pt. 3, intro. On madness and medicine see 25; 59; 143; MC chs. V, VI; HF pt. 1 ch. IV, pt. 2 chs. I, III, IV, pt. 3 ch. IV; AN 12 Feb 1975. On the birth of the asylum in the nineteenth century, see MC ch. IX; HF pt. 3 ch. IV; PP. On the silencing of madness by Reason, see HF pt. 2 intro, pt. 3 ch. IV; OD. On madness as a scientific object, see HF pt. 2 ch. I, pt. 3 chs. III, IV, V. On madness as subsumed by the medical category of mental illness, see MIP, HF pt. 3 ch. III; AN 19 Mar 1975. On the real existence of madness outside of discourse and institutions see 1994; NBP 10 Jan, 4 Apr 1979.

MARX AND MARXISM   Foucault is well known for his controversial statements in 1966 that 'Marxism exists in nineteenth-century thought like a fish in water:

that is, it is unable to breathe anywhere else' and that it was a mere 'storm ... in a children's paddling pool' (OT: 262). See also 85; 163. On Marx and interpretation, see 46. For a brief period after 1968, Foucault's comments on Marxism as a form of political activity became more favourable, see 98; 103; 106; 107; 108. He subsequently returned to his earlier views on the historical specificity of Marxism and to criticisms of the inflated claims made by Marxists in relation to Marx's work. See 119; 139; 152; 156; 157; 169; 235; 281; 330; 1988e. On the oppressive effects of Marxism in university milieux in France, see 2004c. For a critique of the notion that the essence of man is work, see 13; 139; 221; 1976u. The latter item also includes a discussion of how Foucault's approach differs from the 'materialist' or Marxist approach. On the links between Marx's notion of class struggle and post-medieval themes of the 'struggle of races', see SMD 28 Jan 1976. On the absence of a 'socialist art of governing' see NBP 31 Jan 1979. On Marx's economic theories, see NBP 14 Mar 1979.

MEDICINE   Foucault's writings on medicine are extensive. For a detailed study of the birth of modern clinical medicine at the end of the eighteenth century, see BC. For good brief summaries of BC, see 58; 59; 71; 143; AK pt. II ch. 4. For an extended discussion of the relation between medicine and psychiatry in eighteenth and nineteenth-century France, see PP 12 Dec 1973, 16 Jan, 30 Jan 1974ff. In 168; 257, Foucault introduces the interesting idea of a 'noso-politics' and discusses the collective management of the health of populations. See also 170; 196; SMD 17 Mar 1976. On epidemics and their relation to both the development of medical knowledge and social organisation, see BC ch. 2; DP pt. 3, ch. 3; STP 25 Jan 1978. On the medicalisation of urban spaces, see 196; SMD 17 Mar 1976. On the history of hospitals and their role in general social organisation, see 143; 168; 170; 229; 257; BC ch. 1. For a very interesting analysis of medicine in terms of structuralist linguistics, see 44. On eighteenth-century medicine and linguistics, see BC ch. 6. On health as the modern form of salvation, see 46 (discussion); BC conclusion. For definitions on how illness and medicine work within cultures, see 62. On medicine and morality, see 110. On the medicalisation of the abnormal, see AN 19 Mar 1975. On Classical Greek medicine and sex, see 304. On links between medicine, ethics and philosophy in Antiquity, see UP pt. 2; CS pt. 2; HER 20 Jan (a) (b) 1982. On nineteenth-century medicine and sex, see HS pt. 3.

MORALITY AND MORAL SYSTEMS   Foucault defines morality as a set of values and rules for action which are proposed to individuals and groups by diverse institutions such as the family, education systems or churches. See 338. See also 326; UP intro. ch. 3. For a definition of contemporary morality as centred on issues of sex and politics, see 50; 54; 109. On Ancient Greek morality, see 326. On the difficulty of elaborating a contemporary morality, see 326; 344. On the constitution of self as a moral subject, see 326; UP intro. ch. 3. On morality as not being simply a series of prohibitions, see 350. On Ancient Greek morality as less than admirable, 344; 354.

Of the treatment and exclusion of interned persons in the Classical Age as 'moral subjects', see HF pt. 1 ch. II. For Foucault's own description of himself as a 'moralist' and an outline of his own moral code as an intellectual, see 1988e. On the good as something that is practised not discovered, see 1988e. On Christian versus non Christian morality see HER 6 Jan (a), 17 Feb (a), 1982.

MUSIC   In spite of Foucault's professed interest in the most esoteric forms of contemporary classical music, his writing on music is not characterised by the same wealth of ideas as the rest of his work, something he is quite willing to admit himself. On Wagner and Boulez, see 234; 286; 305. See also 50; 336, where Foucault also mentions the importance of music in his personal life. On contemporary music (classical and popular), see 333. On musical cures for madness in the eighteenth-century, see MC ch. VI; HF pt. 2 ch. IV.

NIETZSCHE   On Nietzsche see, 41; 45; 46; 84; 101; 281; 330. On the influence of Nietzsche on Foucault's work, see 156; 354; 362. For references to Nietzsche's notion of tragedy, see 4; 13. For an extended discussion on knowledge and power, using Nietzsche's work as a point of departure, see 139. See OT ch. 9 on Nietzsche's notion of the death of God. On Nietzsche and madness, see MC conclusion; HF pt. 3 ch. V.

NON-DISCURSIVE PRACTICES   In AK Foucault lists non-discursive practices as including 'institutions, political events, economic practices and processes' (p. 162). Cf. SMD 3 Mar 1976. For definitions of non-discursive practices, see 48; 58; 59; 139 (discussion); AK pt. II ch. 6, pt. IV ch 4. For Foucault's response to accusations that he deals with words at the expense of things, see 77; 139 (discussion). For arguments that discourse does not underlie all cultural forms, see 51; 206; FS conclusion; 1994. Foucault also criticises Derrida for reducing discursive practices and events to 'textual traces', and teaching that text is all in 102. For another example of Foucault's distinction between the 'order of discourse' and the 'order of reality', this time in relation to sexuality, see 1989c.

NORMAL AND THE PATHOLOGICAL, NORMALISATION   Foucault argues that contemporary society is a society based on medical notions of the norm, rather than legal notions of conformity to codes and the law. For definitions and discussion, see 2; 50; 52; 161; 170; 173; 194; 212; BC ch. 2; STP 25 Jan 1978. On techniques of 'normalisation' in modern society, see DP pt. 3 ch. 2; PP 21 Nov 1973, 16 Jan 1974. On the 'normal man' as creation, see HF pt. 1 ch. IV. For a series of lectures on the history of abnormal individuals as defined by Western medico-legal expertise and what Foucault describes as 'normalising power', see AN. Also on normalising power see HS pt. 5. On 'monsters', see BC ch. 6; AN 22, 29 Jan, 5 Feb 1975. On the normalisation of certain types of knowledge in the eighteenth century, see SMD 25 Feb 1976. On the 'normalising society' in relation to discipline and biopower, see SMD 17 Mar 1976.

OTHER   On the Other and madness, see MC ch. IX; HF pt. 1 ch. IV, pt. 2 ch. I, pt. 3, ch. V; OT preface, ch. 9. On the care of the self in relation to others, see 356; HER 6 Jan (b) 27 Jan (a) 1982.

OVERVIEWS OF FOUCAULT'S WORK   For an overall description of his work as occupying three domains, or types of problems: knowledge, power and ethics or subjectivity, see 326. Cf. 342; 344; 354; UP intro. ch. 1.

PANOPTICON, PANOPTICISM AND SURVEILLANCE   The Panopticon was a design for a prison produced by Jeremy Bentham in the late eighteenth century which grouped cells around a central viewing tower. Foucault uses this as a model for the operation of power and surveillance in contemporary society. See 169 for some good definitions of Panopticism. See also 127; 139; 153; 221; 238. For extended discussions, see 195 and DP pt. 3 ch. 3; PP 28 Nov, 5 Dec 1973. On surveillance, see 161; DP pt. 3 ch. 2. On surveillance and the gaze in the treatment of mad people in the nineteenth century, see HF pt. 3 ch. IV.

PARRHESIA   On 'free speech' and Ancient Greek practices, rules and obligations in relation to 'speaking the truth', see FS; HER 27 Jan (a) (b), 3 Feb (a), 10 Feb (b), 3 Mar (b), 10 Mar (a) (b), 17 Mar (a) 1982.

PHENOMENOLOGY   For an excellent discussion by Foucault on how his own analysis of discourse differs from phenomenological and ethnomethodological approaches, see 221. For early steps in this direction, see also 1. Foucault also argues that if phenomenology is seeking to discover an authentic, founding subject through the analysis of everyday life, he, on the other hand is aiming at the dissolution of notions of a fixed subject, so that he and others can always be different. See 281. Cf. 80; 295; 306; 339. For other critiques of phenomenology and existentialism, see 85; 242; 1993; 2004c; OT ch. 9; PP 23 Jan 1974.

PHILOSOPHY   Foucault changed his mind many times about the role played by philosophy and the philosopher or intellectual. One thing that remained constant however, was that philosophy should be firmly rooted in a historical context. Foucault frequently emphasised that philosophy should also deal with the question of what is happening right now. See 30; 39; 42; 47; 48; 50; 55; 67; 80; 82; 136; 200; 219; 234; 281; 306; 310; 339; 348. For criticisms of the way philosophy is taught in France, see 78; 104. On philosophy as simply one academic discipline amongst others, rather than underlying them all, see 104; 351. For excellent discussions on the history of the relation between philosophy and the State, and for some suggestions as to how philosophy might relate to State power in the contemporary context, see 232; 356. For discussions on the relation between the philosopher and the Prince in the Roman Empire, see HER 27 Jan (b) 1982. For a useful definition of philosophy as a way, not of reflecting on what is true and what is false, but on our relations to truth and how we should conduct ourselves, see 285. On philosophy as an exercise of the 'care of the self' and self-transformation for the Ancient Greeks, see 1993; UP intro. ch. 1; CS pt. 2; HER. On the philosopher as hero and practitioner of an exemplary life in Ancient Greek thought, see FS ch. 4. On the boundaries between philosophy and non-philosophy, see 1986a; OD.

PHOTOGRAPHY   For a brief history on the relation between painting and photography, see 150. For a review of a photographic exhibition, see 307.

POLAND   On events in Poland in the early 1980s and on the dissident Solidarity union, see 303; 309; 319; 320; 321, 334; 341. Foucault was treasurer for the international support movement for Solidarity. For general remarks on the union movement, see 334.

POLEMICS   Foucault felt very strongly about the destructive effects of polemical discussion and citing Blanchot, he frequently returns to this theme throughout his career. See 163; 254; 262; 281; 282; 285; 342; 356.

POLICE   For a detailed history of early notions of the 'police' and its role in the formation of the modern State and for definitions, see STP 29 Mar, 5 Apr 1978. See also 139; 168; 239; 255; 291; 306; 310; 364; MC ch. II, HF pt. 1 ch. II, pt. 3 ch. III; DP pt. 3 ch. 3.

POLITICAL ACTION AND PROGRESSIVE POLITICS   For a definition of politics, see 197 and for comments on the construction of a 'political dimension' of analysis, see 1993. For a brief history of the notion of politics see STP 8, 15 Mar, 5 Apr 1978. For Foucault's views on how political action might be defined, see 37; 54; 55; 58; 125; 132; 136. For suggestions on how an archaeological analysis of political knowledge might be conducted, see AK pt. IV ch. 6. For comments on a 'new political imaginary', see 235. See also 339 where Foucault says we must turn away from global and radical projects to concentrate on working on our own limits. On the links between theory and political choices, see 341. Here, Foucault argues that his work is not essentially political and is not aimed at realising a political project. On politics as not being the solution to problems such as mental illness, crime and so on, see 342. On not accepting political domination, see 356; 357. On differences between intellectual and political action, see 357. On the problems of political institutions and parties and on social movements, see 358.

POPULATIONS   On the control of populations and individuals, see 139; 206; 239; 255; 257; 297; 364; MC ch. VIII; HF pt. 3 ch. II. On the notion of population as the object of biopolitics, see HS pt. 2. ch. 1, pt. 5; SMD 17 Mar 1976. In relation to power-knowledge see STP 18, 25 Jan 1978. On the State and population see STP 15 Mar, 5 Apr 1978.

POSTMODERNISM AND MODERNITY   Foucault did not comment on the term 'post-modernity' beyond saying how vague and imprecise it was, making a subtly ironic reference to 'an enigmatic and troubling "postmodernity"' (339: 309). He prefers to discuss how 'modernity' has been historically defined See 330; 339; 351.

POWER   Foucault's discussion of power is very extensive, hence this section will be divided into subsections for easier consultation.

General definitions of power   If the term 'power' makes its first appearances in Foucault's work in 1971 with OD and 98, his first extended definition of the notion appears in 106 where he draws attention to the limits of Marx and Freud's theories. See also 1988d. In 194, Foucault outlines five methodological points to consider in relation to the analysis of power. See also HS pt. 4 ch. 2 for detailed definitions. For an excellent critique of traditional notions of power and for a point-by-point definition of Foucault's version of power in 1977, see 218. For some examples of how power operates, see 212. For a brief history of different theories of power, see 297. For some very useful and reworked definitions of power and for what are perhaps Foucault's most nuanced and detailed methodological discussions on the subject, see 291; 306. See also 356; 359; 1988d; 1988e; STP 11 Jan 1978.

Power is not a thing but a relation   On the idea that power is not a substance, but a network of relations, see 193; 194; 206; 291; 306; HS pt. 4 ch. 2; 1988d; 1988e; DP pt.1 ch. 1; PP 7 Nov 1973; STP 11 Jan 1978. For Foucault's rejection of criticisms that his notion of power is a metaphysical one or a founding principle or 'theory' which explains all, see 161; 233; 238; 330.

Power is not simply repressive but productive   In the early 1970s, Foucault still adhered to classical definitions of power as oppressive and negative. See 119. For a detailed discussion of why he subsequently rejected this idea, see 139 (discussion). See also 163; 1988e; DP pt. 1 ch. 1; SMD 21 Jan 1976. On power as productive rather than repressive and for critiques of traditional and Marxist analyses of power, see 157; 160; 192; 193, 194; 197; 218; 233; 297; 1988e; HS pt. 4 ch. 1; AN 15 Jan 1976; PP 7 Nov 1973.

Power is not simply a property of the State   In 132 and NBP 31 Jan, 7 Mar 1979, Foucault criticises the notion of power as something that is localised in government and the State (which he says is not a universal essence). Rather power is exercised throughout the social body. Cf. STP 15 Mar 1978.

The exercise of power is strategic and war-like   For definitions of power as sets of strategic war-like relations, see 161; 175; 187; 192; 193, 194; 232; 235; 2004c; HS pt. 4 ch. 2; PP 7 Nov 1973. For a definition of the notion of strategy, see 306. For Foucault's most extensive discussion of war, the State and power, see SMD. See also STP 22 Mar 1978.

The micro-physics of power   Foucault argues that power operates at the most micro levels of social relations. On capillary power and the microphysics of power, see 139; 156; 194; DP pt. 1 ch. 1, pt. 3 ch. 1; PP 14 Nov 1973; NBP 7 Mar 1979. On power as omnipresent at every level of the social body, see HS pt. 4 ch. 2.

Sovereign power   For a definition of sovereign power, that is, a system of government based on the power of the king, see PP 21 Nov 1973. For a detailed history of the constitution of sovereign State power in Europe, see SMD. See also 1994; HS pt. 4 ch. 1, pt. 5. For an extended discussion of the way 'disciplinary power' gradually took over from 'sovereign power' in the eighteenth and nineteenth centuries and the complex interaction between these two forms, see PP 14, 21 Nov 1973. See also 193; 194; DP pt 1 ch. 2. On sovereign power and governmentality, see STP 8 Mar 1978. On the opposition between economic rationalism and the sovereign, see NBP 28 Mar, 4 Apr 1979.

Disciplinary power   See 'discipline'.

Pastoral power   For useful definitions and a detailed history of what Foucault describes as 'pastoral power', see STP 8 Feb–8 Mar 1978. See also 232; 233; 239; 255; 291; 306.

Normalizing power   See 'normal'.

Power and freedom   For a definition of power as 'the strategic interplays between freedoms', see 356. See also 306.

Power and domination   Foucault is loathe to identify power and domination. Rather he prefers to describe 'states of domination' as particular configurations of relations of power. See 341; 356; 363; 1994; SMD 21 Jan 1976. On techniques of domination, see 1993.

Power and sex   For a critique of the notion of power as repressive in relation to sex, see 1989c; HS pt. 4 ch. 1. On the erotic charge of power, see 140.

Power and ethics in Ancient Greece   On the continuity in Classical ethics between the power the Prince or free man exercises over himself and his power over others (women, subjects, slaves, boys), see UP pt. 1 ch. 4, pt. 3, conclusion. On the relation between the care of the self and power, see HER 6 Jan (b) 1982.

Power and the law   On 'juridico-discursive' power, see HS pt. 4 ch. 1.

POWER-KNOWLEDGE   Foucault first uses the specific term 'power-knowledge' in 115 (along with a useful definition). See also DP pt. 1 ch. 1; HS pt. 4 ch. 2. For other general discussions on the relation between power and knowledge, see 119; 139; 156; 169; 1989c; OD. On the non-hierarchical relation between power and knowledge, see 231. Foucault refutes the idea that he makes the claim 'knowledge is power'. See 330; 350. On the relation between science and structures of power, see 356. See also SMD 25 Feb 1976, where Foucault criticises the notion that truth and knowledge only start when power and violence stops.

PRACTICES   Foucault notes that he is interested in analysing 'regimes of practice', not institutions, theories or ideologies. See 278. See also 339; 345; UP intro. ch. 1. Foucault makes a distinction between discourses and practices in 95.

PRISONS   On the history of prisons and punishment in France, from around 1760 to 1840, see DP. See also NBP 21 Mar 1979. On the continuing failure of imprisonment as an adequate form of penal justice, see DP pt. 4 ch. 2. Also on prisons see 105; 108; 131; 137; 139; 144; 151; 152; 153; 156; 346; 353; 2004b. For very brief summaries of some of the ideas of DP, see 127; 151; 153; 156; 277; 278. On the Groupe d'Information sur les prisons (GIP), see 86; 87; 88; 90; 91; 94; 95; 105; 125; 273; 282; 1988b. On internment in the eighteenth century, see HF pt. 3 chs. I, II, III, IV.

PROBLEMATISATIONS/THE HISTORY OF PROBLEMS   Foucault explains that he is more interested in writing a history of problems rather than a history of solutions or in writing the comprehensive history of a period or an institution. For definitions of 'problematisation' see 350; 1988b; 1994. See also 277; 278; 326; 339; 342; 344; UP intro. pt. 1; FS ch. 2, conclusion. For an early formulation of this idea, see 80.

PSYCHOANALYSIS   For comments, see 1, 2; 8; 139 (discussion); 141; 143; 157; 160; 173; 197; 233; OT ch. 10; PP 16 Jan 1974. For a brief definition, see 349. On psychoanalysis and systems of power, see 163; MC ch. IX; HF pt. 3 ch. IV; HS pt. 4 ch. 4.

PSYCHIATRY   For an extensive treatment of the history of psychiatry and its relation to organic medicine, science and disciplinary mechanisms, see PP. See also 143; 143; 161; 202; 205; 342; 2004c; MC ch. IX; HF pt. 3 ch. IV; AN 26 Feb, 19 Mar 1975. On psychiatry and social control, see 163; 209. On psychiatry and the judicial system, see 156; 220; 301; HF pt. 3 ch. IV; AN 8 Jan, 15 Jan, 5 Feb, 12 Feb 1975. On the response of psychiatrists to Foucault's work, see 160; 281. On nineteenth-century psychiatry and monomania, see AN 12 Feb, 12 Mar 1975. On psychiatry and sexuality, see AN 12 Mar, 19 Mar 1975.

PSYCHOLOGY   Foucault's initial university qualifications and his first university posts were mostly in psychology. For definitions, criticisms and the history of this discipline, see 2; 3; 30; MIP; OT ch. 9. On the historical origins of psychology, see HF pt. 3 ch. III.

PUNISHMENT   On torture and punishment as spectacle in the legal systems of the eighteenth century, see 2004b; DP pt. 1; AN 29 Jan 1975. On the shift to less spectacular and less corporal methods of punishment in the nineteenth century, see DP pt. II. On penal 'rationalities', see 346. For an extremely useful discussion on the problem of punishment in contemporary society, see 353. For a classification of the types of punishment found in various societies into four categories, see 107; 131. For a definition of punishment and penal practices, see NBP 21 Mar 1979.

RACE, RACISM, HEREDITY   For brief discussions on the biological notion of race, see 179; HS pt. 4 ch. 4, pt. 5; SMD 28 Jan, 17 Mar 1976; For brief comments on the history of racism, see 206. On racism and eugenics, see AN 5 Feb 1975. For a very useful discussion on the nineteenth-century view that heredity and race are important causal factors in social and individual abnormality, see AN 19 Mar 1975. On social normalisation and racism, see SMD 21 Jan 1976. On the origins of an oppositional discourse of history centred on the struggle of races as opposed to Roman and Medieval discourses of history centred on the legitimation of sovereign power, see SMD 21 Jan–3 Mar 1976. On the Nazis and racism, see SMD 28 Jan, 17 Mar 1976; HS pt. 5. On anti-Semitism, see SMD 4 Feb 1976. On the question of genetic heredity and human capital, see NBP 14, 21 Mar 1979.

REALITY   For remarks on how reality and the real are defined, see 277; 278; 296.

RECEPTION OF FOUCAULT'S WORK   For comments by Foucault himself on the reception of his work, see 95; 96; 97; 100; 152; 160; 161; 163; 272; 277; 278; 280; 281; 285; 331; 336; 350; 359; 2004c.

REASON, RATIONALITY AND IRRATIONALITY   Foucault criticises the notion that Reason is synonymous with truth and that it offers the solution to all social problems. He notes that repressive systems of social control are usually highly rational. For an extended discussion on the historical division between Reason and madness, see 4 and HF, and on madness as silenced by Reason, HF pt. 3, ch. IV. On the history of Reason, see 58; 330. For a definition of the 'rationalisation of the empirical', see 70. On the moral division between Reason and unreason in the Classical Age, see MC chs. III, IV; HF pt. 1 chs. III, V, pt. 2 ch. 1. On the historical origins of a mutually exclusive opposition between Reason and madness, see HF pt. 1 chs. I, II, pt. 2 ch. I. On spurious divisions between 'rationality' and 'irrationality', see OT ch. 10. The notions of rationality and irrationality, as they were posed by the Frankfurt School, became a fashionable topic of discussion in the late 1970s. On the Frankfurt School, see 281; 330; NBP 7 Feb 1979. On the dangers of describing Reason as the enemy and the equal danger of claiming that any criticism of rationality leads to irrationality, see 310; 330; 339. On Kant and Enlightenment thought, see 219; 339; 351; OT ch. 9. On the links between power, domination and rationality, see 215; 277; 291; 306; 330; 339. For definitions of 'rationalities', see 278; 279.

On the links between violence and rationality see 215; 272; 280; 291; 364. On political rationality and Raison d'Etat, see 291; 339; STP 8 Mar 1978ff. Foucault argues that no form of rationality is equivalent to Reason in 330. On examining specific 'rationalities' as opposed to 'rationalisation' in general, see 306.

REGIMES OF TRUTH Foucault defines 'regimes of truth' as the historically specific mechanisms which produce discourses which function as true in particular times and places. See 192 and NBP 10 Jan 1979; See also 194; DP pt. 1 ch. 1. For a detailed discussion of what Foucault means by 'regimes of veridiction' see NBP 17 Jan 1979. Foucault eventually replaces 'regimes' with 'games'. For definitions of 'games (jeux) of truth', see 338; 345. See also 356; 363 and for an early example, PP 7 Nov 1973. In 356 Foucault explains what he means by 'games.' For similar notions concerning a `politics of truth', see 139.

RELIGION If Foucault's discussions on 'sprirituality' (self-transfomation) are well known, it has often been remarked that he seldom discusses organised religion at any length. However, recent publications of his lectures reveal fairly developed accounts of the history of Christianity both as a social institution (Church) and in terms of its internal conceptual apparatus (sacraments, the division between clerics and the laity and so on). See STP 8 Feb–8 Mar 1978. Foucault also examines resistances to the pastoral power exercised by the Church such as mysticism, asceticism, and various Gnostic and other heresies. See STP 1, 8 Mar 1978. See also 20; 52; 212; 222; 363; HER 17 Mar 1982. A number of writings by Foucault which include comments on religion are collected together in RC. See also 'salvation', 'confession'.

REPRESENTATION For discussions of different historical perspectives on the way words connect with things, see 10; 80; 139. On punishment and representation, see DP pt. 2 ch. 2. On language, representation and art, see 2004a; OT chs. 1, 3, 4, 7, 9, 10. On non-representational literature, see 1986a.

RESISTANCE TO POWER AND THE LIMITS OF POWER Foucault suggests a number of ways in which the exercise of power can be resisted. He argues at one point (200; HS pt. 4 ch. 2) that resistance is co-extensive with power, but only in the sense that as soon as there is a power relation, there is a possibility of resistance. See also 216 and 358. If there is no society which exists without relations of power, this does not mean that existing power relations cannot be criticised. See 306; 356; 358. Foucault further emphasises (238) that it is not a question of an 'ontological opposition' between power and resistance, but a matter of the description of quite specific and changing struggles in space and time. See also 152; 157. On the necessity of examining relations of power at an empirical and local level in order to effect change at a general level, see 281. For a curious discussion about a quality of 'plebness' which, Foucault argues, exists in individuals across all social classes, see 218. Cf. 107; 108 for a discussion of the 'non-proletarianised pleb'. Foucault subsequently rejected this notion in 127. For a description of relations of power as always reversible, see 216. For a detailed and most interesting analysis of historical resistances to pastoral and governmental power in terms of what Foucault describes as 'counter-conduct', or revolts and insurrections of conduct, see STP 1, 8 Mar, 5 Apr 1978. For a critique of the notion of dissidence, see STP 1 Mar 1978. On the idea of using resistance to power as a starting point for discussion and for a useful division of struggles into three general categories, see 306. On the possibility of resistance no matter how oppressive the system, see 291; 310; 356. For definitions which draw attention to the limits of the exercise of power, see 291; 306. On constructing rules, moralities and practices of the self which limit the dominating effects of power in societies, see 356.

REVOLUTION   On the notion of revolution, see 137; 163; 204; HS pt. IV ch. 2; SMD 28 Jan 1976. On the historical origins of the term see STP 22 Mar 1978. On terror and revolution, see 174. On Marxist ideas of revolution, see 108; 157. On the idea of revolution in relation to Iran, see 259; 260; 269. On local and anarchic struggles as opposed to revolutionary resistance, see 306. On Kant's ideas of revolution, see 351. On revolutions as 'insurrections of conduct', see STP 8 Mar, 5 Apr 1978. For some interesting ideas on 'revolutionary subjectivity' and on a relation between notions of conversion and revolution from the nineteenth century onwards, see HER 10 Feb (a) 1982.

RIGHTS   On problems concerning the notion of human 'rights', see 325. See also 313; 355 and HS pt. 5. On notions of natural rights since the sixteenth century and the rights of the governed in relation to government and the State see NBP 10, 17 Jan 1979.

SALVATION   For interesting historical definitions and comparisons of the Ancient Greek and Christian notions of salvation, see HER 20 Jan (b), 27 Jan (a), 3 Feb (a) (b) 1982. See also STP 22 Feb 1978.

SCIENCE   Foucault deals extensively with questions relating to the history of science in the work he produced before 1970. For a particularly good overview of his ideas on scientific knowledge, see 85. On the history of science as a form of knowledge and on the distinctions between scientific knowledge and other forms of knowledge, see 3; 59; 69; 119; 132; 234; 1993; OT ch. 10; AK pt. IV ch. 6; OD; SMD 25 Feb 1976. On the thresholds of 'systematisation' that knowledge passes through in order to become scientific, see 77; AK pt. IV ch. 6. For an excellent discussion on the distinction between science as 'knowledge' and science as 'research', see 3. On the way the history of science has been practised in France, see 219; 281; 330. Foucault offers a definition of 'scientific practice' in 281. On method in the history of science, see OT preface. On science and the notion of the author, see 69. On the historical constitution of science, see 71; SMD 25 Feb 1976. On science and truth see 169; PP 23 Jan 1974.

SCIENCE AND SOCIETY   Foucault frequently draws attention to the complex interrelationship between the disciplinary content of science and social, economic and political practices. His view is that power, knowledge and truth are not mutually exclusive terms. See 3; 58; 85; 132; 139; 356; 2004c. See also AK pt. II ch. 4, pt. IV chs. 4, 6. For an early formulation of structural similarities between scientific theories and institutional practices in the Classical Age, see HF pt. 2, ch. I.

SELF/SELF-TRANSFORMATION   On the government of the self, particularly in relation to sexuality, see 304; 326; 338. On Baudelaire, modernity and self-transformation, see 339. On the culture of self as being a social as well as an individual project, see 348; 356; CS pt. 2. On the cultivation of the self in relation to political and public activity in the Greek, Classical and Roman period, see CS pt. 3 ch. 2; HER 6 Jan (b) 1982. For descriptions of techniques relating to the care of the self and self-knowledge from Plato to the early Christian era, see 363; CS pt. 2, conclusion; FS; HER. On self and the truth, see 336; CS pt. 2; HER. On the differences and similarities between Christian and pagan practices of the self and ethics, see 1993; UP pt. 1 chs. 3, 4; FS ch. 4; HER 6 Jan (a), 20 Jan (b), 17 Feb (a) 24 Feb (b), 3 Mar (a), 24 Mar (b) 1982. For Foucault's first ideas along these lines, see STP 22 Feb 1978. On the differences in the ways Buddhism and Christianity approach the self and the truth, see 295. On the Ancient Greek emphasis concerning the need for constant ethical practice and training, see UP pt. 1 ch. 3. On the historical techniques of the examination of conscience, see 289; 291; 1993; CS pt. 2; HER 24 Feb (a), 24 Mar (b) 1982. For a definition of what Foucault means by techniques, technologies and practices of the self, see 1993. See also 295; 304; 312; 326; 330; 332; 344; 350; 356; 363; 364; UP intro., conclusion; HER. On the shift produced by Descartes in the historical relation between the truth and the self in the West, see 326; 344; HER 6 Jan (a) (b), 3 Feb (b), 24 Feb (a) 1982. On the difference between the care of the self (self-constitution) and knowing oneself (self-discovery), see HER 13 Jan (b), 24 Mar (a) 1982. On notions of 'conversion', see HER 10 Feb (a) 1982. On the genealogy of the self and the subject, see 1993.

SEXUALITY   Foucault's discussion of the history of thought and ethics in relation to sexuality is extensive, with one volume on the history of modern sexuality and two volumes dealing with the Ancient Greek, Roman and early Christian eras. He also wrote numerous articles on the subject.

Modern sexuality   On sexuality, limits and transgression, see 13. For comments on how an archaeology of sexuality might be conducted, see AK pt. IV ch. 6. For comments on the historical appearance of the word 'sexuality', see UP intro. ch. 1. On sexuality as a political problem, see 138. For a very brief summary of some of the themes of HS, see 181. On the relation between sexuality and truth, see 276; 287; 295; HS pt. 1, pt. 3, pt. 5. For early claims by Foucault that sexuality has been repressed since the nineteenth century, see 82; OD. On sexuality and repression, see 200; 336; 1989c; HS pts. 1, 2, 3, 4. On the proliferation of discourse, theory, science and knowledge around sexuality since the nineteenth century (contrary to more common arguments concerning the historical repression of sexuality), see 233; HS; AN 19 Feb 1975. On ars erotica (the erotic arts) versus scientia sexualis (the science of sex), see 233; HS pt. 3. Foucault revises his views on this front in 326; 344. On sexuality and architecture, see 310. On sexuality as an all-pervasive social danger in contemporary society, see 263; HS pt. 2 ch. 2. On sex and power, see HS pt. 1, pt. 2 ch. 2, pt. 4 ch. 1. On hermaphrodites, see 165; 287; AN 22 Jan 1975. On masturbation, see 160; 165; 336; 1989c; AN 22 Jan, 19 Feb, 5 Mar 1975. On sexuality as a problem of personal conduct, see 336. On marriage from the Middle Ages to the nineteenth century, see HS pt. 2 ch. 2. For comments on sexuality in the Classical Age, see HF pt. 1 ch. III. On psychiatry, sexual anomaly and 'perversion' in the nineteenth century, see HS pt. 2 ch. 2, pt. 4. ch. 3; AN 19 Feb 1975;. On incest, see AN 12 Mar 1975. On sexuality and biopower, see SMD 17 Mar 1976. Foucault argues that if there should be freedom of sexual *choice*, this does not imply that there should be freedom of sexual *acts*. See 317. On the issue of pornography, see 317.

Ancient sexuality   For statements debunking the myths about Ancient Greek sexual tolerance versus Christian repression, see 295; 304; 311; 326; 344; 350, UP intro. ch. 2, conclusion; CS conclusion; HER 17 Feb (a) 1982. On monosexual societies, see 311; 313. On early Christian ideas concerning sexuality and the regulation of sexual practices and the notion of chastity, see 312. On Ancient Greek, Roman and early Christian ideas in relation to virginity, see 312; 326; CS pt. 6 ch. 3; HER 17 Mar (a) 1982. On sexuality, Ancient Greek dream interpretation and 'techniques of existence', see 332; CS pt. 1. For critiques of an Ancient Greek ethics of sexuality based on purely masculine attributes of virility, penetration and domination excluding women, see 332; 326; 344; UP pt. 1 chs. 1, 4, pt. 2 ch. 4, pt. 4 ch. 3; CS pt. 1 ch. 3. For comments on how individuals came to recognise themselves as sexual subjects, see UP intro. ch. 1, conclusion. On Ancient Greek and early Christian moral and ethical discussions in relation to sexuality, see 326; 338; 344; 350. On sex as central to the techniques of the self, see 349. On Classical, Greek and Roman views on marriage, see UP intro. ch. 2, pt. 3; CS pt. 3 ch.1, pt. 5, pt. 6. On medicine and sexuality in Ancient Greece and Rome, see CS pt. 4. On why sexuality is the object of moral concern, see UP intro. chs. 1, 2, conclusion. On the 'flesh' and sexuality, see UP pt. 1 ch. 1.

SOCIAL SECURITY   For a detailed discussion on the history of social security, see 325. See also 170; 364; HF pt. 3 ch. II; SMD 17 Mar 1976; NBP 14 Feb, 7 Mar 1979.

SOCIETY   Foucault argues that the theoretical opposition between the State and civil society, between public and private, is a problematic one. See 281; 325; 274; NBP 7 Mar 1979. On the history of the notion of 'civil society', see STP 5 Apr 1978; NBP 4 Apr 1979. For a brief discussion of sociology see OT ch. 10.

SPACE   For a discussion by Foucault on his use of spatial metaphors, see 169. For an analysis of space in dreams, see 1. On the use of space in the new novel and writing, see 24. On the emphasis on time at the expense of space in philosophy and theory since the nineteenth century, see 169; 234. On spatial arrangements of body and disease in the eighteenth century, see BC ch. 1. On the government of space (cities, territories, architecture, railways), see 310; STP 11 Jan 1978. On space and social control see, 195; 234. On the distribution of individuals in space as a means of social control, see DP pt. 3. On the history of space, see 360.

SPIRITUALITY   Foucault defines 'spirituality' as the methods the subject uses to transform him or herself in order to gain access to the truth. See HER 6 Jan (a) 1982. See also 356; HER 6 Jan (b) 1982. On the 'spiritual' experiences of madness and dreams, see 22. On political spirituality, see 245; 251; 278. On the conflict between spirituality and theology as being the important historical issue rather than a conflict between spirituality and science, see HER 6 Jan (b) 1982. Foucault also recasts the standard Church versus State opposition as an opposition between pastoral and sovereign forms of power in STP 15 Feb 1978. Foucault notes a number of differences in the ways pre-Cartesian and post-Cartesian systems approached the problem of acquiring knowledge and the notion of self-transformation. He describes this as the difference between the 'spiritual exercises' and 'intellectual method', see HER 24 Feb (a) (b), 3 Mar (a) 1982.

THE STATE   Foucault argues that the State is a codification of relations of power at all levels across the social body (192: 123). It is a concept which provides a 'scheme of intelligibility for a whole group of already established institutions and realities' (STP: 294). Further, 'the State is a practice not a thing' (STP: 282). For a very detailed pre-history, history and set of definitions of the modern State, see STP and NBP. See also 187; 196; 306; 364; SMD. For criticisms of traditional definitions of the State, see 119; 139; 157; 169; 192; NBP 10, 31 Jan, 7 Mar 1979. For historical definitions of the 'nation', see SMD 18 Feb, 10 Mar 1976. On government and the State, see 239; STP 1 Feb, 8 Mar 1978ff. Foucault emphasises that the State is not the primary source of power. See 231; SMD 21 Jan 1976. For a detailed history of the 'reason of State', see STP 8 Mar 1978ff. See also 255; 274; 291; 364. On the Christian tradition of the State, see 364. On Machiavelli, 239; 364; STP 25 Jan, 1 Feb, 8, 15 Mar 1978. On the State and the individual, see 364. On capitalism and the State see 1994; NBP.

STATISTICS   For a definition and short history of statistics, see STP 15, 29 Mar 1979.

STRUCTURALISM   Foucault is well known in English for his declarations that he was not a structuralist (OT foreword). Less well known, however, are his excellent expositions of structuralism and his remarks on the convergence of his own concerns and those of structuralist thinkers working in other domains. His best writings on the subject are a lecture given in 1967 (1989a) and 281. For other positive treatments, see 37; 47; 54; 66 (this latter article is available in English). For an excellent brief history of the movement and its political context, see 281. See also 330. For an interesting and informative discussion on structuralist linguistics and its relation to the other human sciences, see 70. For good overviews of the relation between the discipline of history and structuralism, see 70; 103; AK pt. I. During the course of 1967, Foucault started to disassociate himself from structuralism. For criticisms of the movement, see 48; 50; 55; 109; 139; 174; 175; 216; 221; 222; 295; 330; 1993; AK pt. V.

SUBJECT   The subject is an entity which is self-aware and capable of choosing how to act. For criticisms of the Cartesian 'cogito' and the humanist idea of man as a unified, universal and transcendent subject and unifying principle in the history of thought, see 13; 28; 38; 48; 50; 58; 59; 68; 69; 80; 84; 85; 109; 132; 139; 192; 234; 345; 356; 357; 1993; OT foreword, ch. 9; AK pt. I, pt. II ch. 1 pt. V; OD. For a comparison of Descartes' version of a unique universal non-historical subject versus Kant's location of the subject in history, see 306. On the subject and truth, see 330; 336; PP 23 Jan 1974. On the subject defined as an entity which makes choices according to self interest in eighteenth and nineteenth-century English empiricist and liberal thought, see NBP 28 Mar, 4 Apr 1978. See also 'phenomenology', 'sexuality', 'self'.

SUBJECTIVITY   For early comments on the freedom that allows a subject to constitute itself as mad in the Classical Age, see HF pt. 3 ch. V. See also 48. For a discussion of the transformation of the subject through writing and meditation, see Foucault's texts on Descartes, 102 and 104. Foucault raises the possibility of a 're-elaboration of the theory of the subject' in 139. On the idea of a historically constituted subject, see 192; 295; 330; 345; 354; STP 22 Feb 1978. For an extremely interesting if brief discussion on the Christian notion of the 'flesh' and techniques of interiorisation, see 233. On 'subjectivation', see 312; 345; 354; UP intro. ch. 3; SMD 21 Jan 1976; STP 22 Feb, 8 Mar 1978. For reformulations of Foucault's entire work as the examination of 'three modes of objectivation' which transform human beings into subjects, see 306; 339; 340; 342. See also 'self'.

TECHNOLOGY, TECHNIQUE, TECHNE   Foucault defines the Greek word *techne* as 'a practical rationality governed by a conscious aim'. For useful definitions of *techne* as opposed to technology (usually understood in a narrow scientific context), see 310. On *techne*, see also 326; 344. Foucault generally prefers the word 'technology', which he uses to encompass the broader meanings of *techne*. For a description of four groups of techniques of practical rationality, see 363. For other uses of the word *techne* to mean knowledge and know-how, see HER 6 Jan (b), 13 Jan (a) 1982. Foucault often uses the words techniques and technologies interchangeably, although sometimes techniques tend to be specific and localised while technologies are more general collections of specific techniques. See 1993 for examples. For a brief discussion of Habermas' notion of techniques, see 1993.

TELEVISION   For Foucault's opinions on television, see 149; 242. Against the popular idea that the media is brainwashing people, see 285. On the media in general, see 285; 330. On the cultural and educational impact of TV, see 330.

TERRORISM   Foucault's comments on this subject have lost none of their relevance today. He argues that terrorism is counter-productive even on its own terms, since it merely entrenches those attacked further in their own world view. He also notes that one of the reasons terrorism is so unsettling is that it undermines the citizens' faith in the capacity of the State to guarantee their security. Those who govern, likewise unsettled, then have an excuse to introduce stricter social and legal regulation as a result. For an extended discussion, see 213. For other remarks on terrorism, see 172; 174; 191; 210; 211; 214; 316.

THEORY   On the idea of theory as practice, see 106 and for a definition of theory, see AK pt. III ch. 3. On theory as a 'tool box' rather than an all-explaining system, see 136; 151; 152; 209; 218; 221; 2004b. Foucault also insists that he does not have a 'general theory' of his own. See 85; AK pt. III ch. 3. If, early on his career, this is a matter for regret, later he comes to see this as a positive attribute. See 216; 278; 306. He argues that what he writes is not prescriptive either for himself or others. See 281; 317. On the line between theory and practices, see 359.

THOUGHT   For definitions of 'thought' and the history of thought, see 34; 296; 322; 340; 345; 350; 362. On thought as an event and action, see 80. See also 301; 342; 362. On the difference between the 'history of ideas' and the 'history of thought', see 1994; FS ch. 2. Cf. AK pt. IV ch. 1. On every human artifact and practice as containing 'thought', see 310; 322.

TIME   For a brief history of the management of time as a means of social control, see 139. See also DP pt. 3 ch. 1.

TOTALITARIANISM   See 306. For a useful analysis and definitions of the totalitarian State, see NBP 7 Mar 1979. On the Nazi state, see NBP 31 Jan, 7 Feb 1979.

TRANSGRESSION   For definitions, see 13; 38; 52. On literature and sexuality as transgression, see 82. On crime, the law and transgression, see 95.

TRUTH   Truth is a major theme in Foucault's work, in particular in the context of its relations with power, knowledge and the subject. For early discussions in relation to truth, see 6. On truth and dreams, see 1; 4. For remarks on the relation between madness and the truth in Western history, see 25; HF pt. 1, chs. I, II, V, pt. 2 intro., pt. 3, intro., chs. I, III, IV, V. On truth and medicine, see BC chs. 4, 5. For an excellent discussion on truth as an event or something that 'happens', and is produced by various techniques (the 'technology' of truth) rather than something that already exists and is simply waiting to be discovered, see 146. Also on the historical origins of 'truth', see 84; 132; 139; 200; 281; UP intro. ch. 1. For a brief 'history of the truth' in the West and two different ways of defining how truth can be accessed, see PP 23 Jan 1974. See also 139. On truth and power, see 139; 192; 356; 2004c; OD. On truth and war, see SMD 21 Jan, 18 Feb, 1976. On the history of truth in relation to science and the division between the true and the false, see 192; 219; PP 23 Jan 1974. For further comments on the division between the true and the false, see 101; 278; 345; OD. On the division between the true and the false using the metaphor of theatre, see 234. On the relation between 'telling the truth' and governing oneself and others, see HER 6 Jan (b) 1982. On historical transformations in what allows people to have access to the truth, see 326; 344; HER 6 Jan (a), 3 Feb (b) 1982. Foucault argues that 'the effect of truth' he wants to produce consists in 'showing that the real is polemical' (238). On the 'obligation' in Western culture and history to speak and search for the truth in general or about oneself, see 295; 349; 356; 1993; FS; HER 10 Mar (b) 1982. On love and truth in Socrates and Plato, see UP pt. 5. Foucault notes that he is not interested in 'telling the truth', in his writing. Rather, he is interested in inviting people to have a particular experience for themselves, see 281. See also 102; 104. For an interesting set of lectures on the problem of how speaking the truth is defined and on parrhesia (free speech) in Ancient Greek and Roman thought, see FS. On discussions in Ancient Greece and Rome on how to become the 'active subject of true discourse', see HER 10 Mar (b) 17 Mar (a) (b) 1982.

UNIVERSAL CATEGORIES   Foucault was firmly and consistently opposed to the notion of universal categories and essences, 'things' that existed in unchanged form in all times and places such as the State, madness, sexuality, criminality and so on. These things only acquire a real (and changing) existence as the result of specific historical activities and reflection. See 84; 345; 2004c; AK pt. II ch. 1 pt. V; FS conclusion; STP 8 Feb 1978; NBP 10, 31 Jan, 4 Apr 1979.

UTOPIAS   Foucault argued that designing a social system to replace the current one merely produced another system which was still part of the current problem. See 98. He also describes the capitalist Utopia of the factory-prison in 130; 139. Also on Utopias, see 356; 360; OT preface.

VIOLENCE   On violence as the limit of power, where power breaks down, see 306; 1988e. See also PP 7 Nov 1973.

WILL TO TRUTH   See 101; OD. On the general notion of 'will' in Western philosophy, see 235.

WILL TO KNOW   For discussion on Nietzsche's ideas on why humans desire knowledge, see 101. See also 139; 330; HS pt. 3.

WITCHCRAFT AND SORCERY   On the history of witchcraft and sorcery in Western Europe, see 52; 62; 85; 173; AN 26 Feb 1975.

WOMEN AND FEMINISM   Foucault is often criticised for his lack of interest in the situation of women. When he does mention the feminist movement, however, it is usually to express his support. See 200. On the male heterosexual imagination and women, see 317. A discussion (209) with a number of others on the law, rape and sex with minors has been the subject of particular controversy within feminist literature. See also 263. For Foucault's response to the misinterpretations of what he said during this discussion, see 349. He also states very clearly in 317 that if there should be freedom of sexual choice, freedom of sexual acts such as rape should not be permitted. Foucault criticises Ancient Greek ethical systems in relation to women and its exclusively male-centred approach in 326, describing it as an 'ethics of men made for men'. Cf. 344; UP intro. ch. 2; pt. 1 chs. 1, 4, pt. 2 ch. 4, pt. 3 ch. 2; CS pt. 1 ch. 3; On the domination of women in Western history and society, see 356. On the role of women as 'Other' in Classical philosophy, see CS pt. 5 ch. 1, pt. 6 ch. 2.

WRITING AS A TRANSFORMATIVE PRACTICE   Foucault often alludes to the process of writing and being a writer and the way in which writing is related (or not) to political activity and social subversion as well as to the formation of subjectivity and the self. See 69; 82; 1985; OD. On writing and intellectuals, see 192; 1985. For comments on his style and the way he hopes his readers will react, see 161; 2004c. At one stage he appears to have found writing particularly difficult. See 149; 150. See also 2004c. On writing as a practice of the self amongst the Ancient Greeks and early Christians, see 326; 329; 344; 363; UP intro. ch. 1; CS pt. 2; HER 3 Mar (b) 1982. On writing, limits and knowledge, see 43. On the notion of writing and the author, see 69; 2004c. For Foucault's comments on writing books as a means of self-transformation, see 102; 104; 281; 296; 336; 343; 350; 357; 362.

Bibliography

Referencing Foucault's work is a complex and arduous task, so I will be adopting a number of conventions. First of all, I have used the common practice of abbreviations for texts referred to frequently. Foucault's work, with the exception of the books listed in the abbreviations section at the beginning of the book is also listed by the date of its first publication whether this is in French, English, or other languages. As Foucault was interested in different things at different times it is useful to know when his individual writings originally appeared. I have also used wherever possible, the most recent English editions of Foucault's work. I am indebted to Richard Lynch's bibliography of English translations of Foucault's work (2004) for providing up-to-date and comprehensive information on this front.

For those who wish to refer to the French originals of Foucault's shorter works, or use them as a point of reference for translations into other languages, I have appended at the end of each reference the number of the item as it is listed in the French four volume collection *Dits et écrits* (1994). So, for example (1963b) 'A preface to transgression' is followed by the appendage DE#8. This means that I have listed items in order of their original appearance in *Dits et écrits*, rather than in the order in which they first appear in the text of the current book. It must be noted, however, that not all these works were originally published in French but appeared in various languages such as English, German, Dutch, Japanese, Portuguese and Italian. Finally, lengthy as it is, this bibliography of Foucault's work is not completely comprehensive. For an exhaustive and frequently updated list of Foucault's shorter works in English translation see Lynch (2004). See also *Dits et écrits* and the www.Foucault.info website (Karskens, 2001) for comprehensive bibliographies of Foucault's work in French.

Introductions to Foucault's work

There are a large number of general introductions to Foucault's work. These include books by Barker (1998); Bernauer (1990); Danaher et al. (2000); Dreyfus and Rabinow (1982): Fillingham and Süsser (1993); Horrocks and Jevtic (1997); Kendall and Wickham (1999); McHoul and Grace (1993); McNay (1994); Mills (2003); O'Farrell (1989); Rajchman (1985); Sheridan (1981); and Smart (1985).

Bibliographies of secondary material

Jeffrey Hearn's (2000) annotated bibliography on the internet is currently the most extensive list of secondary sources referring to Foucault's work in some way. For a huge list of earlier work, see Clark (1983).

Websites

There are now quite a few Foucault resources on the internet. The most comprehensive general sites on Foucault are listed below. These sites include variously: extracts from Foucault's writings, bibliographies, FAQs, introductions to his work, news about conferences and other events, articles, links to other sites, discussion forums and photos of Foucault.

http://www.foucault.info/ – Site title: *Foucault.info.* The owner of this site, having taken to heart Foucault's ideas on the 'death of the author', deliberately maintains anonymity. The main language of the site is English, although it is run from Paris (France).

http://www.foucault.qut.edu.au/ – Site title: *Michel Foucault: resources.* Maintained by Clare O'Farrell (Australia).

http://www.theory.org.uk/ctr-fouc.htm – Site title: *Theory.org.uk.* Maintained by David Gauntlett (UK).

http://www.thefoucauldian.co.uk/ – Site title: *thefoucauldian.co.uk* Maintained by Carl Folker (UK).

http://www.artsci.lsu.edu/fai/Faculty/Professors/Protevi/Foucault/ – Site title: *Coursework materials: Foucault.* Maintained by John Protevi (USA).

http://www.foucaultsociety.org/ – Site title: The Foucault Society. Maintained by the Foucault Society in New York (USA.)

http://www.csun/~hfspc002/foucault.home.html – Site title: The Foucault Pages at CSUN. Maintained by Bernardo Attias (USA).

Journal

An international peer-reviewed online journal with reviews and articles relating to Foucault's work and its applications titled *Foucault Studies* can be found at http://www.foucault-studies.com – The first issue was published in December 2004.

Books by Foucault

B ooks by Foucault are included in the abbreviations section at the front of the book.

Foucault's shorter works

(1954 [1993]). Dream, imagination, and existence (F. Williams, Trans.). In K. Hoeller (ed.), *Dream and Existence* (pp. 29–78). Atlantic Highlands, NJ: Humanities Press. DE#1

(1957a). La psychologie de 1850 à 1950. In DE I. (pp. 120–37). DE#2

(1957b). La recherche scientifique et la psychologie. In DE I. (pp. 137–58). DE#3

(1961a). Préface à *Folie et déraison. Histoire de la folie à l'âge classique*. In DE I. (pp. 159–67). DE#4

(1961b). Madness only exists in society. In FL. (pp. 7–9). DE#5

(1961c). Alexandre Koyré: *La Révolution astronomique, Copernic, Kepler, Borelli*. In DE I. (pp. 170–1). DE#6

(1962a). Introduction to Rousseau's Dialogues. In EW2. (pp. 33–51). DE#7

(1962b). Le 'non' du père. In DE I. (pp. 189–203). DE#8

(1962c). The father's 'no'. In EW2. (pp. 5–20). DE#8

(1962d). Le cycle des grenouilles. In DE I. (pp. 203–4). DE#9

(1962e). Dire et voir chez Raymond Roussel. In DE I. (pp. 205–15). DE#10

(1962f). Speaking and seeing in Raymond Roussel. In EW2. (pp. 21–32). DE#10

(1962g). So cruel a knowledge. In EW2. (pp. 53–67). DE#11

(1963a). Veilleur de la nuit de hommes. Sur Rolf Italiaander. In DE I. (pp. 229–33). DE#12

(1963b). A preface to transgression. In EW2. (pp. 69–87). DE#13

(1963c). Language to infinity. In EW2. (pp. 89–101). DE#14

(1963d). Guetter le jour qui vient. In DE I. (pp. 261–8). DE#15

(1963e). L'eau et la folie. In DE I. (pp. 268–72). DE#16

(1963f). Distance, aspect, origine. In DE I. (pp. 272–85). DE#17

(1963g). Un 'nouveau roman' de terreur. In DE I. (pp. 285–7). DE#18

(1964a). Notice historique, in Kant, E., *Anthropologie du point de vue pragmatique*. In DE I. (pp. 288–93). DE#19

(1964b). Afterword to *The temptation of St. Anthony*. In EW2. (pp. 103–22). DE#20

(1964c). The prose of Acteon. In RC. (pp. 75–84). DE#21

(1964d). The debate on the novel. In RC. (pp. 72–4). DE#22

(1964e). Débat sur la poésie. In DE I. (pp. 390–406). DE#23

(1964f). Le langage de l'espace. In DE I. (pp. 407–12). DE#24

(1964g). Madness, the absence of work (Trans. P. Stastny & D. Şengel). In A.I. Davidson (ed.), *Michel Foucault and his Interlocutors* (pp. 97–104). Chicago: University of Chicago Press. DE#25

(1964h). Pourquoi réédite-t-on l'œuvre de Raymond Roussel? Un précurseur de notre littérature moderne. In DE I. (pp. 421–4). DE#26

(1964i). Les mots qui saignent (Sur *L'Énéide* de P. Klossowski). In DE I. (pp. 424–7). DE#27

(1964j). Le *Mallarmé* de J.-P. Richard. In DE I. (pp. 427–37). DE#28

(1964k). L'obligation d'écrire. In DE I. (p. 437). DE#29

(1965a). Philosophy and psychology. In EW2. (pp. 249–59). DE#30

(1965b). Philosophie et vérité. In DE I. (pp. 448–64). DE#31

(1966a). The order of things. In EW2. (pp. 261–7). DE#34

(1966b). À la recherche du présent perdu. In DE I. (pp. 504–5). DE#35

(1966c). Behind the fable. In EW2. (pp. 137–45). DE#36

(1966d). Entretien avec Madeleine Chapsal. In DE I. (pp. 513–8). DE#37

(1966e). The thought of the outside. In EW2. (pp. 147–70). DE#38

(1966f). L'homme est-il mort? In DE I. (pp. 540–4). DE#39

(1966g). Une histoire restée muette. In DE I. (pp. 545–9). DE#40

(1966h). Michel Foucault et Gilles Deleuze veulent rendre à Nietzsche son vrai visage. In DE I. (pp. 549–52). DE#41

(1966i). Philosophy and the death of God. In RC. (pp. 85–6). DE#42

(1966j). A swimmer between two words. In EW2. (pp. 171–4). DE#43

(1966k). Message ou bruit? In DE I. (pp. 557–60). DE#44

(1967a). Introduction générale aux *Œuvres philosophiques complètes de F. Nietzsche*. In DE I. (pp. 561–4). DE#45

(1967b). Nietzsche, Freud, Marx. In EW2. (pp. 269–78). DE#46

(1967c). La philosophie structuraliste permet de diagnostiquer ce qu'est 'aujourd'hui'. In DE I. (pp. 580–4). DE#47

(1967d). On the ways of writing history. In EW2. (pp. 279–95). DE#48

(1967e). Who are you, Professor Foucault? In RC. (pp. 87–103). DE#50

(1967f). Les mots et les images. In DE I. (pp. 620–3). DE#51

(1968a). Religious deviations and medical knowledge. In RC. (pp. 50–6). DE#52

(1968b). This is not a pipe. In EW2. (pp. 187–203). DE#53

(1968c). Interview avec Michel Foucault. In DE I. (pp. 651–62). DE#54

(1968d). Foucault responds to Sartre. In FL. (pp. 51–6). DE#55

(1968e). Une mise au point de Michel Foucault. In DE I. (pp. 669–70). DE#56

(1968f). Lettre de Michel Foucault à Jacques Proust. In DE I. (pp. 670–3). DE#57

(1968g). History, discourse and discontinuity. In FL. (pp. 33–50). DE#58

(1968h). On the archaeology of the sciences: response to the epistemology circle. In EW2. (pp. 297–333). DE#59

(1969a). Introduction, in Arnauld, A. & Nicole, P., *Grammaire générale et raisonnée*. In DE I. (pp. 732–52). DE#60

(1969b). Médecins, juges et sorciers au XVIIe siècle. In DE I. (pp. 753–66). DE#62

(1969c). Maxime Defert. In DE I. (pp. 766–7). DE#63

(1969d). Ariane s'est pendue. In DE I. (pp. 767–71). DE#64

(1969e). The archeology of knowledge. In FL. (pp. 57–64). DE#66

(1969f). Jean Hyppolite. 1907–1968. In DE I. (pp. 779–85). DE#67

(1969g). The birth of a world. In FL. (pp. 65–6). DE#68

(1969h). What is an author? In EW2. (pp. 205–22). DE#69, 258

(1969i). Interview avec Claude Bonnefoy. Unpublished typescript held at the Foucault Archives at l'Institut Mémoires de l'Edition Contemporain (IMEC) Item number B14. Extracts from this interview are available for download. Retrieved 9 October 2004, from: http://www.radiofrance.fr/chaines/france-culture2/emissions/cultureplus/fiche.php?diffusion_id=25330

(1969j). Candidacy presentation: Collège de France, 1969. In EW1. (pp. 5–10). DE#71

(1970a). Sept propos sur le septième ange. In DE II. (pp. 13–25). DE#73

(1970b). Discussion sur un exposé de F. Dagognet : 'Cuvier'. In DE II. (pp. 27–9). DE#76

(1970c). La situation de Cuvier dans l'histoire de la biologie. In DE II. (pp. 30–66). DE#77

(1970d). Le piège de Vincennes. In DE II. (pp. 67–73). DE#78

(1970e). Il y aura scandale, mais... (sur Pierre Guyotat). In DE II. (pp. 74–5). DE#79

(1970f). Theatrum philosophicum. In EW2. (pp. 343–68). DE#80

(1970g). Croître et multiplier (sur François Jacob). In DE II. (pp. 99–104). DE#81

(1970h). Folie, littérature, société. In DE II. (pp. 104–28). DE#82

(1970i). Madness and society. In EW2. (pp. 335–42). DE#83

(1971a). Nietzsche, genealogy, history. In EW2. (pp. 369–91). DE#84

(1971b). Entretien avec Michel Foucault. In DE II. (pp. 157–74). DE#85

(1971c). Manifeste du G.I.P. In DE II. (pp. 174–5). DE#86

(1971d). Sur les prisons. In DE II. (pp. 175–6). DE#87

(1971e). Enquête sur les prisons: brisons les barreaux du silence. In DE II. (pp. 176–82). DE#88

(1971f). A conversation with Michel Foucault. Partisan Review, 38(2): 192–201. Interview with J.K. Simon. DE#89

(1971g). Rituals of exclusion. In FL. (pp. 68–73). DE#89

(1971h). La prison partout. In DE II. (pp. 193–4). DE#90

(1971i). Préface à Enquête dans vingt prisons. In DE II. (pp. 195–7). DE#91

(1971j). L'article 15 (L'affaire Jaubert). In DE II. (pp. 198–9). DE#92

(1971k). Rapports de la commission d'information sur l'affaire Jaubert. In DE II. (pp. 199–203). DE#93

(1971l). Je perçois l'intolérable. In DE II. (pp. 203–5). DE#94

(1971m). Un problème m'intéresse depuis longtemps, c'est celui du système pénal. In DE II. (pp. 205–9). DE#95

(1971n). Lettre de Michel Foucault. In DE II. (pp. 209–14). DE#96

(1971o). Monstrosities in criticism. Diacritics, 1(1): 57–60. DE#97

(1971p [1977]). Revolutionary action: 'until now' (Trans. D.F. Bouchard & S. Simon). In D. Bouchard (ed.), Language, Counter-memory, Practice: Selected Essays and Interviews. Ithaca, NY: Cornell University Press. (pp. 218–33). DE#98

(1971q). Le discours de Toul. In DE II. (pp. 236–8). DE#99

(1971r). Foucault responds. *Diacritics,* 1(2): 60. DE#100

(1971s). The will to knowledge. In EW1. (pp. 11–16). DE#101

(1972a). My body, this paper, this fire. In EW2. (pp. 393–417). DE#102

(1972b). Return to history. In EW2. (pp. 419–32). DE#103

(1972c). Réponse à Derrida. In DE II. (pp. 281–95). DE#104

(1972d). Le grand enfermement. In DE II. (pp. 296–306). DE#105

(1972e). Intellectuals and power. In FL. (pp. 74–82). DE#106

(1972f). Table ronde. In DE II. (pp. 316–39). DE#107

(1972g). On popular justice: a discussion with Maoists. In P/K. (pp. 1–36). DE#108

(1972h). An historian of culture. In FL. (pp. 95–104). DE#109

(1972i). Les grandes fonctions de la médecine dans notre société. In DE II. (pp. 380–2). DE#110

(1972j). Piéger sa propre culture. In DE II. (p. 382). DE#111

(1972k). Meeting Vérité-Justice. 1 500 Grenoblois accusent. In DE II. (p. 383–5). DE#112

(1972l). Une giclée de sang ou un incendie. In DE II. (p. 385). DE#113

(1972m). Pompidou's two deaths. In EW3. (pp. 418–22). DE#114

(1972n). Penal theories and institutions. In EW1. (pp. 17–21). DE#115

(1973a). Préface, in Livrozet, S., *De la prison à la révolte.* In DE II. (pp. 394–9). DE#116

(1973b). Pour une chronique de la mémoire ouvrière. In DE II. (pp. 399–400). DE#117

(1973c). La force de fuir. In DE II. (pp. 401–5). DE#118

(1973d). De l'archéologie à la dynastique. In DE II. (pp. 405–16). DE#119

(1973e). En guise de conclusion. In DE II. (pp. 416–9). DE#120

(1973f). Un nouveau journal? In DE II. (pp. 419–20). DE#121

(1973g). L'intellectuel sert à rassembler les idées, mais 'son savoir est partiel par rapport au savoir ouvrier'. In DE II. (pp. 421–3). DE#123

(1973h). Foucault, le philosophe est en train de parler. Pensez. In DE II. (pp. 423–5). DE#124

(1973i). Prisons et révoltes dans les prisons. In DE II. (pp. 425–32). DE#125

(1973j). Le monde est un grand asile. In DE II. (pp. 433–4). DE#126

(1973k). A propos de l'enfermement pénitentiaire. In DE II. (pp. 435–45). DE#127

(1973l). Summoned to court. In EW3. (pp. 423–5). DE#128

(1973m). Equipments of power: towns, territories and collective equipments. In FL. (pp. 105–12). DE#129, 130

(1973n). *Ceci n'est pas une pipe.* Illus. René Magritte. Montpellier: Fata Morgana.

(1973o). *This is not a pipe* (Trans. J. Harkness). Illus. René Magritte. Berkeley: University of California Press.

(1973p). The punitive society. In EW1. (pp. 23–38). DE#131

(1974a). Human nature: justice versus power. In F. Elders (ed.), *Reflexive Water: The Basic Concerns of Mankind* (pp. 133–97). London: Souvenir Press. DE#132

(1974b). Sur *La Seconde Révolution chinoise.* In DE II. (pp. 513–5). DE#133

(1974c). *La Seconde Révolution chinoise.* In DE II. (pp. 515–8). DE#134

(1974d). Paris, galerie Karl Flinker, 15 février 1974. Présentation (D. Byzantios, dessins). In DE II. (pp. 518–21). DE#135

(1974e). Prisons et asiles dans le mécanisme du pouvoir. In DE II. (pp. 521–5). DE#136

(1974f). On Attica. In FL. (pp. 113–21). DE#137

(1974g). Sexualité et politique. In DE II. (pp. 536–7). DE#138

(1974h). La vérité et les formes juridiques. In DE II. (pp. 538–646). DE#139

(1974i). Truth and juridical forms. In EW3. (pp. 1–89). Does not include round table discussion. DE#139

(1974j). Film and popular memory. In FL. (pp. 122–32). DE#140

(1974k). Folie, une question de pouvoir. In DE II. (pp. 660–4). DE#141

(1974l). White magic and black gown. In FL. (pp. 287–91). DE#142

(1974m). Psychiatric power. In EW1. (pp. 39–50). DE#143

(1975a). Préface, in Jackson, B., Leurs prisons. Autobiographies de prisonniers américains. In DE II. (pp. 687–91). DE#144

(1975b). (Lettre) in Clavel, M., Ce que je crois. In DE II. (p. 692). DE#145

(1975c). La maison des fous. In DE II. (pp. 693–8). DE#146

(1975d). Un pompier vend la mèche. In DE II. (pp. 698–702). DE#147

(1975e). La politique est la continuation de la guerre par d'autres moyens. In DE II. (pp. 702–4). DE#148

(1975f). A quoi rêvent les philosophes? In DE II. (pp. 704–7). DE#149

(1975g). La peinture photogénique. In DE II. (pp. 707–15). DE#150

(1975h). From torture to cellblock. In FL. (pp. 146–9). DE#151

(1975i). Sur la sellette. In DE II. (pp. 720–5). DE#152

(1975j). La prison vue par un philosophe français. In DE II. (pp. 725–31). DE#153

(1975k). La fête de l'écriture. In DE II. (pp. 731–4). DE#154

(1975l). La mort du père. In DE II. (pp. 734–9). DE#155

(1975m). Prison talk. In P/K. (pp. 37–54). DE#156

(1975n). Body/Power. In P/K. (pp. 55–62). DE#157

(1975o). Aller à Madrid. In DE II. (pp. 760–2). DE#158

(1975p). A propos de Marguerite Duras. In DE II. (pp. 762–71). DE#159

(1975q). Asiles, sexualité, prisons. In DE II. (pp. 771–82). DE#160

(1975r). Talk show. In FL. (pp. 133–45). DE#161

(1975s). Faire les fous. In DE II. (pp. 802–5). DE#162

(1975t). Michel Foucault. Les réponses du philosophe. In DE II. (pp. 805–17). DE#163

(1975u). Sade: sargeant of sex. In EW2. (pp. 223–7). DE#164

(1975v). The abnormals. In EW1. (pp. 51–7). DE#165

(1976a). Une mort inacceptable (l'affaire Mirval). In DE III. (pp. 7–9). DE#166

(1976b). Les têtes de la politique. In DE III. (pp. 9–13). DE#167

(1976c). The politics of health in the eighteenth century. In EW3. (pp. 90–105). DE#168, 257

(1976d). Questions on geography. In P/K. (pp. 63–77). DE#169

(1976e). Crisis of medicine or anti-medicine? Foucault Studies (1) 2004: 5–19. DE#170

(1976f). Paul's story. In FL. (pp. 181–5). DE#171

(1976g). The politics of Soviet crime. In FL. (pp. 190–5). DE#172

(1976h). The social extension of the norm. In FL. (pp. 196–9). DE#173

(1976i). Le savoir comme crime. In DE III. (pp. 79–86). DE#174

(1976j). Michel Foucault, l'illégalisme et l'art de punir. In DE III. (pp. 86–9). DE#175

(1976k). Sorcery and madness. In FL. (pp. 200–2). DE#176

(1976l). Points de vue. In DE III. (pp. 93–4). DE#177

(1976m). Des questions de Michel Foucault à *Hérodote*. In DE III. (pp. 94–5). DE#178

(1976n). Bio-histoire et bio-politique. In DE III. (pp. 95–7). DE#179

(1976o). I, Pierre Rivière. In FL. (pp. 203–6). DE#180

(1976p). Pourquoi le crime de Pierre Rivière? In DE III. (pp. 106–8). DE#182

(1976q). Ils ont dit de Malraux. In DE III. (p. 108). DE#183

(1976r). Le retour de Pierre Rivière. In DE III. (pp. 114–23). DE#185

(1976s). Le discours ne doit pas être pris comme... In DE III. (pp. 123–4). DE#186

(1976t). Society must be defended. In EW1. (pp. 294–9). DE#187

(1976u). Dialogue on power. *Quid*, 4–22. Roneotype edited by Simon Wade.

(1977a). Préface à *My Secret Life*. In DE III. (pp. 131–2). DE#188

(1977b). Preface to *Anti-Oedipus*. In EW3. (pp. 106–10). DE#189

(1977c). Sexualité et vérité. In DE III. (pp. 136–8). DE#190

(1977d). Préface, in Debard, M. & Hennig, J.-L, *Les juges khakis*. In DE III. (pp. 138–40). DE#191

(1977e). Truth and power. In EW3. (pp. 111–33). DE#192

(1977f). Two lectures (first lecture: 7 January 1976). In P/K. (pp. 78–92). DE#193

(1977g). Two lectures (second lecture: 14 January 1976). In P/K. (pp. 92–108). DE#194

(1977h). The eye of power. In P/K. (pp. 146–65). DE#195

(1977i). The birth of social medicine. In EW3. (pp. 134–56). DE#196

(1977j). The history of sexuality. In P/K. (pp. 183–93). DE#197

(1977k). Lives of infamous men. In EW3. (pp. 157–75). DE#198

(1977l). Le poster de l'ennemi public n° 1. In DE III. (pp. 253–6). DE#199

(1977m). The end of the monarchy of sex. In FL. (pp. 214–25). DE#200

(1977n). The gray mornings of tolerance. In EW2. (pp. 229–31). DE#201

(1977o). L'asile illimité. In DE III. (pp. 271–5). DE#202

(1977p). Paris, galerie Bastida-Navazo, avril 1977 (sur le peintre Maxime Defert). In DE III. (p. 275). DE#203

(1977q). La grande colère des faits (sur A. Glucksmann). In DE III. (pp. 277–81). DE#204

(1977r). The anxiety of judging. In FL. (pp. 241–54). DE#205

(1977s). The confession of the flesh. In P/K. (pp. 194–228). DE#206

(1977t). Une mobilisation culturelle. In DE III. (pp. 329–31). DE#207

(1977u). Le supplice de la vérité. In DE III. (pp. 331–2). DE#208

(1977v). Confinement, psychiatry, prison. In PPC. (pp. 178–210). DE#209

(1977w). Va-t-on extrader Klaus Croissant? In DE III. (pp. 361–5). DE#210

(1977x). Michel Foucault: 'Désormais la sécurité est au-dessus des lois'. In DE III. (p. 366). DE#211

(1977y). Le pouvoir, une bête magnifique. In DE III. (pp. 368–82). DE#212

(1977z). Michel Foucault: la sécurité et l'État. In DE III. (pp. 383–8). DE#213

(1977za). Letter to certain leaders of the left. In EW3. (pp. 426–8). DE#214

(1977zb). La torture, c'est la raison. In DE III. (pp. 390–8). DE#215

(1977zc). Pouvoir et savoir. In DE III. (pp. 399–414). DE#216

(1977zd). Nous nous sentions comme une sale espèce. In DE III. (pp. 415–8). DE#217

(1977ze). Power and strategies. In P/K. (pp. 134–45). DE#218

(1978a). Life: experience and science. In EW2. (pp. 465–78). DE#219, 361

(1978b). About the concept of the 'dangerous individual' in nineteenth-century legal psychiatry. In EW3. (pp. 176–200). DE#220

(1978c). Dialogue sur le pouvoir. In DE III. (pp. 464–77). DE#221

(1978d). La folie et la société. In DE III. (pp. 477–99). DE#222

(1978e). Quatrième de couverture in *Herculine Barbin, dite Alexina B.* In DE III. (p. 499). DE#223

(1978f). Eugène Sue que j'aime. In DE III. (pp. 500–2). DE#224

(1978g). Une érudition étourdissante. In DE III. (pp. 503–5). DE#225

(1978h). Alain Peyrefitte s'explique... et Michel Foucault lui répond. In DE III. (pp. 505–6). DE#226

(1978i). La grille politique traditionnelle. In DE III. (pp. 506–7). DE#227

(1978j). Attention: danger. In DE III. (pp. 507–8). DE#228

(1978k). L'incorporation de l'hôpital dans la technologie moderne. In DE III. (pp. 508–21). DE#229

(1978l). Sexualité et politique. In DE III. (pp. 522–31). DE#230

(1978m). La société disciplinaire en crise. In DE III. (pp. 532–4). DE#231

(1978n). La philosophie analytique de la politique. In DE III. (pp. 534–51). DE#232

(1978o). Sexuality and power. In RC. (pp. 115–30). DE#233

(1978p). La scène de la philosophie. In DE III. (pp. 571–95). DE#234

(1978q). Méthodologie pour la connaissance du monde: comment se débarrasser du marxisme. In DE III. (pp. 595–618). DE#235

(1978r). Michel Foucault and Zen: a stay in a Zen temple. In RC. (pp. 110–114). DE#236

(1978s). Le mystérieux hermaphrodite. In DE III. (pp. 624–5). DE#237

(1978t). Clarifications on the question of power. In FL. (pp. 255–63). DE#238

(1978u). La gouvernementalité. In DE III. (pp. 635–57). DE#239

(1978v). Governmentality. In EW3. (pp. 201–22). DE#239

(1978w). The proper use of criminals. In EW3. (pp. 429–34). DE#240

(1978x). L'armée quand la terre tremble. In DE III. (pp. 662–9). DE#241

(1978y). M. Foucault. Conversation sans complexes avec le philosophe qui analyse les 'structures du pouvoir'. In DE III. (pp. 669–78). DE#242

(1978z). Le chah a cent ans de retard. In DE III. (pp. 679–83). DE#243

(1978za). Téhéran: la foi contre le chah. In DE III. (pp. 683–8). DE#244

(1978zb). À quoi rêvent les Iraniens? In DE III. (pp. 688–94). DE#245

(1978zc). Lemon and milk. In EW3. (pp. 435–8). DE#246

(1978zd). 'Paris-Berlin'. In FL. (pp. 292–4). DE#247

(1978ze). Une révolte à mains nues. In DE III. (pp. 701–4). DE#248

(1978zf). Défi à l'opposition. In DE III. (pp. 704–6). DE#249

(1978zg). Les 'reportages' d'idées. In DE III. (pp. 706–7). DE#250

(1978zh). Réponse de Michel Foucault à une lectrice iranienne. In DE III. (p. 708). DE#251

(1978zi). La révolte iranienne se propage sur les rubans des cassettes. In DE III. (pp. 709–13). DE#252

(1978zj). Le chef mythique de la révolte de l'Iran. In DE III. (pp. 713–6). DE#253

(1978zk). Lettre de Foucault à L'Unità. In DE III. (pp. 717–8). DE#254

(1978zl). Security, territory, and population. In EW1. (pp. 67–71). DE#255

(1979a). Préface de Michel Foucault. In DE III. (pp. 724–5). DE#256

(1979c). Iran: the spirit of a world without spirit. In PPC. (pp. 211–24). DE#259

(1979d). Manières de justice. In DE III. (pp. 755–9). DE#260

(1979e). Une poudrière appelée islam. In DE III. (p. 759–62). DE#261

(1979f). Michel Foucault et l'Iran. In DE III. (p. 762). DE#262

(1979g). The danger of child sexuality. In FL. (pp. 264–74). DE#263

(1979h). The simplest of pleasures. In FL. (pp. 295–7). DE#264

(1979i). Open letter to Mehdi Bazargan. In EW3. (pp. 439–42). DE#265

(1979j). For an ethic of discomfort. In EW3. (pp. 443–8). DE#266

(1979k). Michel Foucault: le moment de vérité. In DE III. (p. 788). DE#267

(1979l). Vivre autrement le temps. In DE III. (pp. 788–90). DE#268

(1979m). Useless to revolt? In EW3. (pp. 449–53). DE#269

(1979n). La stratégie du pourtour. In DE III. (pp. 794–7). DE#270

(1979o). 'Le problème des réfugiés est un présage de la grande migration du XXIᵉ siècle'. Interview exclusive du philosophe français M, Foucault. In DE III. (pp. 798–800). DE#271

(1979p). Truth is in the future. In FL. (pp. 298–301). DE#272, 280

(1979q). Luttes autour des prisons. In DE III. (pp. 806–18). DE#273

(1979r). The birth of biopolitics. In EW1. (pp. 73–9). DE#274

(1980a). Préface, in Knobelspiess, R., QHS: Quartier de haute sécurité. In DE IV. (pp. 7–9). DE#275

(1980b). La poussière et le nuage. In DE IV. (pp. 10–19). DE#277

(1980c). Questions of method. In EW3. (pp. 223–38). DE#278

(1980d). Postface, in Perrot, M. (ed.), L'Impossible Prison. Recherches sur le système pénitentiaire au XIXᵉ siècle. In DE IV. (pp. 35–7). DE#279

(1980e). Interview with Michel Foucault. In EW3. (pp. 239–97). DE#281

(1980f). Toujours les prisons. In DE IV. (pp. 96–9). DE#282

(1980g). Le Nouvel Observateur et l'Union de la gauche. In DE IV. (pp. 100–2). DE#283

(1980h). The four horsemen of the Apocalypse and the everyday worms. In EW2. (pp. 233–4). DE#284

(1980i). The masked philosopher. In EW1. (pp. 321–8). DE#285

(1980j). The imagination of the nineteenth century. In EW2. (pp. 235–9). DE#286

(1980k). Le vrai sexe. In DE IV. (pp. 115–23). DE#287

(1980l). Roland Barthes (12 novembre 1915–26 mars 1980). In DE IV. (pp. 124–5). DE#288

(1980m). On the government of the living. In EW1. (pp. 81–5). DE#289

(1980n). Lecture, 9 January 1980. Unpublished audiotape.

(1981a). Préface à la deuxième édition, in Vergès, J., *De la stratégie judiciaire*. In DE IV. (pp. 130–4). DE#290

(1981b). 'Omnes et singulatim': toward a critique of political reason. In EW3. (pp. 298–325). DE#291

(1981c). Lettre à Roger Caillois in *Hommage à Roger Caillois*. In DE IV. (p. 162). DE#292

(1981d). Friendship as a way of life. In EW1. (pp. 135–40). DE#293

(1981e). Le dossier 'peine de mort'. Ils ont écrit contre. In DE IV. (p. 168). DE#294

(1981f). Sexuality and solitude. In EW1. (pp. 175–84). DE#295

(1981g). So is it important to think? In EW3. (pp. 454–8). DE#296

(1981h). Les mailles du pouvoir. In DE IV. (pp. 182–201). DE#297

(1981i). Michel Foucault: il faut tout repenser, la loi et la prison. In DE IV. (pp. 202–4). DE#298

(1981j). Lacan, le 'libérateur de la psychanalyse'. In DE IV. (pp. 204–5). DE#299

(1981k). Against replacement penalties. In EW3. (pp. 459–61). DE#300

(1981l). To punish is the most difficult thing there is. In EW3. (pp. 462–4). DE#301

(1981m). Les réponses de Pierre Vidal-Naquet et de Michel Foucault (l'état de guerre en Pologne). In DE IV. (p. 210). DE#302

(1981n). Notes sur ce qu'on lit et entend (même sujet). In DE IV. (pp. 211–2). DE#303

(1981o). Subjectivity and truth. In EW1. (pp. 87–92). DE#304

(1982a). Pierre Boulez, passing through the screen. In EW2. (pp. 241–4). DE#305

(1982b). The subject and power. In EW3. (pp. 326–48). DE#306

(1982c). La pensée, l'émotion. In DE IV. (pp. 243–50). DE#307

(1982d). Passion according to Werner Schroeter. In FL. (pp. 313–21). DE#308

(1982e). Un premier pas de la colonisation de l'Occident. In DE IV. (pp. 261–9). DE#309

(1982f). Space, knowledge and power. In EW3. (pp. 349–64). DE#310

(1982g). History and homosexuality. In FL. (pp. 363–70). DE#311

(1982h). The battle for chastity. In EW1. (pp. 185–97). DE#312

(1982i). The social triumph of the sexual will. In EW1. (pp. 157–62). DE#313

(1982j). Des caresses d'hommes considérées comme un art. In DE IV. (pp. 315–7). DE#314

(1982k). Le terrorisme ici et là. In DE IV. (pp. 318–9). DE#316

(1982l). Sexual choice, sexual act. In EW1. (pp. 141–56). DE#317

(1982m). Foucault: non aux compromis. In DE IV. (pp. 336–7). DE#318

(1982n). Michel Foucault: 'Il n'y a pas de neutralité possible.' In DE IV. (pp. 338–40). DE#319

(1982o). En abandonnant les Polonais, nous renonçons à une part de nous-mêmes. In DE IV. (pp. 340–3). DE#320

(1982p). The moral and social experience of the Poles can no longer be obliterated. In EW3. (pp. 465–73). DE#321

(1982q). L'âge d'or de la lettre de cachet. In DE IV. (pp. 351–2). DE#322

(1982r). The hermeneutic of the subject. In EW1. (pp. 93–106). DE#323

(1983a). Des travaux. In DE IV. (pp. 366–7). DE#324

(1983b). The risks of security. In EW3. (pp. 365–81). DE#325

(1983c). On the genealogy of ethics: an overview of work in progress. In EW1. (pp. 253–80). DE#326

(1983d). Ça ne m'intéresse pas. In DE IV. (p. 412). DE#327

(1983e). À propos des faiseurs d'histoire. In DE IV. (pp. 412–5). DE#328

(1983f). Self-writing. In EW1. (pp. 207–22). DE#329

(1983g). Structuralism and post-structuralism. In EW2. (pp. 433–58). DE#330

(1983h). An exchange with Michel Foucault. New York Review of Books, 30(5): 42–4. DE#331

(1983i). The cultural insularity of contemporary music. In FL. (pp. 391–6). DE#333

(1983j). La Pologne, et après? In DE IV. (pp. 496–522). DE#334

(1983k). Vous êtes dangereux. In DE IV. (pp. 522–4). DE#335

(1983l). An interview by Stephen Riggins. In EW1. (pp. 121–33). DE#336

(1983m). … ils ont déclaré … sur le pacifisme, sa nature, ses dangers, ses illusions. In DE IV. (p. 538). DE#337

(1983n). Usage des plaisirs et techniques de soi. In DE IV. (pp. 539–62). DE#338

(1984a). What is Enlightenment? In EW1. (pp. 303–19). DE#339

(1984b). Preface to The History of Sexuality, Volume II. In EW1. (pp. 199–205). DE#340

(1984c). Politics and ethics: an interview. In FR. (pp. 373–80). DE#341

(1984d). Polemics, politics, and problematisations. In EW1. (pp. 111–19). DE#342

(1984e). Archeology of a passion. In FL. (pp. 397–406). DE#343

(1984f). A propos de la généalogie de l'éthique: un aperçu du travail en cours. In DE IV. (pp. 609–13) DE#344

(1984g). 'Foucault' by Maurice Florence. In EW2. (pp. 459–63). DE#345

(1984h). What is called 'punishing'? In EW3. (pp. 382–93). DE#346

(1984i). Le souci de la vérité. In DE IV. (pp. 646–9). DE#347

(1984j). Le style de l'histoire. In DE IV. (pp. 649–55). DE#348

(1984k). Interview de Michel Foucault. In DE IV. (pp. 656–67). DE#349

(1984l). The concern for truth. In FL. (pp. 455–64). DE#350

(1984m). The art of telling the truth. In PPC. (pp. 86–95). DE#351

(1984n). Interview with Actes. In EW3. (pp. 394–402). DE#353

(1984o). The return of morality. In FL. (pp. 465–73). DE#354

(1984p). Confronting governments: human rights. In EW3. (pp. 474–5). DE#355

(1984q). The ethics of the concern for the self as a practice of freedom. In EW1. (pp. 281–301). DE#356

(1984r). An aesthetics of existence. In FL. (pp. 450–4). DE#357

(1984s). Sex, power and the politics of identity. In FL. (pp. 382–90). DE#358

(1984t). L'intellectuel et les pouvoirs. In DE IV. (pp. 747–52). DE#359

(1984u). Different spaces. In EW2. (pp. 175–85). DE#360

(1985, 21 June). Pour en finir avec les mensonges. Le Nouvel Observateur, pp. 76–7.

(1986a). On literature. In FL. (pp. 150–3). Interview originally conducted in 1975.

(1986b). La pensée du dehors. Illus. Pierre Tal Coat. Montpellier: Fata Morgana.

(1986c). *Sept propos sur la septième ange.* Illus. d'Ipoustéguy. Montpellier: Fata Morgana.

(1988a). Truth, power, self: an interview with Michel Foucault, October 25, 1982. In TS. (pp. 9–15). DE#362

(1988b). Technologies of the self. In EW1. (pp. 223–51). DE#363

(1988c). The political technology of individuals. In EW3. (pp. 403–17). DE#364

(1988d). What our present is. In FL. (pp. 407–15). Interview conducted in 1983.

(1988e). Power, moral values and the intellectual. *History of the Present,* 4(Spring): 1–2, 11–13. Interview conducted with Michael D. Bess in 1980.

(1989a). Structuralisme et analyse littéraire. *Les Cahiers de Tunisie* (3–4): 21–41. Lecture originally delivered in 1969.

(1989b). Folie et civilisation. *Les Cahiers de Tunisie* (3–4): 43–59. Lecture originally delivered in 1971.

(1989c). Schizo-culture: Infantile sexuality. In FL. (pp. 154–67). Lecture originally delivered in 1975.

(1989d). Schizo-culture: On prison and psychiatry. In FL. (pp. 168–80). Discussion originally conducted in 1975.

(1993). About the beginning of the hermeneutics of the self (1980). In RC. (pp. 158–281).

(1994). Problematics. In FL. (pp. 416–22). Interview originally conducted in 1983.

(2004a). La peinture de Manet. In M. Saison (ed.), *La peinture de Manet suivi de Michel Foucault un regard.* (pp. 21–48). Paris: Seuil.

(2004b). 'Gérer les illégalismes'. A propos de *Surveiller et punir.* In R.-P. Droit, *Michel Foucault entretiens* (pp. 57–73). Paris: Odile Jacob. Interview originally conducted in 1975.

(2004c). 'Je suis un artificier'. A propos de la méthode et de la trajectoire de Michel Foucault. In R.-P. Droit, *Michel Foucault, entretiens* (pp. 88–136). Paris: Odile Jacob. Interview originally conducted in 1975.

Works by other authors

Alt, Casey. (2000). *A very non-Foucauldian history of Michel Foucault.* Retrieved 5 October 2004: from: http://www.stanford.edu/dept/HPS/BirthOfTheClinic/bio home.htm

Althusser, Louis. (1990). *For Marx.* London: Verso.

Althusser, Louis & Balibar, Etienne. (1979). *Reading Capital.* London: Verso Editions.

The Baldness Hall of Fame. (1995). Retrieved 5 October 2004, from: http://www. personal.umich.edu/~pfa/bald/baldhof.html

Barbedette, Gilles. (1984, 28 June). La culture de soi-même. *Les Nouvelles,* pp. 53–54.

Barker, Philip. (1998). *Michel Foucault: An Introduction.* Edinburgh: Edinburgh University Press.

Barthes, Roland. (1972). *Mythologies.* New York: Hill and Wang.

Barthes, Roland. (1974). *S/Z.* New York: Hill and Wang.

Bartos, Michael. (1997). Foucault had to die shamefully. In C. O'Farrell (ed.), *Foucault: The Legacy* (pp. 686–95). Brisbane: Queensland University of Technology.

Baudrillard, Jean. (1994). *Simulacra and simulation*. Ann Arbor: University of Michigan Press.

Baudrillard, Jean. (1996). *The System of Objects*. New York: Verso.

Baudrillard, Jean & Lotringer, Sylvère. (1987). *Forget Foucault; and Forget Baudrillard: An Interview with Silvère Lotringer*. New York: Semiotext(e).

Beauvoir, Simone de. (1952). *The Second Sex* (Trans. H.M. Parshley). New York: Knopf.

Bell, Vikki. (1993). *Interrogating Incest: Feminism, Foucault, and the Law*. London and New York: Routledge.

Bennett, Tony. (1998). *Culture: A Reformer's Science*. St Leonards: Allen & Unwin.

Bernauer, James William. (1990). *Michel Foucault's Force of Flight: Toward an Ethics for Thought*. London: Humanities Press International.

Bernauer, James William & Carrette, Jeremy R. (2004). *Michel Foucault and Theology. The Politics of Religious Experience*. Aldershot, Burlington: Ashgate.

Bourdieu, Pierre. (1971). Systems of education and systems of thought. In E. Hopper (ed.), *Readings in the Theory of Educational Systems* (pp. 159–83). London: Hutchinson.

Bourdieu, Pierre. (1986). *Distinction: a social critique of the judgement of taste* (Trans. R. Nice). London: Routledge.

Bourdieu, Pierre & Adamson, Matthew. (1990). *In Other Words: Essays Towards a Reflexive Sociology*. Cambridge: Polity Press.

Bratich, Jack Z., Packer, Jeremy & McCarthy, Cameron (eds.). (2003). *Foucault, Cultural studies, and Governmentality*. Albany: State University of New York Press.

Burt, Ramsay. (2004). Genealogy and dance history: Foucault, Rainer, Bausch, and de Keersmaeker. In A. Lepecki (ed.), *Of the Presence of the Body: Essays on Dance and Performance Theory* (pp. 29–44). Middletown: Wesleyan University Press.

Canguilhem, Georges. (1978). *On the Normal and the Pathological*. Boston: D. Reidel Pub. Co.

Carrette, Jeremy R. (2000). *Foucault and Religion: Spiritual Corporality and Political Spirituality*. London and New York: Routledge.

Certeau, Michel de. (1967). Les sciences humaines et la mort de l'homme. *Etudes,* 326: 344–60.

Chartier, Roger. (1988). *Cultural History: Between Practices and Representations*. Cambridge: Polity Press.

Châtelet, François. (1979). Récit. In M. Morris & P. Patton (eds.), *Power, truth, strategy*. Sydney: Feral Publications.

Clark, Michael. (1983). *Michel Foucault: An Annotated Bibliography. Tool Kit for a New Age*. New York: Garland.

Col, Cynthia, & Doyle, Sean. (1995). *Foucault and the Power Rangers*. Retrieved 5 October 2004, from: http://www.mit.edu/people/sturkle/PowerRanger.html

La conception idéologique de *L'Histoire de la folie* de Michel Foucault: Journées annuelles de l'Evolution psychiatrique 6 et 7 décembre 1969. (1971). *Evolution psychiatrique: cahiers de psychologies clinique et de psychopathologie générale,* 36(2).

175

Danaher, Geoff, Schirato, Tony & Webb, Jennifer. (2000). *Understanding Foucault.* St Leonards: Allen & Unwin.

Dean, Mitchell. (1999). *Governmentality: Power and Rule in Modern Society.* London: Sage.

Dean, Mitchell & Hindess, Barry (eds.). (1998). *Governing Australia: Studies in Contemporary Rationalities of Government.* Cambridge: Cambridge University Press.

Deleuze, Gilles. (1983). *Nietzsche and Philosophy.* New York: Columbia University Press.

Deleuze, Gilles & Guattari, Félix. (1983). *Anti-Oedipus: Capitalism and Schizophrenia.* Minneapolis: University of Minnesota Press.

Derrida, Jacques. (1976). *Of Grammatology.* Baltimore: Johns Hopkins University Press.

Derrida, Jacques. (1978). *Writing and Difference.* Chicago: University of Chicago Press.

Descartes, René (1993). *Meditations on First Philosophy: In Which the Existence of God and the Distinction of the Soul From the* Body are Demonstrated. Indianpolis: Hacket.

Descombes, Vincent. (1979). *Le même et l'autre: Quarante-cinq ans de philosophie française.* Paris: Minuit.

Donzelot, Jacques. (1986). Les mésaventures de la théorie. *Le Débat,* September, pp. 52–62.

Dreyfus, Hubert, L. & Rabinow, Paul. (1982). *Michel Foucault: Beyond Structuralism and Hermeneutics.* Brighton: Harvester Press.

Droit, Roger-Pol. (2004). *Michel Foucault: entretiens.* Paris: Odile Jacob.

Duncker, Patricia. (1996). *Hallucinating Foucault.* London: Picador.

Ehrenberg, Alain (1998). *La fatigue d'être soi: dépression et société.* Paris: Editions Odile Jacob.

Eribon, Didier. (1991). *Michel Foucault.* Cambridge, Mass.: Harvard University Press.

Eriban, Didier, (1994). *Michel Foucault et ses contemporains.* Paris: Fayard.

Escobar, Arturo. (1999). Discourse and power in development: Michel Foucault and the relevance of his work to the third world. In T. Jacobson & J. Servaes (eds.), *Theoretical Approaches to Participatory Communication* (pp. 309–36). Cresskill, NJ: Hampton Press.

Fairclough, Norman. (2003). *Analysing Discourse: Textual Analysis for Social Research.* London: Routledge.

Ferry, Luc & Renaut, Alain. (1999). *Philosopher à 18 ans: faut-il reformer l'enseignement de la philosophie?* Paris: Grasset et Fasquelle.

Fillingham, Lydia Alix & Süsser, Moshe. (1993). *Foucault for Beginners.* New York: Writers and Readers Beginners Documentary Comic Books.

Frohmann, Bernd. (2000). Discourse and documentation: some implications for pedagogy and research. *The Journal of Education for Library and Information Science,* 42: 13–28.

Gauntlett, David. (n.d.). *Michel Foucault at theory.org.uk.* Retrieved 5 October 2004, from: http://www.theory.org.uk/ctr-fouc.htm

Glucksmann, Andre. (1980). *The Master Thinkers.* Brighton: Harvester.

Goopy, Suzanne. (1997). Repositioning the nurse. In C. O'Farrell (ed.), *Foucault: The Legacy* (pp. 755–63). Brisbane: Queensland University of Technology.

Gordon, Colin. (1999). Under the beach. *Cultural Studies Review*, 5(1): 157–77.

Gordon, Colin. (2000). Introduction. In EW3 (pp. xi–xli).

Guibert, Hervé. (1991). *To the Friend Who Did Not Save My Life*. London: Atheneum.

Hall, Stuart. (1981). Cultural studies: two paradigms. In T. Bennett, G. Martin, C. Mercer & J. Woollacott (eds.), *Culture, ideology and social process: a reader*. London: Batsford with The Open University Press.

Halperin, David M. (1995). *Saint Foucault: Towards a Gay Hagiography*. New York: Oxford University Press.

Han, Beatrice. (2002). *Foucault's Critical Project: Between the Transcendental and the Historical*. Stanford: Stanford University Press.

Hearn, Jeffrey. (2000). *The Untimely Past. Bibliography Project: Michel Foucault*. Retrieved 5 October 2004, from: http://www.untimelypast.org/bibfou.html

Horrocks, Chris, & Jevtic, Zoran. (1997). *Foucault for Beginners*. Cambridge: Icon Books.

Hunter, Ian. (1998). Uncivil society: liberal government and the deconfessionalisation of politics. In M. Dean & B. Hindess (eds.), *Governing Australia: Studies in Contemporary Rationalities of Government*. (pp. 242–64). Cambridge: Cambridge University Press.

Jose, Jim. (1998). *Biopolitics of the Subject: An Introduction to the Ideas of Michel Foucault*. Darwin: Northern Territory University Press.

Karskens, Machiel. (2001). *Chronological bibliography of the works of Foucault*. Retrieved 5 October 2004, from: http://www.foucault.info/foucault/bibliography.html

Kendall, Gavin & Wickham, Gary. (1999). *Using Foucault's Methods*. London: Sage.

Kristeva, Julia. (1992). *The Samurai: A Novel* (Trans. B. Bray). New York: Columbia University Press.

Kuhn, Thomas S. (1996). *The Structure of Scientific Revolutions*. 3rd ed. Chicago: University of Chicago Press.

Lacan, Jacques. (1977). *Ecrits: A Selection*. London: Tavistock.

Lefort, Gérard. (2004, 4 October). Les 24 heures démentes de Foucault. *Libération*. Retrieved 7 October 2004, from: http://www.liberation.fr/page.php?Article=243228

Le Goff, Jacques (ed.). (1978). *La nouvelle histoire*. Paris: CEPL.

Le Goff, Jacques. (1988). *The Medieval Imagination* (Trans. A. Goldhammer). Chicago: The University of Chicago Press.

Léonard, Jacques. (1980). L'historien et le philosophe. In M. Perrot (ed.), *L'impossible prison: recherches sur le système pénitentiaire au XIXe siècle et débat avec Michel Foucault*. Paris: Seuil.

Lévi-Strauss, Claude. (1963). *Structural Anthropology*. New York: Basic Books.

Lévi-Strauss, Claude. (1969). *The Raw and the Cooked*. New York: Harper & Row.

Lynch, Richard. (1997, 2004). *Michel Foucault's shorter works in English*. Retrieved 5 October 2004, from: http://www.michel-foucault.com/lynch.html

Lyotard, Jean-François. (1984). *The Postmodern Condition: A Report on Knowledge*. Manchester: Manchester University Press.

Macey, David. (1993). *The Lives of Michel Foucault*. London: Hutchinson Random House.

Magrs, Paul. (1999). Femme fatale. In S. Cole (ed.), *Doctor Who. More Short Trips: A collection of Short Stories*. London: BBC.

Matisse, Henri. (1994). Letter to Henry Clifford, 1948. In J.D. Flam (ed.), *Matisse on Art*. Berkeley: University of California Press.

Mauriac, Claude. (1976). *Le temps immobile 3: Et comme l'esperance est violente*. Paris: Bernard Grasset.

Mauriac, Claude. (1986). *Le temps immobile 9: Mauriac et fils*. Paris: Bernard Grasset & Fasquelle.

McHoul, A.W. & Grace, W. (1993). *A Foucault Primer: Discourse, Power and the Subject*. Melbourne: Melbourne University Press.

McNay, Lois. (1992). *Foucault and Feminism: Power, Gender, and the Self*. Cambridge: Polity Press.

McNay, Lois. (1994). *Foucault: A Critical Introduction*. Cambridge: Polity Press.

Meadows, Michael. (1999). Cultural Studies and Journalism. *Media Wars*, 90: 43–51.

Miller, James. (1993). *The Passion of Michel Foucault*. New York: Simon and Schuster.

Mills, C. Wright. (1959). *The Sociological Imagination*. London: Oxford University Press.

Mills, Sarah. (2003). *Michel Foucault*. London: Routledge.

Morris, Meaghan. (1979). Fiche Technique. In M. Morris & P. Patton (eds.), *Michel Foucault: Power, Truth, Strategy* (p. 184). Sydney: Feral Publications.

Morris, Meaghan. (1997). The truth is out there … *Cultural Studies*, 11(3): 367–75.

Nettleton, Sarah. (1992). *Power, Pain, and Dentistry*. Buckingham: Open University Press.

Neumann, Iver B. (2002). Forord. In I.B. Neumann (ed.), *Michel Foucault: Forelesninger om regjering og styringsmakt* (pp. 7–38). Oslo: Cappelens upopulaere skrifter. [Three lectures by Foucault translated, annotated and introduced by Neumann in Norwegian.]

O'Farrell, Clare. (1989). *Foucault: Historian or Philosopher?* London: Macmillan.

O'Farrell, Clare (ed.). (1997). *Foucault: The Legacy*. Brisbane: Queensland University of Technology.

O'Leary, Timothy. (2002). *Foucault: The Art of Ethics*. London; New York: Continuum.

O'Malley, Pat. (1998). Indigenous governance. In M. Dean & B. Hindess (eds.), *Governing Australia: Studies in Contemporary Rationalities of Government*. (pp. 156–72). Cambridge: Cambridge University Press.

Packer, Jermy. (2003). Disciplining mobility: governing and safety. In J.Z. Bratich, J. Packer & C. McCarthy (eds.), *Foucault, Cultural Studies, and Governmentality* (pp. 23–46). Albany: State University of New York Press.

Pfister, Thierry. (1981). Ce qui a protégé la France du terrorisme. In N. Muchnik (ed.), *Le Nouvel Observateur: témoin de l'histoire*. Paris: Belfond.

Potte-Bonneville, Matthieu. (2004, 28 June 2004). Michel Foucault: radical et sceptique. *Politis*. Retrieved 7 October 2004, from: http://www.politis.fr/article1009.html

Prado, C.G. (2000). *Starting with Foucault: An Introduction to Genealogy*. 2nd ed. Boulder: Westview Press.

Radford, Gary, Radford, Marie, & Cooper, Stephen. (1997). *Foucault Funk: The Michel Foucault Postmodern Blues*. Retrieved 5 October 2004, from: http://www.scils.rutgers.edu/%7Eband/profs/foucault.html

Rajchman, John. (1985). *Michel Foucault: The Freedom of Philosophy.* New York: Columbia University Press.

Robinson, Paul. (1978, 28 October). Review of *The History of Sexuality, vol 1: An Introduction. New Republic*, pp. 29–32.

Said, Edward W. (1978). *Orientalism.* London: Routledge & Kegan Paul.

Saison, Maryvonne. (2004). Introduction. In M. Saison (ed.), *La peinture de Manet suivi de Michel Foucault un regard.* Paris: Seuil.

Sartre, Jean-Paul. (1966, 15 October). Sartre répond. *La Quinzaine Littéraire*, pp. 4–5.

Seem, Mark D. (2000). *Acupuncture Physical Medicine: An Acupuncture Touchpoint Approach to the Treatment of Chronic Fatigue, Pain, and Stress Disorders.* Boulder, Co: Blue Poppy Press.

Sheridan, Alan. (1981). *Michel Foucault: The Will to Truth.* London: Tavistock.

Smart, Barry. (1985). *Michel Foucault.* London: Tavistock.

Smith Maguire, Jennifer. (2002). Michel Foucault: sport, power, technologies and governmentality. In J. Maguire & K. Young (Eds.), *Theory, Sport and Society* (pp. 293–314). Oxford: JAI.

Stoler, Ann Laura. (1995). *Race and the Education of Desire: Foucault's History of Sexuality and the Colonial Order of Things.* Durham and London: Duke University Press.

Tabard, Claude André. (1967). A propos d'une traduction d'Aristophane. *Etudes,* 326, 361.

Tallis, Raymond. (2001, 21 December). The truth about lies. Foucault, Nietzsche and the Cretan paradox. *The Times Literary Supplement,* 3.

White, Michael. (2000). *Reflections on Narrative Practice: Essays and Interviews.* Adelaide: Dulwich Centre Publications.

Wolfe, Tom. (1998). *A Man in Full.* London: Jonathan Cape.

Index

Abnormal (lectures) 44
Absurdism 26
Aldrovandi, Ulisse 92
Althusser, Louis 14, 27, 28, 74, 123
Ancient Greece 48, 66, 113-14, 115,
  150, 156, 160
anonymous texts 33-4
anti-psychiatry 36, 117, 129, 144
apparatus 7, 65-6, 129, 135
applications of Foucault's work 8-10,
  53, 54-5
archaeology 62, 64-5, 67-8, 72, 127, 129,
  130, 133, 142, 155
The Archaeology of Knowledge 33-4, 41-2,
  68, 78-81, 89, 96-8, 119
architecture 60, 129-30, 156-7
Ariès, Philippe 36
Aristophanes 8
art 2, 7, 15, 17, 51, 80-1, 94, 118, 130,
  144, 153
Artaud, Antonin 92
arts of existence 117-18, 130, 156
ascetics 115
author 4, 21, 23, 27,33-4, 130, 140,
  155, 161

Bachelard, Gaston 6
Barthes, Roland 27, 36, 122, 124
Bataille, Georges 91
Baudelaire, Charles 155
Baudrillard, Jean 2, 123
Beauvoir, Simone de 121
behaviour 109-10
Bell, Vikki 18
Bellour, Raymond 77
Bentham, Jeremy 43, 77, 104, 147
Binswanger, Ludwig 34, 122

biographies 19-24
biopolitics 44, 105, 130, 148
biopower 101, 105-6, 130, 133, 146, 156
The Birth of the Clinic 22, 37-9, 58, 61,
  65, 78, 90, 97
Blanchot, Maurice 4, 36, 144, 148
Braudel, Fernand 36, 75
body 101, 103, 130, 157
Bonnefoy, Claude 19-20
Borges, Jorge Luis 58
Bourdieu, Pierre 4, 13, 59, 125
Breton, André 144
Byzantios, D. 130

Camus, Albert 26
Canguilhem, Georges 6, 36, 57, 123
capitalism 80, 131, 157
The Care of the Self 34, 48, 77
Carette, Jeremy 4
cartesian thought 54, 157, 158
CDA *see* critical discourse analysis
Certeau, Michel de 39chance events 76
Chartier, Roger 16, 60
Chaunu, Pierre and Huguette 74
Christianity 46, 47-8, 132-5, 137, 140,
  146, 153-6, 158, 161
chronology 121-6
Clavel, Maurice 30
colonialism 131
commentary 142
conditions of possibility 69, 72, 134
conduct 131, 138, 148, 154, 156
confession 131
confinement 36-7, 131, 136
constraints 69, 109, 137
continuity 75-6
counter-conducts 47, 99, 154

crime 43, 131–2, 144, 148, 159
critical discourse analysis (CDA) 78
cross-cultural studies 17
cultural analysis 50–60, 132, 143
cultural studies 10, 12–13, 15, 16–18
culture 17–18, 132
cultural traces 76–9
curiosity 21, 116, 132
Cuvier, Georges 4

dangerous individuals 132
death 22, 36–8, 90, 111, 130, 132,
    141, 143
death penalty 132, 116
death of man 140
Defert, Daniel 30
Deleuze, Gilles 30, 123, 124, 132
deontology 115
Derrida, Jacques 5, 112, 117, 123, 132
Descartes, René 14, 54, 77, 83, 112–13,
    132, 134, 144, 155, 158
Descombes, Vincent 84
desire 113, 132–3
Diderot, Denis 144
difference 40–1
disciplinary power 102–5, 130, 133–4,
    136, 150
disciplinary society 43–4, 102, 133, 140
discipline 102–5, 133, 146, 151
Discipline and Punish 4–6, 13, 30, 42–4,
    45, 55, 65, 72, 77, 101–2, 124
disciplines (definition) 12–13
discontinuity 42, 62, 74–82, 133
discourse 13, 16, 41–2, 55, 66, 68, 71,
    74–82, 86, 127, 132, 133, 136, 141,
    143–4, 146, 156, 160
discourse analysis 54, 78
discursive formations 12, 18, 134
discursive practices 60, 66, 72, 79–80, 81,
    127, 134, 146
disease 75, 157
dispositif 7, 65–6, 129, 135
Dits et écrits 6, 19, 34, 49, 82
domination 67, 94, 138, 148, 150, 152,
    156, 161
dreams 34–5, 48, 94, 111, 132, 134,
    144, 156–7, 160
Droit, Roger-Pol 19
Duncker, Patricia 2
Duras, Marguerite 144

economics 130, 132, 134, 143, 145–6,
    150, 155
education 134, 145, 159

empiricism 86–7
Enlightenment period 88, 134, 152
episteme 63–4, 127, 134–5
Eribon, Didier 21, 22, 30
ethico-politics 117
ethics 62, 64, 73, 109–20, 132, 137,
    135, 139, 142, 145, 147, 150,
    155–6, 161
    four aspects of 115
events 74–5, 132–3, 135–6, 142,
    159, 160
evolution 76
examinations 105
exclusion 5, 132, 136, 146
existentialism 24–6, 28–9, 34, 147
experience 118, 136, 85, 143,
    157, 160

family 136, 145
Fearless speech (lectures) 48, 70
feminism 8, 9, 15, 16, 18, 161
Ferry, Luc 14–15
fictions 84–6, 136
film 137
finitude 130, 137
Flaubert, Gustave 144
food 137
formalism 56–7
foundations 55, 59, 137
Frankfurt School 31, 152
freedom 21, 55, 61, 99–100, 109,
    111, 116, 137, 150, 156,
    158, 161
French readership 13–16, 18
Freud, Sigmund 35, 94, 137, 149
friendship 137
fundamental phenomena 59–60
Furet, François 75

Gauntlett, David 1
the gaze 38–9, 138
genealogy 64–5, 67–9, 72, 129, 138
geography 138
Glucksmann, André 31, 125
Gordon, Colin 108
governmentality 16–17, 46, 101, 106–8,
    125, 133, 138
    applications 55, 59
Goya, Francisco 130
Great Confinement 5, 36–7, 136
Guibert, Hervé 2

Habermas, Jürgen 31, 99
Hall, Stuart 13, 60

Halperin, David 1
Hegel, Georg Wilhelm Friedrich 14, 52
Heidegger, Martin 23, 25
hermeneutics 142
The Hermeneutics of the Subject (lectures)
    48, 112, 125, 128
Hesiod 7
heterotopia 138
Hirschhorn, Thomas 2
historical a priori 62-3, 66, 139
historiography 139
history 54, 55, 61-73, 74-82, 139, 158
    of the present 64, 71-2, 139
    of problems 77, 151
    of thought 69-70, 71, 155, 158, 159
    of truth 87-8, 90, 160
The History of Sexuality vol. 1 7, 20, 34,
    44-6, 47-8, 81, 101, 105-6, 137
HIV/AIDS 22-3
homosexuality 1, 15, 16, 22-4, 139
Horrocks, Chris 23-4, 51
human nature 25-7, 75, 140
human rights 32, 111, 154
human sciences 39, 72, 140, 158
humanism 24-6, 41, 111, 140
humanist Marxism 25-6
Husserl, Edmund 25

idealism 70, 86-7
identities 9, 15-16, 40-1, 110-11, 139-41
ideology 96-8, 134, 140, 151
imagination 91-2, 141, 144, 161
individualisation 140-1
individuals 110, 132, 133, 135, 141,
    156, 157
instincts 67
institutions 129, 133-4, 138, 141, 144,
    146, 151, 153, 157
intellectual knowledge 94, 130, 142, 157
intellectuals 9, 101, 141, 147
    specific 9, 77, 141
interpretation 142
the intolerable 116, 135
introductions (nature of) 3-11
Iran 125, 142, 154
irrationality 152-3

Jevtic, Zoran 23-4, 51
Jose, Jim 8
justice 142, 151

Kant, Immanuel 14, 62-4, 152
Kepler, Johannes 113
Klee, Paul 130

knowledge 7, 13, 54, 58, 63-4, 66-9,
    88-90, 93-4, 96-8 , 129, 133-4,
    136-7, 142, 146-7, 151, 153, 159, 161
Kuhn's paradigm 40, 123

Lacan, Jacques 27, 123, 142-3
language (being of) 27, 41, 132, 142-4, 153
law 143, 146,150, 159, 161
Le Goff, Jacques 92, 125
lectures 43-4, 46-7, 48-9
Léonard, Jacques 4, 49
Le Roy Ladurie, Emmanuel 74
Lévi-Strauss, Claude 27, 122-3
liberalism 134, 143, 158
life 143
limits 21, 38, 41, 56, 61, 69, 90-3, 134-5,
    143, 144, 148, 155, 161
limits of power 153-4
linguistics 27, 29, 39, 143, 145, 158
literature 2-3, 16, 91, 144, 153, 159
Lovejoy, Arthur 6
Lyotard, Jean-François 125

Macey, David 9, 21-2
Machiavelli, Niccolo 79, 157
madness 35-8, 75, 91-2, 130, 132-4,
    136-7, 141, 143, 144, 157, 160
Madness and Civilization 5, 18, 35-8,
    65, 85, 90-1, 97, 110, 117, 122,
    124, 128
Magritte, René 81, 130
Mallarmé, Stéphane 144
Manet, Édouard 80-1, 124, 130
Maoism 30-1, 125
marginal experience 90, 116
Marx, Karl 5, 75, 99, 144-5, 149
Marxism 5, 53, 16, 25-6, 29, 40, 59,
    88, 96-8, 122, 131, 139, 140,
    144-5, 149, 154
Matisse, Henri 7
Mauriac, Claude 30
medicine 37-9, 58, 97, 111-12, 132,
    138, 140, 144-6, 151, 156, 160
mental illness 35, 75, 129, 138-9, 144,
    148-9, 154
Mental Illness and Psychology 35, 123
Merleau-Ponty, Maurice 25
methodology 52-60, 78
Miller, James 1, 22
Mills, C. Wright 95
mode of subjection 115
modernity 149, 155
morality 73, 114-17, 135, 140, 145-6,
    152, 154, 156

Morris, Meaghan 9
music 146

Naissance de la biopolitique (lectures)
47, 125
narrative therapy 54
Nerval, Gérard de 92
Nietzsche, Friedrich 65-6, 84, 92, 146
nihilism 2, 119, 135
non-discursive objects 80-1
non-discursive practices 146
non-reductionism 137
normalisation 104, 143, 146, 152

objective truth 51, 83
O'Farrell, Clare 19
O'Leary, Timothy 95
O'Malley, Pat 60
order 11, 54, 56-60, 67, 90, 119, 132,
135, 142, 146
The order of discourse 7, 42, 65, 68, 98
The Order of Things 6, 11-12, 36-41,
57-8, 60, 61, 63-5, 75, 78-9, 85, 89
Other 90-1, 147, 161

painting 130, 148
painting-objects 80-1
Panofsky, Erwin 130
Panopticon 43, 77, 103-4, 147
parrhesia 147, 160
pastoral power 46-7, 107, 141, 150,
153, 154, 157
personal biography 19-24
Pfister, Thierry 30
phenomenology 24-6, 28-9, 34, 110,
136, 147
philosophy 14-15, 18, 55, 136, 138,
141, 145, 147-8
photography 148
Plato 7, 14
Poland 31-2, 122, 125, 148
polemics 4-5, 148
police 46-7, 49, 148
politics 29, 64-5, 67, 89-90, 96, 135,
145, 148
populations 106-7, 130, 138, 148
positivism 109
postcolonialism 9, 15, 16, 53
positivity 79
post-war humanism 24-6
postmodernism 125, 149
Potte-Bonneville, Matthieu 18
Le pouvoir psychiatrique (lectures) 44,
59, 97, 102, 124

power 17, 31, 96-109
definitions 149-50
disciplinary 102-5, 130, 133-4, 136, 150
discourse 42, 133
ethics 119-20
knowledge 10, 54, 67, 96-8, 105,
134, 141, 146
limits of power 135, 143, 153-4
microphysics 100-2, 150
productive 100-1, 149
truth 83-4, 86-7
power-knowledge 67, 101-2, 131,
148, 150-1
practices 70-1, 89, 151, 159
prisons 42-3, 129, 141, 151
problematisations 69-70, 127-8, 151
programmatic texts 77
progressive politics 148
pseudonymous texts 33-4
psychiatry 37-8, 131, 134, 145, 151, 156
psychoanalysis 142-3151
psychology 35, 71-2, 97, 151
punishment 42-3, 143, 151, 152, 153

race 145, 152
rationality 152-3, 158
Raymond Roussel 37, 123, 144
readership 10, 13-16
reality 143, 146, 152
Reason 76, 88, 89, 91-3, 137, 144, 152-3
reductive labelling 28
regimes of practice 70, 141, 151
regimes of truth 65-7, 94, 127, 153
relativism 83
religion 26, 107, 153
representation 16, 78, 80-1, 92, 130,
133, 136, 153
resemblance 40
resistance to power 99-100, 140, 141, 153-4
revolution 142, 154
Rebeyrolle, Paul 130
rights 154
Robbe-Grillet, Alain 27, 144
Rousseau, Jean-Jacques 144

Sade, Marquis de 144
Said, Edward 91
salvation 154
Sartre, Jean-Paul 5, 14, 25, 26, 28, 40, 125
Saussure, Ferdinand de 27
science
definitions 80, 89, 154-5
history 41, 63, 69, 72, 92, 129, 135,
143, 154

science *cont.*
  knowledge 51, 54, 69, 92, 140, 154
  power 87, 96–7, 151, 155
  society 155
  truth 75–6, 88–90, 134, 155,
    157, 160
science fiction 1, 2, 18, 144
Securité, territoire, population (lectures)
    46, 125
Séglard, Dominique 18
self 70, 110–14, 140, 155
  practices of 53, 54, 115, 130, 133, 137,
    138, 140, 145, 147, 155
  self-discovery 113, 115, 155
  self-transformation 135, 137, 148,
    153, 155–7
  truth 130, 138, 142, 155, 157, 160
Serres, Michel, 36
sexual repression 91
sexuality 1, 20, 23–4, 91, 139, 155–6
  social activism 29–31
social context 24
social justice 54, 109, 116
social security 156
society 157
Society Must be Defended (lectures)
    44, 67, 106
Solidarity 31–2, 125, 148
sovereign power 101–2, 107, 136, 143,
    150, 152
space 103, 138, 157
spiritual knowledge 94, 112, 142
spirituality 93–4, 142, 153, 157
Stalin 122
State 46–7, 67, 100, 107, 138, 141, 143,
    147–9, 150, 154,157, 159, 160
statistics 157
Steiner, George 5, 6
Stone, Lawrence 5, 85
structural linguistics 27, 145
structuralism 26–9, 36, 38, 40, 56, 139,
    142, 158
subject 27, 72–3, 99, 101, 107, 110–15,
    129, 133, 135, 137, 140, 143, 145–7,
    149, 155–60
subjectivity 55, 109–20, 136, 147, 154,
    158, 161
surveillance 60, 103, 133, 147

Tallis, Raymond 22
technical vocabulary 11
techne 127, 158–9
technology 127, 158–60
television 159
Terayama, Shugi 118
terrorism 30, 154, 159
theory 60, 71, 129, 148–9, 159
  as tool box 50–60, 128, 159
thought 69–70, 71, 159
time 157, 159
totalitarianism 159
trade unions 31–2, 148
transformation 110, 112, 117–18, 160
  see also self-transformation
transgression 143–4, 155, 159
translation 7–8, 34
travel 20
truth 48–9, 50–1, 54, 83–95, 112–13,
    134, 138, 140, 142–4, 147–8,
    151–3, 155–60
  see also regimes of truth
truth-events 93–4, 136
Tunisia 29, 123
Turkle, Sherry 1

universal categories 160
The Use of Pleasure 47, 72, 77, 114, 115
utopias 105, 160

Valasquez, Diego 130
verbal traces 76–7
Verne, Jules 144
violence 30, 67, 142, 151, 153, 160
vocabulary 11, 127–8
Voltaire 6

war 67, 149, 160
websites 163–4
will to know 66, 161
will to truth 161
witchcraft 161
Wolfe, Tom 2
women 150, 156, 161
words and things 37, 57–9, 86,
    146, 153
writing 11–12, 20–1, 139, 143,
    157–8, 161